MAKING A KILLING

MAKING A KILLING

James Ashcroft

With Clifford Thurlow

IN MEMORIAM

Philip
Jason
Mohanned
Hayder
Riyadh
Khaled

How dull it is to pause, to make an end,
To rust unburnish'd, not to shine in use!

Alfred, Lord Tennyson, *Ulysses*

The rain fell alike upon the just and upon the
unjust, and for nothing was there a why and a
wherefore.

W. Somerset Maugham, *Of Human Bondage*

Never, never, never believe any war will be
smooth and easy, or that anyone who embarks
on the strange voyage can measure the tides and
hurricanes he will encounter. The statesman
who yields to war fever must realise that once
the signal is given, he is no longer the master of
policy but the slave of unforeseeable and
uncontrollable events.

Sir Winston Churchill

GLOSSARY

.50 cal   12.7mm calibre anti-materiel round; also a term used to refer to the **Browning** machine gun.

5.56 5.56×45mm calibre rounds, standard NATO calibre since 1979.

7.62 long 7.62×54mm round, Soviet rimmed cartridge fired in the **PKM** and **Dragunov**; also designated 7.62×54R.

7.62 NATO 7.62×51mm round used in the **GPMG** and rifles such as the **G3** and FAL.

7.62 short 7.62×39mm round used by **AK-47**, **RPD** and **SKS**.

9 milly   British Army slang for 9mm pistol.

AAFES   American Army and Air Force Exchange Service, the welfare shopping organisation establishing shops for US Forces around the world on US bases. Commonly known as the **PX**.

Abrams   US main battle tank M1A2, 120mm cannon, .50cal machine gun and two 7.62mm **GPMG**.

AC-130H/U   Military designation for **Spectre** aerial gun platform based on a C-130 airframe. It has a

40mm cannon, twin 20mm multi-barrelled Gatling guns and an automatic 105mm artillery piece. Computer guidance allows the aircraft to circle and maintain uninterrupted, accurate fire support on to target. Its radar can track its own 40mm and 105mm projectiles in flight, thus allowing pinpoint adjustment of fire. The software will allow two targets up to 1km apart to be engaged simultaneously.

Actions on   Term used to describe standard operating procedures for any given scenario.

AGC   Adjutant's General Corps.

AH-64   See **Apache**.

AK-47   Soviet assault rifle firing **7.62 short**, available folding or fixed stock with 30-and 40-round magazines or 75-round drum.

Apache   US twin-engine attack helicopter military designation **AH-64** with excellent long-range stand-off optics, armed with a wide variety of air-to-air and ground attack anti-personnel and anti-vehicular munitions.

B6/BVI   Vehicle armour grading of a level to withstand a limited level of high-velocity rifle and machine-gun fire up to 7.62mm. Not proof against armour piercing rounds, .50cal rounds or **RPG**.

BIAP   Baghdad International Airport.

Blue-force tracker   A **GPS** tracking unit that will display a vehicle's exact location on a digital display both in the vehicle and in the operations room. Only issued to US Forces and **PSDs** carrying out **CF** taskings.

BMP   Soviet tracked armoured personnel carrier with turret and medium-calibre weaponry varying according to model.

Bradley	Bradley **M2** tracked Infantry Fighting Vehicle, or M3 Cavalry variant, armed with 25mm chain gun, 7.62mm **GPMG** and TOW missiles. Some variants carry anti-aircraft Javelin or Stinger missiles. Three crew and six passengers.
Browning	Browning Hi Power pistol, or GP35, a 9mm automatic pistol with a 13- or 20-round magazine. Made by Fabrique Nationale, the Belgian firearms manufacturer who also produced the MAG, the **Minimi** and many others. Sometimes also used to refer to the Browning M2 **.50 cal** machine gun.
Casevac	Casualty Evacuation.
CF	Coalition Forces.
Circuit	The network of men working as Private Security Contractors.
COP	Close Observation Platoon.
CP	Close Protection, bodyguarding activity.
CPA	Coalition Provisional Authority, the interim government installed by the US government after the invasion of Iraq. Also refers to the Presidential palace compound later to be known as 'the **Green Zone**' or 'the International Zone'.
CQB	Close Quarter Battle, refers to the weapons and tactics used for close-range fighting.
Dragunov	Semi-automatic Eastern Bloc sniper rifle firing **7.62 long**. Also known as SVD.
FOB	Forward Operating Base.
FPS	Facilities Protection Service.
G3	Heckler & Koch automatic rifle, firing 7.62mm NATO.
Glock	Austrian 9mm pistol, most commonly the Glock 17 or 19 models with 17- and 15-round magazine capacity respectively.

GPMG   General Purpose Machine Gun, such as the
                MAG made by Belgian manufacturer,
                Fabrique Nationale. The MAG is an
                extremely reliable design used all over the
                world firing **7.62 NATO** from a
                disintegrating belt with left-hand feed,
                recently adopted by US Forces as the M240
                or M240G.

GPS   Global Positioning System, satellite
                navigation system which can be handheld,
                the size of a cellphone, or vehicle mounted.

Green Zone   Compound surrounding the **CPA** and US
                Embassy palaces, approximately 10 sq. km
                in the centre of Baghdad. Later known as the
                International Zone or IZ.

Humvee   Standard 4 × 4 utility vehicle of the US
                Forces. A variety of models, some soft, some
                with light Kevlar armour and some with
                heavy armour, often with home-made or
                factory-built turrets to protect top gunners.
                Armed with anything from **SAWs** and 240s
                to **.50cals** and **Mk19s**.

ICDC   Iraqi Civil Defence Corps, local troops
                recruited and trained by **CF** to carry out
                military security duties. They had a
                reputation for being corrupt, with a strong
                tendency to desert with all their kit.

IED   Improvised Explosive Device. A bomb.

ING   Iraqi National Guard, replaced the **ICDC**.

IP   Iraqi Police, also known as 'Iraqi 5-Oh' or
                'Baghdad's Finest'.

IRAQNA   Iraqi cellphone network.

Jacky   Derogative term for Arab/Iraqi, as in 'Jacky
                the Iraqi' (they call us 'Mister').

KIA   Killed In Action.

Kiowa	OH58D Kiowa Warrior, single-engine US attack/recce helicopter with two universal weapons pylons capable of accepting combinations of Hellfire missile, the Air-to-Air Stinger (ATAS) missile, 2.75' Folding Fin Aerial Rocket (FFAR) pods, and a .50cal machine gun. The extra weight of weapons and avionics has given this airframe a reputation for difficult auto-rotations in the event of engine failure.
Klick	Military term for kilometre.
Long	Slang for rifle, i.e. a long weapon as opposed to a **short**.
M1	See **Abrams** main battle tank.
M16	Standard battle rifle of US Forces firing 5.56.
M2	See **Bradley**.
M240	See **GPMG**.
M249	See **Minimi**.
M4	5.56 carbine, compact version of **M16** rifle.
MCI	US cellphone network set up and used by **CF** in Baghdad.
Minimi	Light machine gun manufactured by Fabrique Nationale of Belgium, firing 5.56mm from a disintegrating belt left-hand feed, also capable of feeding from **M16** magazines if no belted ammunition is available. A compact and reliable weapon when new. Used by US Forces under the designation **M249 SAW**.
Mk 19	40mm automatic grenade launcher.
MP5	SMG family manufactured by Heckler & Koch, also includes MP5K (short) and MP5SD (suppressed). An excellent 9mm SMG.
NGO	Non-Governmental Organisation, usually a

	humanitarian aid organisation such as the International Red Cross or the UN High Commission for Refugees (UNHCR).
OGA	Other Governmental Agency, i.e. the CIA, but don't tell anyone. It's a secret.
PE	Plastic Explosive.
PKM	Soviet **GPMG** firing **7.62 long** from a non-disintegrating belt fed in from the right-hand side. Also known as 'PKC' or 'BKC' by the Iraqis.
PSC	Private Security Company/Contractor.
PSD	Personal Security Detail, used as a noun or a verb.
PX	See **AAFES**.
QRF	Quick Reaction Force.
Regiment	'The Regiment', slang for 22 SAS Regiment.
RLC	Royal Logistics Corps; aka Really Large Corps.
RMP	Royal Military Police.
RPD	Soviet light machine gun from 1953, very light, fires **7.62 short** from a non-disintegrating belt fed in from the left-hand side. Manufactured and found in most former communist bloc countries. Also known as 'Degtyarev' by the Iraqis.
RPG	RPG-7 rocket-propelled grenade, a common Soviet weapon featuring a reusable launcher tube and a separate rocket with an 84mm High Explosive Anti-Tank warhead.
RPK	Support weapon, a long-barrelled AK rifle with a bipod. The thicker, longer barrel increases muzzle velocity, accuracy, heat dissipation and effective battlefield range. Magazine or drum fed from AK magazines.
RUC	Royal Ulster Constabulary.

RV	Rendezvous.
SAW	Squad Automatic Weapon; see **Minimi**.
Short	Slang for pistol or side arm.
Sig	Sig Sauer firearms manufacturers, who produce the quite excellent P226 and P228 pistols, among other weapons.
Sitrep	Situation report (radio traffic) status report or update.
SKS	Old Soviet semi-automatic rifle firing **7.62 short**.
SMG	Submachine gun.
Spectre	See **AC-130**.
T-62 or T-72	Soviet main battle tanks.
Tasky	Slang for Special Task Force (South African police elite tactical unit) member.
Thuraya	Regional satellite telephony provider, also a term used for their phone handsets.
VBIED	Vehicle-borne **IED**.
VSI	Category given to casualty; Very Seriously Injured.
WIA	Wounded In Action.

ONE

As the three of us fanned out across the empty arrivals hall at Baghdad International Airport I casually disengaged the safety catch on my East German AK-47.

'Talk about the mother of all fuck-ups,' said Seamus, his voice echoing over the high ceiling.

He was stabbing the digits on his mobile phone. He glanced about the empty space.

Les Trevellick had moved to his right. He remained expressionless as he looked back.

I was on the left flank with a good view of the runway. Beyond the plate glass windows were the cannibalised remains of some prize specimens of the Iraqi Airways fleet. No other aircraft were in sight.

The rest of the team was outside, three South Africans guarding our two vehicles and humming along to Freedom Radio, the American Forces channel and the only English language radio station we had found. It was ten weeks before Christmas 2003 and Bing Crosby was dreaming of a white Christmas.

In the months to come Baghdad International Airport, or 'BIAP' as it was better known, would be bustling with hundreds of security contractors flying into Iraq under the cold, watchful eyes of armed ex-Ghurkas. Now, in all that vacant space, our footsteps sounded far too loud and the absence of crowds was an almost tangible presence in itself.

We had unloaded our weapons as ordered by the US soldiers at the Coalition checkpoint at the airport entry gate, but had magged up again as we approached the deserted terminal buildings.

The arrivals lounge was far too lavish with its marble trim and polished floors. It was like wandering through an abandoned cathedral, a reminder of something once sacred that had lost its meaning. When the Iraq War ended on 1 May 2003, the first thing the Iraqis did after toppling the statues was remove the name Saddam Hussein from all the airport signs, although you could still see the faded outline where the sun had bleached the stone around the letters. The tyrant had gone, but his presence was everywhere, as strong as ever. Six months had passed since the end of the war, it was October now, the insurgency had begun to gather momentum and enemy attacks were becoming more effective.

That's why we had been tasked to bring Associated Press reporter Lori Wyatt safely into the Green Zone. This was the interim government, the Coalition Provisional Authority's (CPA) safety zone, a heavily defended, 10 square kilometre area with a dozen or more of Saddam's marble palaces in the heart of the city. Among the palaces you could find all the comforts of home in the shops at the PX – the AAFES, or American Army and Air Force Exchange Service – not to forget the golden-rimmed toilets of the omnipotent dictator where hairy-arsed GIs from Illinois and Tennessee now went to take a leak.

Although the CPA was in the centre of the area known as the 'Green Zone', the two terms became synonymous and it was later renamed the International Zone. This was my first tasking since I'd arrived in Iraq; our first tasking as a team. And our principal wasn't there.

No one was there.

We were working as private security contractors for Spartan, a UK-based outfit set up by a group of ex-officers, one of a clutch of new security firms with savvy bosses aware that the United States didn't have enough boots on the ground.

We were in Iraq for the $500 a day we earned. When President George W. Bush, dressed for battle, announced from the deck of the aircraft carrier USS *Abraham Lincoln* that the war was over, the White House pushed an $87 billion reconstruction package through Congress; 30 per cent of the money was earmarked for security and everyone wanted a piece.

It had turned Iraq into a gold rush.

The country was awash with new cars, air conditioners, new political parties, newspapers, new computers, Internet porn and money; the dollar bills arrived in shrink-wrapped plastic packs of $500,000 and all our needs from Mars bars at the supermarket to machine guns on the black market were paid for in cash. You could get *anything*. The money made you hungry for more money. You couldn't help coveting those plastic packs of $500,000 and wondering how you could fit one into your suitcase and take it home. It would certainly solve all my problems. My girlfriend, Krista, and I had a little girl now. We had a new flat with an extra bedroom. The bills had been pouring in.

I had joined the 1st Battalion, the Duke of Wellington's Regiment as a platoon commander in 1993 after a year at Sandhurst. After six years of attachments and tours including Bosnia, West Belfast and working with American Special Forces, Airborne and US Marines, I resigned my commission to return to my original career path. I had gone up from Winchester, England's oldest public school, to take law at Brasenose, Oxford. I reckoned in two years as a City solicitor I'd be raking it in.

The excitement of civvy street faded in about five minutes and I assumed this was it. This was civvy life. Civilians got up every morning, endured a harrowing commute on London's filthy and inefficient public transport system, detested their jobs for eight or nine hours, then slogged home in time to fall into bed, just so that they could get up next morning and do it all over again. Day after day. For years. I don't think a day passed without me daydreaming about rejoining the army.

I exaggerate? Maybe, but not much. Only Krista made it all worthwhile and I did everything I could to keep my depression from her. Our daughter Natalie was born in 2000. I loved being a father, but it hit me like a religious revelation just how much I detested working in an office on Wednesday, 19 March 2003, Natalie's third birthday. It was the day Coalition Forces (CF) invaded Iraq and with them went the Dukes as part of Operation Telic, the British name for the invasion. I mused on signing up again to join my old regiment, but the war was over three weeks after it started.

The war was over, but the post-war insurgency was growing and private security operators were arriving in Iraq to fight it. There was a fortune to be made. Fortunes were being spent! In the last three weeks we had broken the seals on two plastic packs of $500,000 and spent the lot on equipment, guns, ammunition, vehicles, bribes and baksheesh. Three weeks of spending like millionaires. Now, it was time to put some black ink in the account books. One of the contracts to chaperone reporters around the fractured country had been awarded to Spartan through the US Department of Defense. It was as interesting as PSD missions get and had come at the right moment.

Iraq was *the* story. Al Qaeda's attack on the Twin Towers on 11 September 2001 was one of those defining moments in history. If the Iraq War was a direct response to 9/11 – most US soldiers I'd met certainly believed it so – its implications would affect every aspect of our lives: the price of oil, peace in the Middle East, US relations with Europe, the trust gap between the people and their governments. In Britain, Italy and Spain people had marched in their millions against the war but Blair, Berlusconi and Aznar still followed Bush to Baghdad.

Why? And what next?

I'd always stayed in contact with my army mates and one morning three weeks before, while I was hurrying to catch the 8.10 into the City, the phone rang and my pulse started to race when I heard the voice of Angus McGrath on the other end of the line. Like myself, Angus was a former infantry officer in the Duke of Wellington's Regiment, a great barrel-chested, Scots brute of a man and not famous for wasting 50p on a phone call.

He was in Baghdad working for Spartan and when he asked me if I could drop everything and be there in a week it dawned on me that my Hermès tie was choking me to death.

'Is it going to be dangerous?' I asked him.

'Absolutely. You're replacing some poor sod who got slotted two days ago.'

I glanced at Krista. She was doing a poor job pretending not to listen as she put on her make-up in the mirror. I could see her eyes in the reflection.

'Not dangerous at all, a desk job you say?'

'You're joking, mate. I got contacted this morning, there's fucking bullet holes in my windscreen.' He paused. The penny must have dropped. 'Is Krista in the same room as you?'

'Yes she is, and she's very well thanks. Count me in.'

This was the answer to our dreams. Before my late entry into law, I had done one tediously safe security job in Tanzania where I was instructing the locals in the art of guarding a cement factory. I assured Krista it would be the same in Iraq. Big money, I said, no danger. My attitude was that what Krista doesn't know she's not going to worry about.

I was going back into action. I spent a frantic few days running around the Army and Navy surplus stores looking for kit. I bought a couple of pistol holsters, which Angus said were hard to come by in Iraq, sand-coloured shirts and trousers, two pairs of desert boots, torches, batteries and a daysack to carry everything.

I spoke to Angus again and he told me that there had only been a handful of casualties among security men at this time, with the highest scoring killer of contractors being friendly fire from the US contingent of Coalition Forces.

The Americans themselves were taking hits on a daily basis in a conflict they could never win. Declaring a War on Terror may have played well at home on Fox News and CNN, but the very notion was a miscalculation. For every insurgent rendered inoperative, two more or five more or ten more were crossing the porous borders to fill the ranks. The same went for every civilian killed or tribesman embarrassed while being body-searched in front of his family. The next morning would see dozens more recruits to the insurgency.

It was easy to forget, and even American colonels and oilmen I knew sometimes forgot, that we had come to Iraq to oust their wicked dictator and remove his weapons of mass destruction (WMD). We were *not* an occupying force safeguarding the second largest oil reserves on the planet. We were rebuilding Iraq to bring security to the Iraqis.

I imagine that's why a hefty 30 per cent of that first $87 billion reconstruction package was for security and why there were more than 15,000 private contractors in Iraq when I arrived; about 10,000 from the UK in various companies; ex-Special Forces Americans, Australians, South Africans; no French firms but a motley assortment of Frenchmen, and there was the usual bunch of adventurers who looked as if they'd stepped off the set of *Apocalypse Now*.

The number would double, as would the number of un-armed civilian contractors rebuilding the country. At that time, an extraordinary 100,000 people were employed in Iraq by reconstruction company KBR, a branch of the American giant Halliburton, CEO'd once upon a time by the US Vice-President Dick Cheney. War was being privatised. It made perfect sense.

Al Qaeda and radical Islamists had been banned under Saddam. Now, they were flocking into the country, praying in the mosques, intoxicating themselves with jihadi zeal and dreaming of the seventy virgins said to greet martyrs in heaven the day they die. Iraq was on the slippery slope to chaos. October had come with a welcome respite from the oven heat of a long summer and I had a feeling that with the cool the chaos would deepen.

We had armed ourselves during the two weeks I'd been in Iraq with whatever we could lay our hands on. The quest for ordnance would be ongoing throughout my eighteen months in Baghdad. In the meantime, we packed four Browning pistols and two Austrian Glocks, the latter a prestige side arm in South Africa so our Afrikaners were ecstatic. We had acquired a pair of RPD light machine guns made in Egypt, a weapon which first appeared in the Korean War in the 1950s and was carried by Fidel Castro and Che Guevara into the Cuban Revolution. We had binned the bipods to reduce the weight, chopped four inches from the butts and cut the barrels down, leaving four inches beyond the gas port to allow enough pressure to cycle the weapons. More powerful PKM machine guns had been available but due to their bulkiness in covert vehicles, and the short engagement ranges we anticipated within the urban Baghdad area, we had opted for the RPDs instead. We had tried and discarded a sorry assortment of faulty Iraqi AKs that hadn't inspired confidence at around $100 a piece and instead acquired some Romanian and other Eastern Bloc AKs that cost up to $350 and were far tastier. Like Germans with coffee brands, you quickly become an AK connoisseur.

Iraqi munitions described perfectly the Iraqi army. It was hardly surprising the third biggest military force on the planet was overrun in three weeks. The soldiers were mainly petrified conscripts who had laid down their weapons the moment they saw the Stars and Stripes on the horizon. It wasn't a war, as one American colonel had told me, it was a cakewalk. Having said that, I was pretty sure he hadn't been with the frontline grunts who had watched their mates bleed and die on the long road up from Kuwait. Maybe doing a few night patrols through Sadr City would have given him a sense of reality.

Only the Republican Guard and the Fedayeen Saddam had put up a decent stand. Those who escaped the coalition offensive were the battle-hardened veterans leading the insurgency and were now generally known as the 'fedayeen' by Coalition Forces. There were a few foreign fighters, but the majority were home-grown Iraqis.

Seamus Hayes, our team commander, was still trying numbers on the cellphone. The American MCI network was dodgy at the best of times. It would be more than six months into the new year before the Iraqi network was up and running, to the delight of Western contractors and Iraqi insurgents both. He shook the MCI violently.

'Piece of shit,' he said, his gruff voice lifting the sour mood somehow. 'I'll try the Thuraya,' he added, and stamped out to get the satellite phone. He would need a clear view of the sky for it to work.

Les Trevellick pointed at the exit and made his way out to join Seamus. I listened as his footsteps receded.

I took one more look around before joining the rest of the group outside.

It was surprisingly cool. The air tasted ancient and dusty. I could hear the sound of birds over the hum of traffic on the main highway. While Seamus was abusing the satellite phone, I was absently wondering what to prepare for dinner that night. It was my turn to cook.

Far fewer emotions were surfacing in my mind than might be expected. Emotions, fears and feelings are all buried away in the deepfreeze, ready to be thawed out when you need them. The type of character who dwells on the thousand and one ways one could get killed or maimed in Iraq doesn't last long in the job. The average security contractor tends to concentrate any intellectual focus on close observation of potential threats in the immediate area, combined with as much forward planning and anticipation as possible. That and the sad choice between lamb or chicken, and I was bored to tears with roast lamb.

I made eye contact with Hendriks as he stepped out of the space between the two vehicles. He shrugged as if to say, 'What the hell's going on?' and I returned the gesture.

'What's up?'

'Fuck-up,' I said and he smiled.

Hendriks was one of the three South Africans keeping guard over the Opel and Nissan Patrol 4×4. With seventy years' experience between them fighting bush wars in Namibia, Angola and Mozambique I imagined it would take a regiment to wrest the vehicles from their hands. Hendriks and Cobus had RPD light machine guns out with the belts loaded. Cobus had his propped on the bonnet of the Nissan and was slowly scanning the terminal building. Hendriks had his RPD on its sling at his hip. Etienne was in the driver's seat in the 4×4 humming along to Bing.

The company you keep takes care of any feelings of fear. The raised pulse is the adrenaline kicking in and what I felt most as I continued passing my gaze over the rooftops was a sense of frustration. We were in the wrong place at the wrong time. Someone had screwed up. Looking on the bright side, at least I knew it wasn't the guys I was with.

Seamus Hayes, with his toned muscles and icy stare, was the archetypal professional soldier who had done fourteen years with the Paras, leaving as a Colour Sergeant. He knew his stuff. So did Les; he was stamped from the same mould, a former Royal Engineer Staff Sergeant who had done both the Para and Commando course and had been an instructor on the latter. They were men just into their forties, British soldiers of the old school and as hard as coffin nails.

As for myself, I was used to giving orders and ready to react when things went bad. I'd had the brass on my shoulders after passing out of the 'chap factory', as we called Sandhurst, and had been relieved to see that under contact from the enemy during operational tours I had remained calm and focused. Did Seamus and Les have the same leadership skills? Would they be watching my back when the bullets were flying?

Damn right they would.

It was a relief to be out of that office and working with men who knew what they were doing. In the world of private security, ex-sergeants and ex-officers were keen to know a man's prior rank because it revealed their skills in a single word. Reading a guy's CV told you the rest: he was a sniper, for example, a jungle or arctic warfare instructor, or both. You knew with British soldiers and Royal Marines that you were with a modern-day Tommy Atkins and could have complete confidence. In a hostile environment, in my experience, Brits consistently displayed qualities of character, loyalty, toughness and humour that could get you out of most trouble spots as well as giving Johnny Foreigner a damned good hiding at the same time. After all, as an Empire we had ruled the world once, hadn't we?

Speaking of colonies, I glanced back at the South Africans.

Our Afrikaners all had big families and were paying off their mortgages; bonds they called them. They had no employment future in the new South Africa and had taken to the life of soldiers for hire. Etienne and Cobus were fair-skinned, ruddy-faced typical Boers with moustaches and blond hair. Etienne was a bluff, cheerful, naïve man and a devout Christian. Cobus, the youngest, was the prankster of the group. Hendriks was sharp and cynical. He had short cropped brown hair, a scarred face with skin burned black by the African sun and cold grey eyes like chips of frost. The trio were utterly reliable and crack shots with anything that fired bullets. We Brits were more than happy to point out that that was because in their backward country if they didn't hit what they shot their families went hungry. An old joke that brought a satisfied smile to Hendriks's face every time he pocketed his winnings from our team's weekly shooting competition. I had lost ninety dollars to him in the last two weeks. Dai Jones, a Welshman who was back in the UK on leave, had lost twice that amount and he had been a British Army sniper.

Six of us at an empty airport.

Contractors, that was us, and although there was nothing in the contract about regimental spirit or patriotic duty, there was definitely a high standard of team loyalty and personal pride in one's skills. We avoided the word mercenary with its villainous connotations and clothed ourselves in new acronyms – we were a PSD on CP: a Private Security Detail on Close Protection. This was a new kind of conflict. A new kind of war. We were writing the rules as we went along.

It was basic maths: that with more reporters covering Iraq, more were being killed and the media digging in their pockets for security was a bottomless new source of income for Spartan.

When thirteen Red Cross workers were killed in Afghanistan, the International Red Cross switched 20 per cent of its budget to security; other non-governmental organisations (NGOs) followed suit. The UN building in Baghdad had been bombed in August. A week later, the HQ of the Red Cross would also be blown up. In this war, the enemy would accept no one as neutral. Not journalists, Christian peacekeepers, not humanitarian aid workers. For security companies it looked as if business would be very good indeed.

High-ranking US officers, even Coalition supremo Ambassador Paul Bremer, were using private contractors to chaperone them around Baghdad because the US government lacked adequate Special Forces to do the job. As war goes private, a nation's defence capabilities become less important than its security arrangements, especially for the people who matter. Tony Blair's holiday destination in summer 2005 was top secret. Hollywood stars, Saudi princesses and the Beckhams can't shop without bodyguards. There was a time when the rich would say, 'I'll send my butler,' when there was something urgent to attend to. Now they send their SAS man.

We had rehearsed our drills and bonded over barbecues with crates of black-market lager and Johnnie Walker, swinging the lantern and swapping campfire tales of old battles. There had been some confusion when Hendriks kept referring to his battles in 'Vambuland'. Upon questioning he clarified unhelpfully that this was 'the land of the Vambus'. When we were still none the wiser, he informed us that it was also known as South West Africa.

'Namibia, you mean?'

'*Ja*, that is what the blacks call it now.'

We slapped our sides and refilled our glasses.

Now the team was in the field for the first time I had every reason to believe we were a team and not just a bunch of chancers. The South Africans seemed solid. The Brits I knew were reliable. As the months passed and I came into contact with many more contractors, I would meet some good guys, good at their jobs, as well as some total losers, and would come to appreciate how lucky we were to have our particular Afrikaners. They were bloody amazing cooks for a start.

'What the fuck's going on –'

Seamus had finally got through to HQ on the satellite phone and was giving someone an earful. I removed my shades and as I gave the lenses a polish I gathered through the barrage of invective we'd been sent to the civilian airport in error. Turns out there was a military side to the airport and we now had detailed directions how to get there.

No big deal. But in my experience, when things start out bad, even just a tad, they tend to get worse.

TWO

We piled into the vehicles and skirted the perimeter fence heading for the military airfield on the other side.

Seamus was in a bad mood. 'Give it some gas, *Rupert*,' he said and I dropped a gear and put my foot down.

I was driving the Opel, Seamus at my side, Les in the rear. The Yaapies were in the Nissan behind; there was no discrimination in this, no apartheid, it was just easier for them to be able to speak their own language. We called the South Africans Yaapies, pronounced 'Yar' – as in 'yard' – because they were very agreeable guys who said *Ja, Ja*, no matter what the question, no matter what the answer. For some reason, young British officers got the moniker *Rupert*, which was unfortunate if you happen to be named Rupert.

We screamed to a halt at the Coalition Forces checkpoint where a pair of soldiers from 82nd Airborne, who looked about twelve years old, chewed their gum as they checked out our Ray-Bans and Oakleys with a lot more interest than our IDs.

'Have a good one,' said one of the guys and waved us through.

'Fuck me, does his mum know he's out here?' asked Les as we drove off.

It was another ten-minute drive through the sprawling environs of Camp Bristol, Camp Slayer and Camp Victory, named I'm told without irony. GIs with tattoos and jackets tied around their waists, were shooting hoops, tossing balls, smoking and looking bored. War's a cakewalk, the colonel had said to me, but bringing democracy to the lucky people of Iraq was going to cost – money, time and lives. There were almost 10,000 soldiers based at the airport, where the containers stamped Department of Defense and the prefab warehouse full of army issue coffins gave a distinct feeling of permanence. There were few planes that we could see, compared with the number of land forces, and the big Abram M1 tanks were lined up as if ready for the apocalypse.

By the time we reached the military airport we were long overdue and a solitary woman was waiting outside on the tarmac with two pieces of luggage at her feet and a cigarette burning in the crook of her fingers. I leapt out of my seat looking contrite the moment I stopped.

'Lori Wyatt?' I asked.

'That's me.'

'James Ashcroft. Spartan,' I said. 'We're late, I'm so sorry.'

She glanced at the two vehicles and the six of us manning them.

'It happens,' she replied, and stamped out her cigarette.

Lori Wyatt was a slender brunette of around thirty with pixie hair and inquisitive dark eyes. She was looking relaxed in sand-coloured cargo pants and a tan safari jacket. She had a deep, East Coast accent and was by far the most attractive woman I'd seen in Iraq since I'd crossed the desert from Jordan three weeks before with Les Trevellick and an Iraqi driver who drove with the gritty determination of the deranged.

Lori had hitched a ride out of Kuwait on a military transport plane. She had covered the aftermath of the war in Afghanistan for Associated Press and was in Iraq on the same kind of assignment, not embedded, which gave her less access but greater freedom, although freedom in a limited sense. All news from Iraq was filtered through a soft-focus lens. Journalists may have wanted to get to the heart of the story, but had neither the time nor the autonomy to make lasting contacts and interview the insurgents to tell their side of the story. What drives young men to leave their own country and become suicide bombers in Baghdad? There were probably as many answers as there were volunteers but the big picture, the underlying cause, had yet to be fully explored. Reporters who got too close ended up being kidnapped, ransomed or beheaded for Internet snuff movies.

Lori travelled with a laptop, a satellite phone and a Bergen, a hiker's rucksack – lightweight kit. With the introductions sorted, Les slung the gear in the back of the Opel. Just as Lori was a stunner, Les Trevellick was something of a ladies' man and grabbed his place in the back seat beside her. When we had told him he was going to be the nominated bodyguard for the job we had not expected Lori to be quite as attractive.

As I fired the engine, he began his briefing.

'Nothing is going to happen, but if it does, just do exactly what I say. You get down flat. Make yourself as small as possible. You only move if I tell you to move.' He softened his voice. 'Don't worry about a thing, I'll look after you, all right, love?'

'Got it,' she said.

Les took a Glock from the pocket behind the driver's seat. 'Are you familiar with firearms?'

'No. And I don't want to be,' she replied. 'It makes us a target.'

In the first two years of the 'peace' in Iraq, more journalists would be killed than in twenty years of guerrilla war in Vietnam and five years of civil war in Yugoslavia. New millennium. New war. New rules.

'If you've got a white face you're a target,' Les told her and we all took a beat to wonder if she truly realised what she had got herself into.

I was driving slowly through the shuffling army of off-duty soldiers back to the checkpoint where the guys chewing gum waved us straight out on to the BIAP road, the Baghdad International Airport Highway, or Route Irish, to give the road its military designation. This was the main feeder highway into the west of the city and stretched between the US beachhead at the BIAP and the Coalition Provisional Authority. It was the most dangerous stretch of road in the world and despite a massive deployment of Coalition troops and armour, people were dying on this road every day.

The sky was low and oppressive, the same dull, uniform grey it was every day. 'Reminds me of bloody Dartmoor,' Les had said on our journey from Jordan. I had expected to see blue skies, especially in the desert, but the wind whips the dust into the air and spins it into a fine layer that hangs over Iraq like a veil.

Highways from airports in the developing world are often wide, well made and designed to impress visiting dignitaries. Route Irish was no exception. Along each side of the road there was waste ground and scrubby bush. The nearest buildings were between 100 and 200 metres away, terraces of three-storey blocks with flat roofs in muddy brown, the same colour as the local stone, the same as every building in the city.

There were flyovers crisscrossing the highway, the cement ramparts ideal for mounting an assault or dropping unpleasant items on Westerners driving underneath. The principal danger was close-quarter attacks from other vehicles or from an IED (improvised explosive device) planted on the side of the road: a buried artillery shell, a parked or abandoned car packed with explosives, or a device concealed in debris, a dead dog, tumbleweed, a plastic bag, of which there was an endless supply skipping across the open spaces.

Most of the locals were incredibly ignorant, but I never confused this for a lack of intelligence. Over the next year we would see the insurgents move from basic IED attacks on Coalition cordons to more complex, well-planned ambushes with multiple elements, secondary shoots and additional IEDs or mortars. What we had seen the IRA over the water develop during thirty years of the Troubles would be learned by the jihadis in a matter of months.

In an urban environment the thing to expect is to be hit anywhere in a 360° arc, another lesson learned in Northern Ireland, where I had been shot at for the first time and discovered that it isn't so bad as long as you hear it coming. Soldiers are told to welcome the sound of explosions and incoming shots, the premise being that, if you can still hear, the enemy must have missed, so you are alive and free to react and fire back.

Along some sections of the highway the undergrowth was dense enough to conceal rebel bands who opened up on the traffic with RPGs (rocket-propelled grenades) and machine guns. Another danger was the have-a-go Johnny who had grown fed up with the occupation and was taking pot shots with an old Kalashnikov normally used for weddings, although the traditional wedding day gun salute was dying out in Baghdad after a number of patrols had mistaken the festivities for attacks and returned fire, killing brides and guests alike.

Then they wonder why the insurgency was growing rather than flagging.

In close-quarter attacks on the road, it is awkward getting the long barrel of a rifle up to the window; you lose a second and you can lose your life. With the stock folded, our AKs were only just short enough to be usable as car weapons. To save time, Seamus had the safety selector set to fire and his rifle muzzle rested on the crack between dashboard and door, ready for him to flip it up to either windscreen or the side with a flick of the wrist.

To prepare the team for any eventuality, Seamus, as convoy commander, was giving a running commentary on the radio to the Yaapie wagon with positions and approximate ranges when appropriate.

'*Abandoned vehicle left. Bodies in the fields, right 100 metres. Two piles of rubbish right. Dead dog right. Bridge 200 metres. Bridge is clear. Two kamikazes left . . .*'

Lori started, 'Jeez, what the hell?' Two cars were on the wrong side of the road speeding directly towards us.

I angled sharply into another lane and looped back into the middle as they passed. Etienne at the wheel of the 4 × 4 did the same, like a shadow always exactly two metres from my back bumper.

Les explained in his sardonic way that a kamikaze was a local driver who had chosen to drive on the part of the road that appealed to him at that particular moment. It made journeys more interesting. If a driver had missed his turn, he'd just turn round and drive back against the flow of traffic; if someone had a flat tyre, they didn't pull over, they stopped in the middle of the highway and calmly changed the wheel ignoring the consequent chaos around them.

I could see the two speeders in the rearview mirror and thought it might be interesting to witness what would happen when they reached the trigger-happy Americans at the CF checkpoint travelling at high speed from the wrong direction.

Once Saddam fell from power, Iraqis became very touchy and literal over what freedom actually meant and concluded that they were free finally to do whatever they chose, whenever they chose, in any way they chose. If they felt like driving on the wrong side of the road like the Brits, who was going to stop them? Fights would break out in shops where people were now refusing to pay for groceries because they were 'free'.

Like the military, the police had been disbanded by the Americans, so reckless driving was the least of it. Petty crime, organised crime, profiteering, racketeering, extortion, arms and people trafficking, rape, pillage and kidnap for cash were all new career options. So was politics, but more dangerous.

As we passed under the bridge I swerved violently into another lane, eliciting a squeal from Lori. I had done this so that I would go under the flyover in one lane but emerge in another. The Yaapies performed the same manoeuvre with the addition of hanging out of the windows with rifles pointed up and back as they emerged, ready to gun down any enemy lurking on the bridge. Although we were driving with a covert profile, i.e. with mixed vehicles, not with two or three identical 4×4s in an obvious PSD packet, we had only just left the airport road and it would be obvious to anyone that we were connected to Coalition Forces.

Seamus was keeping up the commentary:

'*Merging traffic right, 100 metres. Group of kids right. Big plastic bag left. Two women carrying gas cylinders, right . . .*'

Gas cylinders are heavy, even when empty, but the local women carried them miles for refills. You saw women working in the fields in the blazing sun, women carrying prodigious loads of firewood on their backs; stocky, thick-bodied women who managed to remain graceful carrying urns of water on their heads, their young daughters with mini-urns, learning from the age of three that if there was work to be done or something to be carried, the women do it. The men grow fat and spend their time chatting, smoking and drinking sickly sweet *chai*.

As we passed the two women with gas cylinders, one of

them put hers down and started rolling it, kicking it with her sandalled feet.

Seamus continued scripting the way ahead, keywords warning the rear driver what to expect in about five seconds. He described everything as left and right. As the rear gunner was facing backwards, watching our backs, it is natural to get mixed up, so pasted on each side of his rear window frame there were big signs with LEFT and RIGHT reversed to remind him to look in the direction of the sign.

Like sex and comedy, as Les liked to say, PSD driving required a keen sense of timing. The lead driver would only take openings when there was space for both vehicles, or all three vehicles in a three-car packet. The rear driver would stay on your tail through hell if that was en route and would not allow queue-jumpers to squeeze in the gap.

The Opel and Nissan were dusty white vehicles indistinguishable from the stream of Iraqi cars on both sides of the road and we soon blended into the flow. We had chosen not to have an overt signature as Westerners, in contrast to some PSDs that imitated the military patrols and barged through the traffic with horns blaring and ears deaf to the Arabic blasphemy that followed in their wake. An ambush group would spot these miles away and be ready to engage by the time they passed.

With the threat of suicide bombers months in the future, our main danger was from an IED or the fedayeen armed with RPGs. We were more than happy to use the local traffic as cover if need be and by the time any locals realised we were Westerners we would be right next to them. And Jacky the Iraqi doesn't like close-quarter shootouts, not if he's looking into the cold grey eyes of Hendriks ready to gun him down like a tribe of Vambus.

There is an odd contradiction inside your head when you are on the job. You are concentrating fully, instincts buzzing, but at the same time, you can find yourself daydreaming about the past and future. With the constant threat of danger, the fact that there are men out there who want to kill you, there is a need for normality and a part of your mind would be running through silly, personal things like the pink smears on Krista's cheeks that day when she painted Natalie's bedroom.

I was musing, too, on my prospects with Spartan. I was content to start at the bottom as a hired gun. With my kind of background: public school, Oxford and Sandhurst, ex-officers often expected to walk into jobs and instantly be the boss. That's the way it had always been. But the War on Terror was a new kind of war and the operatives who rose to management prominence on the Circuit were going to be men who had not merely proved themselves in the field, men with soldiering skills and training, but those who also possessed the business acumen to gouge profitable contracts from the project managers of their client companies or governments.

Did I have these two different and vital talents?

There was no way of knowing, but if I was going to pursue this life as a career, I would want to move speedily from the guns and jeeps sector to project management, risk assessment, due diligence and – the *crème de la crème* of the security game – fraud investigation.

I was maintaining a steady speed, watching for kamikazes, IEDs, escape routes, boys on lookout; 'dickers' as we Brits called them. Cellphones would come online in the coming months. The mobile was the modern equivalent of smoke signals; crucial to the new generation of terrorists and a key tool in the Madrid train bombings six months later. They had said Al Qaeda was a spent force, but it had done what it had set out to do and its influence was growing as far as I could see, not diminishing.

We carried a couple of remote-control car transmitters with a switch taped permanently on SEND with the hope that any remote-controlled bombs would be detonated before we got to them. We had heard that some CF units had had good results with transmitters, but we had yet to set anything off. Terrorists tend to use the same frequency bands as toy manufacturers when they are unable to build more sophisticated devices; if they used normal radio frequencies the device would detonate as soon as anyone in the area used a radio, often when the bomb was still being set by the hapless bomber. We were aware that carrying remote-control car transmitters was a cheap trick and had a limited lifespan. The enemy was learning fast and would move quickly to more sophisticated transmitters and detonation initiation methods.

While Seamus at my side and Les in the back were focused on potential threats, I was keeping an eye out for access routes for my vehicle in case of trouble. The kerbs were high and although the 4 × 4 could mount them and go off road, the Opel wouldn't have a hope.

In the event of a contact we had agreed a predetermined set of horn blasts to alert the rear driver what action to take: one blast meant the lead vehicle was disabled and (as long as the driver remembered to stick it into neutral) expected the rear vehicle to shunt it forward through any obstacle or at least out of the danger area. Two blasts told the rear driver that both vehicles were to turn around and head back in the opposite direction. Three blasts was the signal to de-bus, suppress the enemy with fire if required and await orders on the ground, which would either be to commandeer a local vehicle or house, or to withdraw on foot in a direction chosen by the team commander.

Straps were attached to towing points on both vehicles at all times and spare tyres were always the last thing to be loaded; easy to discard and for quick access when needed. We had agreed that the 4 × 4 would pull into the danger zone during any contact, and either block the traffic or shield the front vehicle from incoming fire with its own chassis and protect the principal by putting down a shitload of return fire from its two belt-fed guns.

Good security requires prior preparation, planning and drills combined with training, stamina, shooting practice, intuition, an eye for detail and physical strength coupled with an instinct for knowing when to use it. You have to know your maps, the local geography and conventions.

For example, if you are driving in the UK, you don't eyeball other drivers. It's impolite. In Iraq, it was the national pastime. On the street, people would stop and stare. On the road, old men cleaned their specs, women peered over their veils (guess they don't see men as good-looking as us that often) and entire carloads of people would lean forward and gaze unblinkingly until you were out of sight.

As the driver in the lead vehicle, I was observing the custom, scrutinising everyone and looking for likely terrorists, which was a problem as most of the men looked exactly how you would expect terrorists to look: fierce and tribal with chequered headcloths, hard eyes and beards. Every man and boy over the age of thirteen had a moustache, a sign of masculinity, and something I couldn't help finding amusing: a whole nation of Saddam Hussein lookalikes. You had to get used to the fact that not everyone was a terrorist.

THREE

I had allowed that evil insect doubt to creep into my mind during the initial screw-up at the empty airport. Now, everything was flowing along as it should be, even the traffic on Route Irish.

I was aware of the reassuring lump of the 9mm Browning on my chest; it was stuffed into a spare mag pouch as it was easier to draw from than the thigh rig while I was driving. My 'long', the AK, was stuffed between my left leg and the door, useless to me unless we de-bussed. My job was to drive not shoot. If an enemy did happen to pop up at my window I would use the 9 milly to give him the good news.

Seamus's brand of army cockney resonated over the radio.

'*Two geezers, 100 right. Static car 100 feet left. Derelict building 200 metres right.*'

His stream of observations was interrupted by Cobus in the Yaapie wagon.

'US patrol apprroachink vrom da rear.'

I hit the brakes and skidded into the dust at the side of the road along with the rest of the cars.

An armoured command vehicle and three soft Humvees raced by at about 100 *klicks* down the middle of the road. The gunners on the Humvees were exposed in open hatches, their weapons trained left and right, front and rear. They were blasting their horns and Iraqi traffic peeled over to the side like the Red Sea parting. They had learned that non-compliance resulted in warning bursts followed quickly by disabling bursts. Sometimes so quickly, in effect, that there was actually just one long burst of fire.

Lori seemed shaken by the sudden halt. 'Do they have to do that?' she asked.

'It's standard procedure,' said Les.

'That's why the locals hate us,' Lori remarked. 'It's the same in Kabul.'

'At least they're clearing the road for us,' Les explained. 'If there are any ragheads planning to take a pop at the cars, they'll hit the patrol first.'

Lori was taking it all in. I caught her eyes for a moment in the rear-view mirror. I couldn't believe that Les had been picked randomly to be bodyguard that day.

An old man on a donkey cart glided by, oblivious, as I pulled back on to the highway, Etienne on my tail. Dust swirled through the air. I could taste grit in my mouth even though my window was only down an inch. I would almost have preferred rain to clean the air, but in a desert country unused to rainfall there was no drainage and the roads flooded instantly, hence the high kerbs.

Before we were back up to speed, the rest of the traffic curved off the exit ramp leading into the city and we carried straight on through a channel of NO ENTRY signs. The road narrowed and twisted through concrete blocks laid out in traffic-controlling chicanes.

Seamus taped the plastic, A4-sized American flag in the windscreen; the South Africans would be doing the same. We didn't show the flags when we were on the open road.

As I snaked my way through the concrete barriers towards the Green Zone I recalled that ten women and children had been shot to pieces a week before when the van they were in failed to stop at an entry gate. The driver had ignored the US soldier's hand signals and had continued moving towards the checkpoint. 'We're sorry about that, but there's bound to be some spillage,' US General Richard Myers was reported to have said.

Collateral damage had become spillage and either way it meant more dead innocents.

The road swung in a final curve and Gate 12 came into view. 'Nearly home,' Les said to Lori.

This was the BIAP road's main access to the Green Zone. The BIAP Gate consisted of two checkpoints, 40 metres apart, one for entry and one for exit; they were part of the one-way system. Across the concrete barricades to our left, a line of cars were exiting. The process was slow.

A disused flyover, also on our left, was pressed tight against the BIAP exit gate. Beyond the flyover stood a long terrace of three-storey, flat-roofed buildings. Like many buildings in Baghdad, they seemed abandoned, half built or half demolished, the washing hanging from windows and the occasional potted magnolia adding a melancholic air. The building nearest the gate was a concrete skeleton gutted in the war.

To our right was a wall and beyond stood a derelict palace bombed during the invasion and needing severe restoration. I could tell that Les's sapper heart was dying to get out there and put a decent roof on the place.

With the disused flyover crossing the road between the gates and good cover from the buildings, this entry point was popular with the insurgents and had been hit so many times the guards had learned to shoot first and answer questions later.

The gates were each manned by a squad of six US soldiers supported by M1 Abrams battle tanks with mine-clearing bulldozer blades bolted to the front and pet names scrawled down the barrels in white paint; 'Al Qaeda Killer' and 'Al Capone' were normally on the gate but today two different tanks were on duty.

About 100 metres behind each checkpoint, well inside the Green Zone, both facing down the highway towards us, were two Bradley M2 armoured fighting vehicles crewed by a commander, gunner and driver, and capable of carrying six battle-ready infantrymen in the stuffy interior. If a rebel driver did get through either one of the gates, he'd be going head to head with an M1 and a Bradley.

I was crawling along, aware of the glint of binoculars above the turret on the nearest Abrams. The American flag moved leisurely on the breeze, the guards observing our approach.

At the exit gate, a car facing the wrong way had stopped and appeared to be trying to enter against the flow of traffic. The guards were waving the car away, directing it towards the correct gate, towards us.

Suddenly, the driver leapt from the vehicle and sprinted away, weaving between the stopped cars waiting to be waved forward by the troops. The sprinter headed towards the buildings. He was running fast, but the scene appeared to be in slow motion and in silence.

The silence ended with a terrific explosion as the car vanished in a violent cloud of smoke and flame.

I was momentarily deafened.

The soldiers at the far exit gate instantly disappeared and I wasn't sure if they had taken cover behind the earth-filled chest-high Hesco barriers or whether they had been blown back by the blast. Either way they were not doing anything constructive at that moment.

The car bomb was followed instantly by small arms fire from the flat-roofed buildings.

My hearing had obviously come back because I could hear the whine of ricochets in the still air. The muzzle flashes came from inside the rooms which told me two things: these guys had had some training, they weren't just leaning out of the windows and shooting wildly; and they were firing AKs, guns notorious for their muzzle flash.

We were the only vehicles on our side of the road. Neither the Opel nor the Nissan were armour-plated. As this thought ran through my mind and I prepared to gun the engine to get us out of there, Seamus gave a different order . . .

'De-bus!' he yelled.

He was diving out of the door as he spoke. He rolled over several times, his AK trained on the buildings. First rule when there's enemy contact is to return fire. You match aggression with aggression. Various studies say that the initiative in firefights is won in the first three to five seconds.

I gave three toots on the horn to warn the South Africans to de-bus, then scrambled out behind Seamus dragging my AK.

In my haste, the Browning slipped from the mag pouch and clattered on to the road. I ignored it. I dashed to cover behind the concrete blocks and opened up on the windows from where I had seen the sparks of muzzle flash. If you hit the enemy that's a bonus. The British Army constantly drills in emphasis on aimed fire and the use of sights, even during suppressive fire. Even if you don't hit anyone, there had better be enough lead thumping whatever cover the enemy has to stop him from sticking his head up, which allows you to retain control of the firefight.

Etienne pulled up to cover our left. In this way, the Nissan would act as a blocking vehicle and would avoid us becoming the inviting target of vehicles in a straight line. As the South Africans piled out of their vehicle, I judged that they were just on the edge of the killing area: the arcs of fire coming from the buildings.

Les hauled Lori out of the car like a sack of potatoes. She wasn't screaming and seemed in control. She clung to Les as he dragged her behind the front tyre and engine block, the safest place. She spread out on her stomach, hands over her head. Les straddled her, knees either side of her shoulders, his body protecting her torso, his AK trained on the rooftops as he looked for a target.

Short bursts of fire peppered the wall behind us but I didn't hear any hits on our two vehicles. Vehicles are bullet magnets and although our standard drill was to get away from them as fast as possible, in this situation there simply wasn't anywhere to go. At least we had the cover of the low concrete barriers and Seamus and I were tucked up behind them.

A lot of security contractors had been killed in friendly fire and, as I glanced around the killing zone, my main concern wasn't the insurgents, but the US soldiers on the gate and the gunners on the Abrams 100 metres away. The Abrams carries two 7.62 machine guns, a .50 cal heavy machine gun and, the main armament, a 120mm cannon with enough power to blow our little convoy off the road without leaving a grease spot behind.

As I was thinking about this, my thoughts appeared to provoke the Abrams commander. He released a single round from the .50 cal which exploded through the front windscreen and out of the rear window of the Opel with a colossal bang before disappearing down Route Irish at twice the speed of sound. If this had been a movie, the Stars and Stripes Seamus had taped on the screen would now have a neat hole in it, but the flag remained untouched on the surviving section of cracked glass.

The shell missed the Nissan. Etienne had done a good job parking.

I was partially deafened from the shooting and was hearing everything through the muffled filter that descends as soon as you fire your first shot without ear defenders, but I was *very* aware of the bullets cracking over my head from the other side of the road. Bullets shot *at you* have a completely different tone to the thousands of rounds I had fired down the range. The familiar smell of cordite flared in my nostrils.

Time goes into a strange state when your adrenaline is pumping. Only a few seconds had gone by, but those seconds were stretched like elastic. All your training and experience kicks in as the temperature heats up. Seamus and Les were shouting at the checkpoint, waving their CPA pass-holders and pointing at the enemy. They were obviously Westerners, but the air was full of dust, the day was grey, and the Americans were taking no chances.

I was counting rounds as I poured fire back at the enemy. It is a cliché to say that you never feel more alive than when you hear bullets whizzing by your ears, but it's true. Your back's wet. Your armpits are sopping. You're sweating but oddly cool. Your mind is racing as your training prioritises your actions and every second is charged with control and focus. When the next second may be your last, I would like to say that the present second is long and lusty and precious. But all you are really thinking about is your next magazine and *did I get that bastard or did he just drop into cover?*

Maybe at the very back of your mind there is a flitting promise to yourself that if you get out of this alive you'll go home to some shitty civilian job and never complain about being bored again. You are concentrating on keeping your front sights posted on the bad guys and your peripheral vision on the men at your side, shouting to co-ordinate your fire and your next potential move. It was bad news that we were stuck in the middle of the road with nowhere to move to. The good news was that the enemy was catching it far worse than us.

The Americans at the gate were under fire from the buildings, but they were anxious about us in case this was some ingenious twin-pronged assault. They could see that our weapons were pointed at the buildings, not them. But they had been trained to recognise AK-47s, the trademark terrorist weapon, and conditioned to open fire the moment they saw one.

We couldn't move towards the Americans. They would just gun us down without a second thought. I didn't really want Seamus to suggest heading back down Route Irish and out of the killing area, since there could well have been a cut-off group waiting for us, and there were no concrete blocks there either, just an empty road.

I estimated there were between eight and a dozen rebels in the buildings and an unknown number in the surrounding area. They had almost certainly worked out that we were foreign contractors, even if the Americans hadn't, and were beginning to lay down more accurate fire. There was at least one gunman at street level, probably the sprinter who had set off the car bomb. His rounds were hitting the concrete wall behind us. I reckoned that with the low standard of marksmanship, at the most we would take one hit, or maybe we'd get lucky and not take a hit at all.

Hendriks and Cobus were pouring fire into the buildings with their RPDs. Not to be outdone, after the initial shock period, a lull of several seconds, the US guard at the near gate opened up with his M249 light machine gun and shot up the row of cars stranded in front of the exit gate. He let off the entire 200-round box in one long burst, shattering windscreens and drilling holes in the vehicles that had survived the car bomb. In a few seconds the front few cars had turned into colanders. I remembered reading that for every 15,000 rounds of ammo the US military fires there is one fatality. This guy was doing his best to lower the average.

Tracer ricocheted into the air and I thought it would be a miracle if none of the civilians out there was hit. The people had either rushed from their vehicles into the buildings or were lying flat on the road with their hands over their heads. It was the rebels who had started the firefight, but the way the US troops had reacted would ensure that the families of the dead would blame the Americans and transfer their sympathies to the fedayeen. The people at home in the US may have believed the War on Terror would wipe out the insurgency but that day in October 2003 I was certain that it was going to get worse. A lot worse. This wasn't the end of the uprising. It was the beginning.

The soldiers on the near checkpoint were silent again. They must have been reloading. From the far checkpoint there was no fire at all. The soldiers were either dead or had been knocked unconscious from the car explosion. Either way, they remained ineffective throughout the contact.

Cobus and Hendriks were now firing controlled bursts into the windows on the top floor of the buildings. Seamus, from his cover behind the concrete blocks, was waving his mobile about hopelessly trying to get a reception. As was common in the city, especially around the CPA, which we suspected was filled with jamming equipment, our radio comms were down and we had been unable to send a contact report to our HQ.

Les and I, from our better viewpoint, snapped off shots whenever we saw a target. It was impossible to know if we had hit anyone. You think you have made a hit and he goes down, then later a gunman pops up from the same spot. Is it the same one or a new one?

My eyes flicked back and forth over the scene like I was following the erratic movements of a mosquito. The enemy sniper was well hidden, his shots now striking the road about three feet to my left and getting closer. The Americans at the near gate were back into it and were pouring fire into the apartment buildings. The noise was cacophonous, like a continual train crash.

I caught the barest flicker of movement above on the disused flyover 50 metres in front of us. I snapped off two rounds into the parapet.

'Up on the bridge,' I yelled over the racket to Les.

Three rebels popped up in baggy camouflage pants and *shemaghs*. They were young and ragged and could have been any faces in the crowd. They had obviously seen us approach down Route Irish but, hidden behind the parapet, had not known exactly where we had stopped.

The rebel in the centre carried an RPG on his shoulder. It cracked noisily as he released the rocket, but it was badly aimed and fired far too early. He was spooked by my shots, by the intoxication of the moment, and the rocket screamed over us, over the wall behind us, and exploded somewhere in the CPA near the ruined palace. The pounding of the launch and the detonation as it exploded behind us were almost instantaneous.

I trained my front sight on the insurgent on the left of the RPG gunner and squeezed the trigger as he was bringing his weapon to bear.

I gave him a triple tap.

He definitely went down as I saw the blood spray from one head shot; pure luck, I was trying to put all three in his chest.

Then I slotted the guy with the RPG.

At the same time, Les fired three rounds at the insurgent on the right.

As he went down, Les shot the guy with the RPG.

It was instantaneous. Like a drill. I shoot left to right. Les shoots right to left. It was the way we had been trained.

The rebel we had both shot remained standing, which gave me a spark of panic as we pumped rounds into him. It was incredible, these were 7.62mm rounds we were firing and bloody great lumps were coming off the guy but he was still fumbling with a new rocket trying to reload. I was aware that he was not a trained soldier, or he would have first dropped behind cover.

After five rapid rounds from myself and the same from Les, he finally fell.

I had been counting rounds and had got through half a mag.

FOUR

Civvies often ask if you enjoy killing people. They assume killing someone means wandering along the high street and slaughtering an innocent passer-by with a loving family at home. But it's not like that. The people I end up killing are always in the act of actively trying to kill me in some murderous, violent and agonising fashion. So, no, I don't enjoy killing people, but, yes, I feel great afterwards because I feel the initial and immediate exhilaration at realising that I am alive and that the man who tried to kill me has failed.

The other common mistake civvies make is that once they feel they 'understand' how I 'enjoy' combat, they assume that I must actively seek that thrill again and again. The only reply I have to that is that if a mother and her children are happy when they survive a terrifying car crash, that does not mean that she is going to load her babies into a new car and drive off at high speed looking for the next crash just so that she can re-experience the joy of survival all over again. This is the heart of the misconception people have about security. The purpose of the job is to avoid trouble, not look for it. But no matter how good you are, if trouble finds you, the other part of the job is to ensure that the bad guys don't try it again.

You may ponder more deeply on the act of taking another man's life, but if that time comes, it comes later. You may ask

yourself what you are doing there on an autumn day in
Baghdad, a privately hired contractor licensed to kill by the
United States Department of Defense. You may reassure
yourself that you are just a PSD doing essential security work
in the aftermath of a just war. You are bringing 26 million
Iraqis the gift of democracy. All these thoughts run through
your mind. You may dig them up later for review. Maybe you'll
just bury them deep as usual and, in the meantime, you're just
a guy having a very bad day at the office.

There was no more action on the flyover above us. Les and I
exchanged looks that lasted maybe a fraction of a second and
then looked back over our front sights.

As I focused again on the buildings, I realised I was smiling.

Something had been nagging away inside me for the last
three weeks: I had been afraid of being left behind. I wasn't
afraid of dying, not more than anyone else; not more than any
soldier. I was afraid of falling into the hands of this army of
religious zealots and getting my head cut off on TV.

It was chilling to contemplate and that brief nod from Les
Trevellick told me I wouldn't be left behind. If there was
absolutely no chance of escape a head shot from one of my
team-mates would make sure I wasn't taken alive.

It also occurred to me that any reservations Seamus and Les
may have had working with an untried Rupert would also have
gone. The kind of men who gravitate to security work tend to
be those who showed the best qualities when they were in the
military: determination, initiative, guts, pride, loyalty. Seamus
and Les would definitely be watching my back, the same as I
would be watching theirs.

Now, we were still being shot at and continued answering
fire with fire, picking out shadows that moved along the
rooftops, while the Yaapies were putting random bursts into
the flyover wall above.

I was reasonably certain the three insurgents we had shot
were dead but they were out of sight and there was no way to
be sure. When you hit an enemy you want them dead, none of
this shooting them in the leg rubbish; an injured man who is
still armed is still just as dangerous. I know I bloody would be.

'Magazine.'

I shouted this out to let the guys know that for the next few seconds I would be inoperative. I had shot perhaps 15 or 16 rounds from my second mag of 30, but during the lull it was time to change to a full mag. You don't keep firing until the last bullet, then change. If badness popped its ugly head up again I wanted a full mag good to go. I also scooped up my pistol, gave it a cursory wipe and holstered it on my thigh.

'Back in.'

Enemy fire was becoming untargeted and intermittent.

Les went through his mag-changing ritual. I could hear him saying to Lori, 'It's all right, love. It's over now.' She turned and half wriggled out from under him. There was dust on her cheeks and her dark eyes were shiny in the dull light.

Seamus had quit trying to get reception on his mobile and was giving a concise contact report to Ops on the Thuraya satellite phone.

The soldiers at the near checkpoint had finally stopped shooting up the buildings and traffic with their light machine guns.

Once the noise had died down, I could hear the familiar rumble of an armoured vehicle. I assumed at first that it was one of the Abrams, but then realised it was the Bradley on the other side of the highway nosing its way through the checkpoint to get a better view.

The fire from the buildings had fallen to no more than a sporadic shot or two. We could not see the firing point, and as the Americans were not firing back, then it was probably just shots let off into the air as the rebels fled to fight another day. Only the dead were left. Amazingly about a hundred civvies in the middle of the road were still alive and started raising their heads from the tarmac. They began to stand up, but shouts from the American soldiers got them to change their minds and they laid back down again.

'I dink vee got three confirmed,' shouted Cobus to us.

'Glad you managed to learn something in Bongo Bongo,' shouted Les.

'If vee don't hit vot vee shoot vee don't eat,' shouted Cobus, repeating our own joke.

'Speak the bloody Queen's, will you. Christ, do this lot come with subtitles?'

'*Ja. Ja. Ja.* The Queen's Own Bloody English vee kick out of Africa. Vee kick the bloody Rooinek ass.'

The Americans had their weapons trained on the buildings and their binoculars trained on us. I was relieved they weren't listening in on this outburst of banter, the release of tension that comes after a contact.

I used this moment to crawl back in the car for my daysack. In the front pouch there were two four-foot flags: a Stars and Stripes and a Union Jack. By the time I got back out of the Opel, Seamus had come to his feet and was brandishing his pass at the Americans. I unrolled Old Glory, stepped away from the car and waved the flag for all I was worth.

The Bradley had stopped and two soldiers popped out of the vehicle to take a look at us. One of the guards at the checkpoint had his M249 trained on us and the gunner on the Abrams, safely buttoned up inside his tank, still had the long barrel of the main armament pointed in our direction. The squat armoured vehicle was like a giant insect emerging out of the dust and smoke. A fucking huge, monstrous insect the size of a whale.

Seamus took a few steps forward, removed the CPA pass from around his neck and held it up again.

'We're British,' he shouted.

'Freeze. Don't fucking move, motherfucker,' came the reply.

'Listen, you wanker. We're British. We're coming in.'

'Don't fucking move,' shouted the American.

It seemed like half an hour had gone by since the start of the shooting but it was probably no more than five minutes. My pulse was racing and as I stood there in the open with the US flag I began to visualise hordes of hostile Iraqis pouring out of the buildings and regrouping around the backstreets ready for another assault. I had watched this scene in Ridley Scott's film *Black Hawk Down* and the image had printed itself on my mind like a photograph.

I gave the flag another flutter, all to no effect. As far as I could see, we had three lousy options: (1) sit in the middle of the killing area with no cover and wait for either the enraged

horde to arrive or for this dickhead at the gate to calm down
and realise that we are on the same side; (2) get back in the
vehicles, swing under the bridge through the killing area, shoot
past the Bradley on the far gate with its deadly 25mm and
drive off into Baghdad to circle around to another gate; (3)
reverse back down Route Irish, the most dangerous road in the
world, hoping that the enemy cut-off group had scarpered,
catch lunch at Burger King in Camp Victory and come back
later.

Seamus must have been contemplating the same options.

He shouted to the American corporal: 'We are going to get
back in the vehicles and drive away. Don't shoot.'

As he made his way towards the Opel, the guard at the
checkpoint sent a couple of warning shots cracking over our
heads. Lori was on her feet. She screamed, but at the same time
her hands were busy unclasping a pouch at her waist. I then
heard the click and buzz of her digital camera as she snapped
off picture after picture of the contact area. She was shaken but
doing her job. Good girl.

'I said, freeze you motherfucker!'

It was a standoff. The guard had told us to freeze and we
stood there, sweating like pigs.

It should have been blatantly obvious that we were security
contractors: six white men, four of our number with fair hair.
We were wearing bulletproof vests, thigh rigs and Ray-Bans,
Western trappings shunned by the holy warriors waging *jihad*.

But we were carrying Kalashnikovs and the guys doing the
peacekeeping were taking no chances. They had fought their
way across the desert from the Kuwaiti border to Baghdad
City. They weren't exactly trigger-happy, but they were not
shy of letting loose with a few rounds if there was a sniff of
danger. They had seen their buddies get shot. Their president
had told them the war was over, and their buddies were still
getting shot. They knew about the coffins waiting at the
military airport and they didn't want to be going home in one.

Seamus was back on the Thuraya seeing if anyone in HQ
had comms with anyone in the CF who could come up to the
gate and sort this mess out. I gave the flag the occasional flick
and stood straight-backed, shoulders square, getting bored

with this impasse. I was relieved when a patrol of four
Humvees, the standard 4 × 4 vehicle used by the US forces,
came rolling round the chicanes behind us on Route Irish.

'Don't worry, love, here comes the cavalry,' I heard Les
saying, and I couldn't help wondering if Lori got the irony in
his tone.

What the Humvee drivers saw as they turned the last bend
was absolute carnage, trashed and smoking vehicles on the far
side of the road, dead bodies sprawled out, glass everywhere,
the Bradley looming over the checkpoint. And there we were,
armed with AKs with Americans on the gate pointing a battery
of guns at us.

I raised the flag as high as I could and gave it another jiggle as
the Humvees deployed in a zigzag. There was another intermis-
sion. This was normal. Everyone was being cautious. In South
Armagh, if you shoot two rounds from your rifle there's a
Board of Inquiry. The Americans don't bother with that sort of
thing in Iraq unless you raze a couple of towns. They had a
shoot-first policy, a shoot-first mindset. Still, they didn't want
to get a reputation for wiping out their allies with friendly fire.

As the Humvees stopped, the rear gunner was facing back
down Route Irish, the two middle gunners were pointing into
the buildings to their left and the gunner on the lead vehicle
was pointing his Mk19 grenade launcher straight at us.

The door on the lead Humvee cranked open and two US
soldiers climbed out, a black sergeant with four stripes on his
helmet and an Hispanic sergeant with three stripes. They took
a look at us, they studied the shot-up vehicles, they gazed at
the peppered buildings across the way, then the four-stripe
sergeant sauntered slowly towards us, alone, M16 pointing at
the ground.

'I'll take this,' I called to Seamus.

He nodded. It's normal. Security isn't top-heavy. Everyone
deals with outsiders at all levels from the dustman to government ministers.

The sergeant stopped about ten feet from me. He was closely
shaven with sparkling eyes like a Baptist minister. He was
wearing 3rd Infantry insignia and the name 'Willows' was
embroidered on a patch on his broad chest.

'You want to break out some ID?' he said.

I showed him my pass. 'We're escorting an American reporter into the zone, Staff Sergeant,' I explained.

'Uh-huh.'

He glanced at Lori. Les stood with his arms protectively around her shoulders.

'They're getting younger,' he said and I smiled. He continued, 'OK, that's no problem, sir. You probably had some hassle because these guys aren't used to dealing with civilian contractors and they have to shut the gates down if there is an incident. I'll go ahead and sort them out.'

A whole bunch of guys had climbed out of the Humvees, rifles covering their sergeant. He waved that everything was OK and they turned their rifles towards the street. He slung his rifle over his shoulder but I kept mine pointing left, just in case, you know, for the hordes from *Black Hawk Down*. We ambled unhurriedly towards the checkpoint.

'These guys are cool,' said Willows when we reached the gate, indicating us with a thumb.

The soldier behind the 249 didn't look too convinced, so I went into my Rupert routine and laid on a frightfully, frightfully accent.

'That was a very worrying contact,' I said. 'I do understand. We are under a lot of stress and I do so hope that everyone over here is all right. What I'd really like to do is get our principal inside. *An American reporter*,' I emphasised. *'She's really rather shaken.'*

The Americans usually responded to all this British stuff and I laid it on thick for good reason: I didn't want us to have to go through the standard procedure of them shutting down the gate and sending us to another entry point. With the delays in picking up Lori at the BIAP we were in real danger of missing free lunch in the CPA canteen.

Meanwhile down the road the commander on board the Abrams popped out of his hatch grinning and punched the air.

'Way to go!' he howled up at us.

Yeah, way to go, you tosser, I thought to myself. *You just fucked our windscreen.*

The guys on the checkpoint were jumpy still. They all looked frightened and very young and kept their weapons trained on our two-car package. They only calmed down when Willows finally said he was going to escort us in. I turned and circled my index finger rapidly: the sign for my people to prepare to mount up.

I walked back with Willows. This guy was in no hurry. He asked me how much we contractors earned. I assured him that I didn't get out of bed for less than two grand a day and that during the time it had taken to stroll back to our cars I had just earned another $100.

'War's good business,' he said.

Seamus was scooping out the glass from the Opel.

'Staff Sergeant Willows is going to escort us in,' I told him.

'Thanks, Sergeant.'

'Uh-huh,' he said.

Lori Wyatt was smiling, the danger forgotten. She had lived through a real gunfight in Baghdad and would get to write about it. She was writing something in her notebook that moment. I would learn later that it was the number of her satellite phone which she passed to Les. Les Trevellick, also known as Studley von Goodshag, scores again. Bastard.

When we reached the lead Humvee, I made a point of shaking Willows's hand and saying thanks to his men. I really felt for these guys; the 3rd Infantry were still taking huge numbers of casualties. A lot of GIs who had earned combat ribbons in the first Gulf War (1991) thought the second war was about the second Bush getting revenge for the errors of the first. They wanted to serve out their time and get home with a pension. The situation was even worse for the thousands of National Guardsmen who had never expected to be posted to Iraq and were there because they couldn't pay back their college loans to the army. You take the shilling and you serve your time.

Staff Sergeant Willows pulled himself up into his vehicle. I raced back to the Opel. Seamus climbed into the passenger seat and I got in beside him. The engine had been running the whole time.

'Nice one, Ash,' he said. Ash was my army nickname and that's what people called me when Krista wasn't around. She hated the army.

Two Humvees passed us and, with two CF vehicles front and rear, we were escorted the last 20 metres down Route Irish into the BIAP Gate.

I stopped and leaned out of the window. 'Thanks once again, gentlemen, I will see that you are highly commended in my report.' I flashed a winning smile at the guard on the gate.

Les had got his window down. 'You fucking cunts,' he bellowed. 'Couldn't you fucking see who we were? You blind cunts.'

Hank the Yank doesn't like the 'C' word. The soldier's face turned sour.

'Excuse me, sir –'

'Don't fucking stand around here with the *sir* bollocks,' said Seamus, leaning over me and shouting out of my window, 'you want to get up there into those buildings and make sure they're secure. Go and see if there's any fucking injured ragheads and bring 'em in as well as any weapons. See if there are any wounded civvies that need help. And get your arses over the road and see if your mates on the other fucking gate are all right.'

'As I said, thank you so much for your assistance,' I added, interrupting Seamus seamlessly. I was still beaming brightly at the soldier. 'Good day.' Before international relations were strained beyond breaking point, I put my foot on the gas, only for Les to join Seamus as we drove past the Abrams and both of them leaned out of the right-hand windows to give the commander a similar piece of their mind with much gesticulating, use of the 'C' word and pointing at the shattered windscreen.

We carried on towards the CPA building. Les and Lori were whispering together in the back seat. Action is a drug. It gives you a high.

I zipped into a space in the parking lot big enough for Etienne to pull in beside me. We locked our longs in the Nissan, seeing how the Opel had a bloody great hole in the windscreen. We unloaded, firing off the pistols into one of the big oil drums full of sand, and strode through the marble halls of Saddam's palace slapping each other's shoulders as we followed the smoky aroma of burgers on the grill in the canteen.

'What do you fancy for dinner tonight?' I asked Hendriks.
'What about roast lamb?'
'For a change!'
'You can never have too much lamb, Ash.'
'You want to bet on it?'
'I only bet on my shooting.'
Hendriks almost smiled. It had been a good day. First contact. No casualties. Not on our side. I'd been in Iraq for a fortnight and in that time Spartan had started to nail down some attractive contracts. Close Protection was a start, especially if all the journalists were going to look like Lori Wyatt.

We collected our burgers and found seats.
'You done good,' said Seamus. 'This round's on me.'
On the table he dropped an armful of Cokes he'd taken from the free cooler.
The guys in the squad raised their cans.
'The future.'
It was looking rosy. It wouldn't stay like that. The Americans were getting itchier trigger fingers as more boxes draped in the flag were flying home. The suicide bombers were learning their deadly craft, and if we had half a mind to, we could already hear the stamping boots of Moqtada al-Sadr's Al Mahdi Army. They were coming. But that autumn day we raised our Cokes and, while we were contemplating the future, maybe I should wind back to my arrival in Iraq two weeks before.

FIVE

The shopping plaza at Amsterdam's Schiphol airport was smaller than I had expected, although I did manage to get a good price on a digital camera to take some photos when I got to Basra.

I had treated myself to a pair of duty-free shades in Heathrow; nothing fancy, these were a black, utilitarian pair of mountaineering sunglasses that would keep the desert dust and sun from creeping in around the edges. I was relieved to see that the same pair wasn't any cheaper in Amsterdam.

With only forty minutes to go before my flight to Jordan, I made my way to the departure gate and was appalled to find two dozen Texan oil workers on their way to Iraq filling the seating area. Any terrorist worth his salt could have had a field day, or would certainly have been able to call ahead and let any contacts in Jordan know that a busload of infidels was on the way.

You didn't need the brains of an archbishop to spot these guys. Five of the men were wearing cowboy hats. The rest of them were wearing baseball hats glorifying either 'Houston' or 'Dallas', with one exception, but he made up for it by wearing a Stars and Stripes T-shirt. I also counted four large belt buckles in the shape of the state of Texas, six of those silver-tipped leather thong neckties that cowboys wear and one T-shirt that said 'NYPD 9/11, Proud to be a Patriot'.

But there was another reason why I knew they were going to 'Goddamn *I-raq*' and that was because they were talking about it at the tops of their voices – and the *entire* group were wearing transparent wallets around their necks containing labels with their names in bold and 'KBR IRAQ' in letters two inches high.

I slunk away to the far corner of the lounge where I noticed another man standing with his back to the wall, sneering at the Americans. He was in his late thirties, sandy-blond hair, average height, stocky and well-muscled with a dark tan marred only by pale skin around his eyes and in narrow strips from his eyes to his ears where he had been wearing shades. He sported a grey polo shirt, sand-coloured combat pants, tan hiking boots, an expensive diving watch and on his forearms were depressingly familiar British squaddie tattoos. A daysack with a multitude of little pouches sat at his feet. Another security man, and as obvious as the Texans.

I looked down at my sandy-coloured cargo pants, diving watch, daysack and hiking boots.

The squaddie and I ignored each other. I mentally made a note that on future trips I would dress like a tourist.

I had printed out some of Angus McGrath's emails and on the flight I read them through. The insurgency was spreading in the north and in central Iraq, but I was heading for Basra, in the southern sector, and it was less volatile thanks to the professional restraint of the British troops in occupation, something I had witnessed in several operational theatres. Hundreds of years of colonial policing had left the experience of interacting with indigenous peoples in the bones of the British Army.

Despite the fact that the Brits were mostly to blame for creating the mess in Iraq by imposing a Sunni monarch, Emir Faysal ibn Husayn, at the end of the First World War, I would discover that the Iraqis respected the British and considered us harsh, a sign of strength, but fair – in spite of the fact that the British had gassed the Kurds when they revolted in the 1920s, and had built most of the country's petrochemical infrastructure in order to better plunder the rich resources.

The British learned the local languages and showed respect to the sheikhs and imams. The old adage that an Englishman's word is his bond still rang true for Iraqis whether Assyrian Christian, Sunni, Shia, Turkman, or Kurd. When arranging meetings later in the year I would be puzzled that my Iraqi interpreters would ask whether the meeting was at British nine o'clock or Iraqi nine o'clock. The latter meant any time before lunch, whereas 'British' time meant you sat down at nine with notebooks ready.

The Shia uprising against Saddam after the first Gulf War in the early nineties had been brutally subdued. The Shia had been jubilant to finally see an end to the dictator and Shia militias were now prowling the southern cities slaughtering every former Ba'ath Party official they could lay their hands on. There were about 130,000 American troops in Iraq, ten times as many Brits, but statistically, a British soldier in the south had the same probability of being killed or wounded. It was shocking to me that so few British troops had been deployed to maintain order over such a vast area of the country. Once again Tommy Atkins was being stretched to the limit by his oblivious masters in Whitehall.

As a private security contractor, I was going to be a lot safer in Basra, where there were only three attacks a day, than in Baghdad, where there were now as many as fifty. In fact, most attacks in the south were not anti-British, but turf wars between rival militias. As one contractor told me, when you were driving in the south, as long as you stayed out of Basra itself, the biggest danger was falling asleep at the wheel, whereas driving in Baghdad was 'like Stalingrad', he said, with everyone shooting at each other.

The chaos should have been expected after the despotic rule of Saddam Hussein, a virtually illiterate tribesman from Tikrit who had worked his way through the ranks of the Revolutionary Command Council after the monarchy was toppled in 1958. He had been the de facto ruler of Iraq for some years before officially being made head of state in July 1979. His initial popularity for ridding the country of the last vestiges of colonialism quickly faded and the people suffered through nearly thirty years of tyrannical fascism and a horrific eight-year war of attrition with Iran which had killed an estimated one million people.

Despite having his arse kicked back into Iraq after invading Kuwait in 1990, Saddam had achieved a heroic status among Arabs by going toe to toe with America and surviving in battle against the much vaunted army of the Great Satan.

The flight passed without incident and darkness shrouded the countryside as we approached the golden sparkle of lights that was Amman. Upon arrival at Queen Alia International Airport I was very glad that Angus McGrath had briefed me on the procedure for Jordanian immigration.

'Make your way straight to the passport control desks,' he had said. 'The far right-hand desk sells visas to foreigners and no one knows because the sign's so fucking small you cannae see it. But don't go there yet because you have to buy the visa with ten Jordanian dinars. Go to the back of the hall where there's a bureau-de-change and change some money first.'

I had already exchanged some JDs at Heathrow so I went straight to the right-hand side of the hallway and joined the queue at the last passport desk. The tattooed squaddie was right in front of me.

The effects of the war in Iraq had touched the airport hallway in Jordan if you knew what to look for. There were several earnest young men and women who could have been aid workers, some journalists laden with laptops and cameras, the Texan KBR tour group with their booming voices and a few others who may or may not have been security men, but they were all fit, muscular, tanned, travelling alone and wearing sand-coloured cargo pants and hiking boots. The Westerners were spread throughout the hall with the exception of the security guys. They were in the right-hand queue behind me.

I watched contentedly as the first three people in the line were turned away when they couldn't produce the necessary dinars. They wandered off searching for the bureau-de-change. I saw Westerners being sent off from other desks and being directed to the back of our queue. In short order there was a long snake of people behind us and a large knot of grumpy

Europeans hanging around the bureau-de-change desk waiting
for someone to turn up.

Queen Alia International is a modern airport, but it was
obvious that I was back in the Middle East with the smell of
tea and dirty bathrooms, cigarette smoke and cheap aftershave
mingling in the air. The Jordanian officials had rigid epaulettes,
small medal ribbons and neat moustaches. There wasn't a
female official in sight.

The squaddie stepped up to the desk and handed over a
British passport and a 10JD note. He knew the drill.

'*Salaam alaikum*,' I said as I stepped forward to the desk
with my passport and 10JDs.

I had picked up an Arabic phrasebook in Heathrow.

'*Wa alaikum salaam*.' The official beamed back at me.

He licked, peeled, scribbled and stamped a striking visa into
my passport. I began to wonder if I was going to do the Circuit
long term whether I would need to get one of those sixty-page
passports.

The immigration officer smiled again. 'Welcome to Jordan,'
he said as he handed my passport back to me.

'*Shukran*.' Thank you.

I walked two steps further and presented my passport to
another officer who was unmoved by my *salaam alaikum*. He
gravely inspected my passport and visa and handed it back. I
smiled, *shukran*'ed him and went downstairs to baggage reclaim.
Four dirty boys in cream overalls fought to take my daysack for
me. I waved them away and turned towards the luggage trolleys.

'Ten JDs, Mister.'

One of the boys was indicating the trolleys. I didn't know
whether he was telling me the fee for his portering services or
whether the trolleys cost 10JDs to push the 20 yards into
customs. I had been warned that the baggage allowances were
strict so despite all my last-minute shopping I was travelling
light.

My holdall was one of the first pieces of luggage to slip out
of the chute and circle towards me on the carousel, always a
good sign, and I carried my two bags through customs into the
unimpressive arrivals area. I looked around, grinning like an
idiot. There was no one there to meet me.

I turned on my mobile phone.

No coverage. Fuck.

I had thought from the start that my phone provider's claim of 'complete worldwide roaming coverage' was nothing more than advertising fluff and before leaving London I had bought a different pay-as-you-go SIM Card from another company that guaranteed coverage throughout the Middle East. British officer training, you see, always well prepared. I slotted that in and turned my phone on. And waited. No coverage.

This was Jordan, for God's sake, not some village in the Western Sahara. Maybe there was just no coverage around the airport area? I watched as the squaddie came into the arrivals area lugging his bags. He was chatting on his mobile. No problem. Fuckfuckfuckfuckfuck.

I needed a new phone contract with reliable service. No way was I going to carry on paying some grasping monthly charge when I was stuck in Iraq and only back in the UK for a couple of months a year. I was cursing my bad luck when I saw a middle-aged man jogging breathlessly through the terminal carrying a dirty handwritten sign with the word 'Spartan' on it.

We *salaam alaikum*'ed each other and he apologised.

'Two terminals, sir,' he puffed and lit up a cigarette to help him regain composure. 'I am not sure which one you are arrive to.'

I slung my bag in his car. We drove thirty minutes into Amman and I checked into the Marriott. In the future, I would try the Grand Hyatt, which was OK, and a couple of other hotels that were on the Circuit, but the Marriott would always remain my favourite.

Spartan gave us a travel allowance but I was happy to pay the extra $60 just to treat myself to the steak sandwiches from room service and to eat at the Library, a place that for me became a haven outside of time, the twilight zone between the normal world and the world of war in occupied Iraq.

On my way into Iraq, I would enjoy the exquisite Chateaubriand steak and a few glasses of red wine knowing that this might be my last decent meal before getting slotted by a terrorist. On my way out, I would enjoy the same ritual, knowing that I had cheated death again and arrived back in

civilisation with fine dining and bubble baths after months of
appalling food and dribbling cold showers.

The hotel receptionist was looking at me with a puzzled
expression. I was miles away.

'Two a.m., sir,' he said.

'What?'

'Your message from Mohammed. He will meet you in the
lobby at two o'clock in the morning, sir.'

'*Shukran*,' I mumbled, and went upstairs to lie fully clothed
on the bed. It was already getting on for midnight. No point
unpacking. I had enjoyed my steak and a few drinks in the bar.
The Amman Marriott illustrated perfectly the Middle East.
The Library with its leather chairs and the smell of polish
belonged to the colonial past. The Sports Bar with its chrome
and high stools was 100 per cent Americana

At one-thirty my alarm went off. I felt like a dead man. I
called room service and ordered a sandwich, a coffee and a
large bottle of water, then lay back down again. Twenty
minutes later a knock at the door woke me and a waiter
brought in my order. I gave him a 10JD note and he seemed
happy enough as I shushed him out of the room. Christ, I was
tired. I felt as if I had been run over by a bus.

I wrapped the sandwich and stuffed it into my daysack with
the bottle of water and complimentary fruit basket. That was
lunch sorted. I downed the cup of coffee with three sugars.
That was breakfast taken care of. I grabbed my bags and
headed down to reception to check out. One other Westerner
was already down there. I knew from Angus that two of us
would be crossing the border into Iraq that day.

He eyed me for a moment, then stepped forward to shake hands.

'Les Trevellick,' he said.

He had a firm, dry grip, fierce blue eyes and close-cropped
hair silver-tipped at the sides. I guessed he was in his early
forties but he looked younger with the kind of fitness that you
see in good career soldiers. I imagined he could run all day,
probably ran the London marathon every year, but at the same
time he had a solid chest, shoulders and forearms that said

anyone who stepped into the boxing ring with him was going
to have his work cut out. He was clean-shaven and was
wearing jeans with army desert boots and a fleece.

'James Ashcroft,' I replied.

He looked me up and down. I don't know what he saw but
if I looked half as bad as I felt, it was not impressive. I hadn't
shaved or changed in two days and had slept in the clothes I
had been wearing on two flights. I looked and felt like a sack
of dirty laundry.

'Officer?' he asked.

'Captain, Duke of Wellington's. Been out five years. And
you?'

'Staff Sergeant, Royal Engineers. I came out twelve years ago.'
He had an accent I would come to learn was a Derbyshire accent.

We were quiet for a moment. He looked reliable, tough and
competent. I was glad I was heading over the border with him.
As for his opinion of me, I couldn't tell.

The moment passed and I went to check out. I paid by credit
card. I had changed £50 into JDs and seemed to have spent the
lot on nothing.

Mohammed arrived and loaded our bags into the taxi. It was
bitterly cold out, colder than London. England had been
balmy. Krista had been wearing a sleeveless dress when she'd
left me at Heathrow.

'Five hours,' Mohammed grinned, showing off his three
remaining teeth.

'To Baghdad?' I asked, surprised.

'To the border. Then five, maybe six hours to Baghdad.'

Les and I looked at each other, then shrugged.

'Not being rude, mate, but do you mind if I catch up on
some sleep?' I said to him.

'Fill your boots. I'm going to do the same.'

We snuggled into our fleeces, the driver shut the windows,
put the heating on full and lit up the first of about four hundred
cigarettes. I closed my eyes. One of the things you learn in the
army is to catch your sleep when you can. It seemed like no
time at all before Les was nudging me in the side.

'Wake up, Jim, we're at the border. Momo here needs our
papers.'

I cracked an eye and looked out. A beautiful dawn was breaking over the desert. We were parked up in a big line of lorries laden with goods; the UN sanctions had been lifted by the Coalition Provision Authority. The car was throbbing with Arabic music and thick cigarette smoke. It was like a nightclub in Manchester.

'Jesus wept.' I stepped out and stretched, filling my lungs with good fresh diesel fumes. After the inside of the ashtray that ingeniously functioned as our taxi I felt as if I were breathing in the finest Highland mountain air. Les got out the other side and we both coughed up enough tar to coat the motorway back to Amman. I felt a bit more alive now. We gave Mohammed our passports.

'Let's see where he goes with them,' I said.

'Roger that.'

Mohammed set off into the main building. We followed and the noise when we entered the passport hall hit us like a wall. There must have been a hundred or more Arab truckers standing in crowds and stretched out on rows of old wooden chairs. It was a bare concrete room with a million fag butts flattened in the dust on the floor. The smoke was so thick it made your eyes water. Mohammed pushed his way through the shouting throng to the chaos at the front of the wooden counter at the far end of the room. He shoved our passports together with his through the grille with a fat wedge of dinars. The official looked bored as he stuffed a few bills in his top pocket and passed the remainder with the passports to some underling who disappeared into a back office.

Les and I stood at the back studying the drivers. They lit cigarettes from the butts of their cigarettes and stared back. They didn't seem belligerent, just curious. Still, they were a good-sized mob and there were only the two of us out there in the middle of nowhere.

We wandered back outside. We weren't sure if we were at the Jordanian or Iraqi passport control. Some of the buildings were whitewashed, most were just concrete blocks stripped to the bare essentials. No clues there, until I saw a soldier with a Beretta assault rifle and wearing a beret the size of an aircraft carrier's landing deck.

'Jordanian,' I said.

'Then we'll have to do all this again on the other side.'

We popped our heads in and out of the passport hall during the course of the next hour and a half. I had no idea how the system worked but every so often an official who sounded like he had a sore throat would appear with a handful of passports and start shouting out names. A dozen truckers would push their way through to the front of the counter and claim their documents.

We visited the toilets, which were bog-standard holes in the ground jobs, went back to the car and had breakfast. I offered to share my lunch with Les but he pulled out an identical package from his bag.

'Room service,' he said, 'PPP. Prior Preparation and Planning.'

We munched our sandwiches while the sun rose higher and began to throw out a bit of heat.

Les removed the new Oakleys he'd bought at Heathrow the day before. They were bright silver with icy blue mirrored lenses: very cool. I looked at them enviously and reminded myself that I was not going into a fashion show as I slipped on my black mountaineering shades. Shit. His definitely looked better.

Eventually Mohammed retrieved our passports. We drove forward about a hundred yards and stopped under a massive concrete awning. Mo turned and made dragging motions as he fired away in Arabic. I glanced out the side window. Between each lane of the highway there was a concrete ledge about waist high and three feet wide. In the next lane an Arab family was pulling the bags from the roof of their car and laying out the contents on the ledge where an official poked about looking for anything worth having.

'Do they need to check our bags?' I asked Mohammed.

'*Na'am*, yes. Bags.'

Les and I got out and hauled our kit on to a similar ledge under the awning. An official came over, went perfunctorily through our belongings and waved us through without touching anything.

'Waste of fucking time,' Les commented as we drove on.

They hadn't bothered to check the car boot and we could have smuggled anything in under the mess of bags and jackets on the back seat. We passed along a barbed wire chicane and approached a group of cement buildings. Snapping in the wind above us was a red, white and black flag with green stars and 'God is Great' in Arabic script.

We were in Iraq.

SIX

Two fresh-faced American soldiers checked our baggage thoroughly and efficiently when we stopped under the awning. As we drove on to another, smaller building, we saw several heavily armed GIs watching the traffic with weapons ready, although they seemed more concerned with administrative duties than foreign fighters concealed among the traffic.

I didn't know whether that meant that the threat level was low in this region or whether they were poorly trained. I said as much to Les and we agreed to be optimistic and say that the threat level was low.

As there had not been a substantial influx of American soldiers since the war ended, it was highly likely that these guys had seen active combat fighting their way through Iraq. They would be on the ball and, if they had thought for one minute that there was a threat out on the border, they would have been looking more wary.

We showed our passports and were disappointed when they were handed back without 'IRAQ' stamped on the pages. It would be a few months before the Iraqi government had a functioning immigration service and even then it only occurred because some sharp minister had seen an opportunity to make money out of the growing volume in cross-border traffic.

Another car was waiting for us on the other side of the border with four Iraqi escorts from Spartan HQ. They were from the same tribe and wore matching *shemaghs* folded stylishly around their heads, Ray-Bans and dish-dashes, a floor-length shirt with a small collar, usually grey in Iraq, always as white as snow when worn by the sheikhs of Saudi Arabia. We could see AK-47s on the seats next to them.

The leader came out and introduced himself to us as Hayder. He had a pistol tucked into his belt.

'Fred Karno's fucking army,' muttered Les under his breath.

We had been led to believe there would be weapons for us upon arrival in-country and were annoyed that there were none. Fuck-ups are normal. There was nothing to be done and we carried on as the escort car pulled in behind us and Mohammed led the way into Iraq.

It looked a lot like Jordan.

We were on a multi-lane highway that crossed the Mesopotamian Plain and on either side of the road there was nothing but flat stony ground as far as the eye could see. It was grey. Even the sky was grey. I was fully awake now, and as Mohammed lit up the first of his next four hundred cigarettes I realised it was going to be a long five hours to Baghdad.

Les opened the window a crack and we sat back, breathed in the dust and exchanged stories, as soldiers do.

Les's military career was impressive. He had done both the 'P' (Parachute) Company and the all-arms commando course, and had been an instructor on the latter as well as an arctic warfare instructor. He was intensely proud of having been with airborne troops, but was far prouder of being commando-trained than of his para wings. He had found 'P' company 'easy' after doing the commando course. Oh and yes, he had run the London marathon three times. And boxed for the army. Holy shit.

I'd been sitting on my arse in an office for three years. Hill-walking in Scotland and cross-country running had kept me in shape but it was time to start thinking seriously about physical fitness if I was going to be working with guys like this. We talked about what threats we might face on our upcoming contracts and amused ourselves imagining the number of ways foolish white-eyes like ourselves could get blown up.

All this time, Mohammed had been well in the lead for the acting mad competition, but even he was rolling his eyeballs

worriedly as Les screamed 'Ally Akbar, KABOOM' every time
he saw a driver who looked like a potential suicide bomber. It
was curiously prescient of Les Trevellick because up until then,
in September 2003, there hadn't been any suicide bombers in
Iraq.

I glanced back. Our escorts were still behind us, their car so
full of smoke I was surprised the driver could see through the
windscreen.

Mohammed pointed at the buildings on the outskirts of a
city in the distance.

'Fallujah,' he said.

This was a hotbed of criminals and insurgents. The United
States Marines would flatten it eventually, but the name at the
time meant nothing to me and could have been Arabic for 'I
was born there', or 'crappy brown buildings' for all I knew.
Mo lapsed into silence and nodded along to the wailing music
on the radio. The songs all sounded the same. I wondered if
we were listening to a special club mix that lasted a full five
hours.

We carried on talking threats and tactics.

'They don't care if we are Brits or Yanks, mate,' Les said.
'They take one look at us and think we're American-Jewish
peeegs taking the dollar to come and dishonour their women
and steal their country.'

We began spotting potential enemy positions overlooking
the highway, and vehicles that could have been full of
explosives parked on the side of the road. We overtook a taxi
crawling along under its heavy load.

'Look at that fucker, the wheels are scraping the arches.'

'He must have a ton of Semtex on board,' I replied. 'And
he's cunningly disguised the bombs as a family of twelve.'

'Suicide bombers,' said Les knowingly, 'fresh from Gaza.'

'Don't make eye contact –'

'Too late . . . Ally Akbar, KABOOM!'

Mohammed winced and drove faster.

Les and I had both been to Northern Ireland several times and
we discussed what tactics we would use to counter the threats
we might face. We talked over several scenarios and seemed to

see eye to eye on most things. This was what we were being paid for: for the experience and training we had in dealing with counter-insurgency and guerrilla tactics. It was good to know that I would be (a) doing work I was good at and (b) working with people who were just as good. We agreed on several 'actions on' and drills we should train in, and were looking forward to meeting up with Les's mate Seamus, who was already in-country, to confirm them.

Like me, this was Les Trevellick's first proper contract. He knew a great deal more about the Circuit though, as he had quite a few Regiment mates. The SAS to the public is *the Regiment* to everyone in the army.

'It's a close group,' he told me. 'Everyone knows everyone, so you fuck up more than once and no one will hire you. All they have to do is call around and people will say, "Oh yeah, I remember that cunt, he was useless," and that's you.' He looked me up and down for a second as though already filing me under that category.

There was a large pool of ex-soldiers who did short-term contracts for a relatively small group of companies. When I thought about it, it was obvious that you not only had to be a good operator, but you had to get on well with the men you worked with. If much of the recommendations were based on word of mouth then even someone with a dull personality or poor personal hygiene might find it difficult to get recommended by former team-mates. Having said that, with the sudden explosion in demand for security contractors in Iraq, there were some companies hiring men by the yard, barely even scanning CVs before offering contracts.

We were passing through the little towns and villages on the outskirts of Baghdad. As we pulled off the highway and turned on to another substantial road, I could see destroyed Iraqi tanks dotted along the way. Most had their turrets blown off and were in such a terrible state I couldn't tell whether they were T-62s or T-72s. We were silent for a while.

'All still dug in, hull down,' Les then grunted. I stared back at a pair of tanks that looked untouched but had scorch marks on the side. 'Probably never knew what hit them.'

'Apaches, you reckon?'

Les was referring to the American AH-64 gunships, a familiar sight in Iraqi skies to anyone who followed the television news during the weeks of war. They were armed with Hellfire missiles with a range of eight kilometres. At that distance death would have dropped out of the sky on unsuspecting Iraqis who wouldn't have had a clue that there were any helicopters out there. Especially if the attack had come at night.

'Probably,' I said. 'A10s would have left them looking like Swiss cheese.'

We were both acquainted with those slow-flying American tank-hunting jets armed with a fearsome Gatling gun that chewed through tanks as if they were tin cans. I had seen the remains of target tanks on American ranges up in Yakima and you could hardly tell that they had once been tanks.

We could follow the traces of the battle through the remains of the Iraqi army. Half a dozen Russian-built BMP personnel carriers were spread out across the fields to our right between the protection of the berms nearest the road and the palm plantation 200 metres away. To civvies they would just have looked like destroyed vehicles. To our eyes they told another story.

Most likely American ground forces had claimed these. We could not say whether they had been caught in the open withdrawing from the road to the safety of the tree line, or whether they had made a suicidal attack towards the advancing Americans. Both Les and I tended towards the former theory. The fact remained that they had still been moving as a group in one direction, and that meant that they had seen what killed them.

'Tanks,' I said to Les.

'You sure?'

'Aircraft would have destroyed them before the crews knew what was going on. Look how far they got. They didn't do too badly, so they must have had time to think and act. Most of the men would have known what the Apaches had done to their tanks in the first Gulf War. If you came under attack from American jets or helicopters what would you do?'

'Run like fuck as far from the vehicles as possible,' Les replied. He was thinking it through. 'They'd destroy the

vehicles and not bother picking off the poor fuckers if any
survived.'

'And these guys tried to drive out of it,' I said. 'If they'd
come under air attack they would have de-bussed and fucked
off on foot. They probably saw the American armour coming
for them and thought they were far enough away from them
to make a withdrawal in vehicles.'

He nodded. We both knew the scenario. An M1 tank would
have been able to engage these guys from a couple of Ks away,
easy. The Iraqis weren't used to long engagement ranges like
that and probably would have thought they could escape in
their vehicles.

I remembered the instructors at Sandhurst telling us that
Abrams during the first Gulf War in 1991 had reported
successful engagement ranges of up to four kilometres against
static targets. There was always the possibility that artillery,
the biggest killer, had taken them, but it was unlikely, bearing
in mind that the huddle of modest houses and the trees nearby
were untouched. One way or the other, the Iraqi troops hadn't
stood a chance.

I remembered slowly patrolling through an abandoned village
in Bosnia. We could tell the direction that the attack had come
from because all the walls on each house were peppered with
bullet holes on one side only. After our eyes had adjusted to
truly recognise what we were seeing we could even trace the
course of the battle, seeing which houses had been taken first
and then used as points for covering fire for assaults on the
next house.

We even fancied that we could tell the differing characteris-
tics of each squad as they leapfrogged past each other, since
alternate houses showed either more accurate strikes around
the windows where the defenders would have been, as opposed
to every other house which had been saturated with small-arms
fire. Lateral striations zigzagging across the road showed the
strike of bullets as teams covered each other from each side
of it.

The house at the end of the village was clearly where the last
stand had been mounted, and the houses nearest it bore

evidence of that fact on their walls. They were riddled with bullet holes, not only from the direction in which the attackers had come when they took them, but also on the other side, facing towards them coming from the defenders. This last house had been completely flattened to rubble, and tank tracks in the field next door told us how that particular fight had ended.

The destroyed vehicles were behind us and we started seeing more and more built-up areas with shops, gas stations and family houses. We had left the flat barren desert behind and were soon driving in the middle of a substantial city.

'Is this Baghdad?' I asked Mohammed.

'*Na'am*, Baghdad,' he grinned and lit a cigarette.

The buildings were all two-storey blocks, residential houses or apartment buildings with flat roofs flying flags of washing. In some areas, the buildings had shops on the ground floor. All of them were a uniform mud-brown colour lacking features or architectural interest. A friend of mine at Oxford had once told me that Baghdad was the most beautiful city in the world. She must have been dreaming. In biblical times, maybe. Burned out cars, car tyres and broken masonry littered the streets. Men stood around on street corners and goats grazed on rubbish dumps.

Eventually we drove up to an American checkpoint. Mohammed showed them a laminated ID card and Les and I showed our passports. Behind us I noticed Hayder's team all showing ID as well. This was the entrance to the CPA, the Green Zone, where many of the private security companies were based. Two minutes later we were pulling up outside a walled villa.

'Spartan,' Mohammed said, grinning at us. Two white men walked out of the house to greet us. Angus McGrath was one of them. I pointed him out to Les.

'That's Seamus Hayes,' he said, pointing to the other one.

He looked as fit as a butcher's dog and sported a massive, 70s-style Mexican moustache.

Both Angus and Seamus were wearing mirrored Oakleys which looked both cool and mean.

Bollocks.

SEVEN

The four guys in the escort car jumped out and lined up to unload their rifles with the muzzles pointing into an oil drum filled with sand: a primitive but effective loading/unloading bay.

'I'm impressed,' I said to Angus as he came to shake hands.

'We had a couple of NDs in the early days.'

An ND (negligent discharge) is someone accidentally firing off a round from his weapon; a serious offence in the army and potentially lethal for any poor sod standing nearby.

Angus was the Ops officer in charge of organising the house security force among other things.

'You should sort out some uniforms or armbands,' I said, 'or your locals are going to get slotted by the first American patrol that sees them.'

'I've had a word with the local CF unit and let them know where we are, but you're right, some uniforms are on order.'

'CF?'

'Coalition Forces. The Yanks.'

Of course. Silly me.

Seamus shook my hand. 'Nice to have you on board,' he said, and turned away as Les pulled a bottle of Jack Daniels and a couple of magazines about triathlons out of his bag.

'Here you are,' he said.

'That's fucking great, Les. Nice one.'

Angus led us inside and of course I felt like shit that I hadn't thought to bring him some small gift. In a narrow corridor he pointed out a couple of rooms. Les was sharing with Seamus and I was in a room with a Welshman named Dai Jones. They had prepared everything for us; sheets, duvets and towels were already laid out on the beds like in boarding school. We each had a bulletproof vest. I tapped mine. Soft with no ceramic plates. We dumped our bags and came back out. Both of us went straight to the lavatory. Five hours in a taxi tends to strain the bladder.

Seamus waved us over towards him.

'Come on, let's get you to the armoury and sort some weapons out.'

'Ash, I'll see you later at scoff. I have to get back to the office,' Angus called as he disappeared into another doorway at the end of the hall.

Les and I followed Seamus out of the house, through a courtyard with several 4 × 4 vehicles and into a steel shipping container with a doorway cut in the side. The armoury was basic but functional. AK-47s filled the racks of crude wooden shelves and in one corner a rack on the floor held several RPD light machine guns. Half a dozen Heckler & Koch MP5 submachine guns were on a separate shelf as well as two Sterling SMGs.

Les and I ignored them. I had used the HK weapons a great deal when in COP (close observation platoon). I liked them, but when you're battling through an urban environment you want a full-calibre battle rifle to punch through doors, walls, windscreens and especially the enemy. We both examined the AKs carefully.

Some of the weapons were in a shit state, some looked new. We each chose a decent-looking AK, both opting for folding stocks. Seamus unlocked a steel cupboard with a key from the armourer, a quiet man who introduced himself as Phil Rhoden. Seamus pulled out two Browning pistols for us.

'The last two decent shorts in the armoury,' he said. 'Until we get the permits sorted and get some Glocks and Sigs the best we can get so far on the black market are Brownings. Otherwise we have a handful of Tariqs.'

He also gave us three mags each for the pistols. We stuffed the mags into pockets and checked the pistols were clear.

I'd never seen a Tariq before and Seamus obliged me by pulling out what looked like a cheap and nasty Beretta. They were locally made, single-column magazine and the mag release was in the butt of the pistol grip. He showed me a magazine, then replaced them both in the cupboard.

'What state do we carry these around in?' Les asked.

Seamus indicated his rifle.

'Longs to be unloaded or made safe while you're in the compound, make ready only as you leave, and unload into the drums when you get back,' he replied. He tapped the Browning 9 milly in his own waistband. 'Shorts you can carry how you want but they go everywhere with you at all times, in the bog, in the shower, everywhere.'

'Have you got any holsters?' asked Les.

'No, mate,' replied Seamus. 'We have a load sitting in a container in Kuwait ready to be trucked up once the passes are stamped.'

'You can borrow one of mine. I've got a couple,' I said and turned back to Seamus. 'What about plates for our vests?'

Without them the vests were only good for stopping shrapnel and pistol rounds. Hard plates front and back were essential for protecting the lungs and heart from high-velocity rifle fire.

'In Kuwait. In the Golden Container.'

The arms permits from the US State Department that would allow us to import decent weapons were signed, sealed and, according to our logistics team, would be in our hands 'within the week'. But something we would quickly come to learn in Iraq was the legend of the 'Golden Container'.

Anything that was mission critical you would be assured by HQ was sitting in a box in Kuwait or Jordan and would be in Iraq in the next ten days. Bullshit. If we had waited for the Golden Container we would have been mooching around Baghdad without vehicles and with nothing but steak knives to defend ourselves.

Instead we had acquired our weapons on the black market and would later barter for the hard plates in our Kevlar vests from a Lieutenant Colonel in the CPA. We would get fourteen plates in exchange for two bottles of Jack Daniels and five of our faulty Iraqi AKs that the guys in his unit wanted to take home as souvenirs.

Les and I took a moment to sign for weapons and ammunition from Phil, each taking eight magazines for the AKs. I cleared my rifle, pointing it at the floor away from the others, placed the safety catch on and put on a full magazine. Les did the same. I loaded my pistol, cocked it, put the safety on and shoved it into the back of my belt.

'Let's go get some lunch and meet the rest of the gang.' Seamus jerked his thumb at the door.

We trooped out with Phil locking up behind us.

Seamus waited while Les and I dumped our rifles and magazines on our beds. I gave Les the holster from my bag and we both threaded them on to our belts and holstered the Brownings. I had a double mag pouch as well, for my spare 9mm magazines. I put the spare AK mags into a bum bag with a strong waist belt in case I needed them to be handy later.

In the communal dining room, Seamus introduced us to the rest of the gang. There were two teams of Brits and South Africans on their way down south to Basra. We all shook hands and I tried to remember their names.

As for HQ staff there was Phil, who functioned as the storeman, armourer and company accountant in-country. There was Angus, my mate from the Dukes, who had got me over there, just as Seamus had brought in Les. It was all very incestuous. The only woman was Jacky Clark from Yorkshire, who was in charge of all administration.

Jacky and Phil covered for each other when one of them was on leave, but her primary task was to deal with the vast flow of paperwork and phone calls generated by having to get us in and out of the country, obtain passes, travel warrants, insurance and a million other details I was only too happy not to know about. Jacky and Phil also dealt with procurement of materials, supplies and equipment. Angus teamed up with the managing director to go out on sales pitches and win contracts.

We helped ourselves to plates of food, but before we could get tucked in, the MD got to his feet and introduced himself.

'My name's Adam Pascoe. Welcome to Baghdad and welcome to Spartan. It's good to have you on board.' He looked
cheerful and professional. He glanced at Jacky. 'Jacky here will
see you contracted and documented right after lunch and then
I think you're off to the range.'

He looked at Seamus who gave an affirmative nod.

'Things are fluid right now. We are in a good position with
quite a few contracts coming through, so be as flexible as you
can.' He glanced across the room at me. 'The first change
concerns you, James,' he said, 'I know you expected to be
going down to Basra after being processed here, but we have
a new tasking coming up that may need a man of your
experience. I'd rather like to keep you in Baghdad.'

'Aye,' said Angus. He had sworn blind I would be sent down
to Basra, not that I actually cared. The action was in Baghdad
and that was where I wanted to be.

'My pleasure,' I said.

By the time Adam Pascoe had sat down, Dai Jones had
scoffed his food. He finished his Coke in one long swig and got
up from the table.

'Seeya losers,' he announced. 'I'm off home.'

'Give her one for me,' Seamus said, and Dai gave him the finger.

Dai liked to think of himself as Welsh but I would learn that
his father had been in the army and Dai had grown up all over
the UK learning to speak the generic brand of army cockney.
He disappeared along with two other men headed out on leave.

I could hear Hayder's escort team loading magazines and
starting engines outside. I also noticed that as the three
outgoing men filed past the hallway with their bags, they were
fully armed. I asked Seamus about that.

'We have a Spartan locker at the Jordanian border and leave
weapons there,' he explained. 'The CF boys get a bit shitty
sometimes and Hayder just brings the lot back with him if that
happens.'

I turned back to my lunch, which was distinctly under-
whelming. Cold hotdogs.

The men around me were tanned, fit and in their forties.
Seamus did the introductions. Etienne, Hendriks and Cobus
were ex-South African Defence Force officers, the Yaapies.

They stuck out big scarred gnarled hands the size of dinner plates and crunched the bones in my hand one after the other.

'*Gut* to have you, James . . .'

There was a mixture of Jim and James and I put everyone straight once and for all.

'Ash,' I said. 'Everyone just calls me Ash.'

'Izzit?' said Hendriks, and he fixed me with his cold grey eyes.

Spartan at that time was unusual in that it would only take on ex-army South Africans. Many companies were hiring South African policemen. Later, this policy would change as security boomed and the manning requirements went through the roof. Just like all the other firms operating in Iraq, we then signed on dozens of former Special Task Force officers, 'Taskies', we called them, and I would discover that after a career on the tactical unit for the police force in South African cities, these guys had had more contacts and firefight experience than I had dreamed of.

As we munched away, Seamus explained the course of events for the afternoon.

'Right, Les and Ash,' he said, tasting the name for the first time. 'You'll need to get administrated by Jacky after lunch and then we're heading out to the All American range to zero personal weapons and test-fire some kit from the armoury. It's one o'clock now, we'll aim to be wheels up at two.'

People assume that you get a weapon out of the box and it will work just fine. A firefight in downtown Baghdad was not the place to discover that you have a bum rifle or a faulty magazine. Each weapon and each magazine has to be tested.

We handed our plates to the Iraqi housekeeper in the kitchen. Les and I went into the admin office where Jacky was waiting. She was a petite, pretty girl in her mid-twenties. She was ex-army as well, from the AGC (Adjutant's General Corps) and had been running her own human resources business before taking this job. She had a small-calibre Beretta in a cross-draw position on her left hip and an MP5 tucked under her desk.

We added our signatures on various contracts and filled in bank details for our salaries. We had both gone through the complicated process of setting up US dollar offshore accounts, which is not as easy as you might think and had hardly seemed worth the effort at the time. Now we were in Iraq, it was eminently sensible. We also signed insurance policies. The monthly premiums were paid by Spartan. If I got greased Krista would get £250,000.

'Best not to let her know that,' Jacky said. 'She can hire a hitman here to take you out for a hundred dollars.'

'For fifty I'll do it myself,' said Les. 'Bit of all right, is she?'

'Don't even think about it,' I said. 'She's got taste.'

I guess we were becoming mates.

We went back to our rooms. I grabbed a shower to get rid of the sweat of two days' continuous travel and the vestiges of the driver's cigarette smoke. Passive smoking in Iraq was as big a risk as friendly fire. As I was getting dressed, Seamus came in with a Motorola radio and a spare battery.

'Here's your comms, mate, stick it on channel two. Put your name on it with tape and every time we come back in just stick it in the charger in the front room.'

'Callsigns?' I asked.

'Just our first names for the minute. Our team callsign is Sierra Five Zero and the Ops room here is Sierra Zero. Obviously if Zero Alpha comes up on the net that's Adam.'

'Do we have a team medkit?'

He pointed at a bin-liner next to my bed. 'Every expat has a standard trauma pack – do you know how to put an IV line in?'

I did. I upended the bin liner on to my bed with the kit in my daysack. I checked the medkit, then put it back in the bin-bag, rolled it up and stuffed it into the daysack. I added a pair of ear defenders, which I had thought to bring out, the radio battery and a large plastic bottle of water, which I'd snagged from the carton of bottles in the dining room. In the top pocket of the daysack I put a Maglite torch, Silva compass, my passport, wallet and digital camera. I dug around in my baggage and found another three army-issue field dressings and zipped them in my fleece pocket.

Seamus watched me pack, nodding thoughtfully.

'We need to get you and Les some MCI phones, but they're limited at the moment, I'll tell you about it down on the range,' he said. 'I'll get booted and spurred and meet you in the front hall, Ash.'

MCI was an American cellular phone network set up to ease comms within the city because they had trashed the entire Iraqi comms infrastructure during the war.

Seamus was cut from the same piece of fabric as Les, a Colour Sergeant who had spent fourteen years in the Parachute Regiment. Like Les, he also ran marathons, each always trying to beat the other's best time. I wouldn't have laid a bet if you put the pair of them in a boxing ring.

I slipped into my Kevlar vest, took it off and adjusted the straps. The last guy to wear it must have been one fat bastard. It sat just above my pistol holster, but my mag pouches on the other side were digging into me. I undid my belt, readjusted them and retightened the belt again. I put my fleece on over the whole lot, including the vest, buckled on my bum bag with the AK mags, grabbed my rifle and daysack and headed for the front door.

Seamus appeared with Les and I followed them through a door marked 'Ops Room'. Inside was a well-ordered operations room with several radio base stations, a scattering of telephones and a large-scale map of Baghdad on the wall. Angus sat there with an Iraqi, also called Hayder. He was wearing a neat shirt and a tie.

'We sign out here every time we leave the house,' Seamus said.

He pointed at a white board with a grid taped to it. With a marker pen he noted our first names, destination 'AA range', the vehicles we would be taking and the time we were heading out.

'We call in when we arrive at the location, and when we set off on our way back, as well as giving the Ops officer a rough trace of our route.'

It was like being in the army.

Seamus walked over to the map of Baghdad and pointed out Spartan HQ. It was marked by a red pin in the middle of the city, inside the clearly marked Green Zone, just north of a massive loop in the Tigris river. The Tigris made a large oxbow loop in the shape of a penis with a huge bulbous head, pointing from east to west. Seamus pointed to a large complex just above the penis. 'This is the CPA or the Green Zone where we are. This is the main CF base in the area, the centre of new government and is well defended by armour and troops.'

'There's the PX for shopping and you can eat in the canteen in the CPA palace itself, but first of all we need to sort you out some CPA passes.'

He then indicated a swathe along the body of the penis. 'This is Karrada. It's relatively upmarket and is supposed to be the best place in the city for shopping.'

Angus came and joined us at the big map. 'The route we take today is to familiarise you with this section of Baghdad,' Seamus continued. Angus was following the route. 'We'll head south, straight down over the 14th July Bridge, over this bit of Karrada,' he indicated us cutting south over the body of the penis, 'straight over the roundabout and the next bridge and past Dora refinery. Then we'll take the six-lane highway and come off here at the range.'

There was a large motorway running east–west just south of the city and it looked like it was a major route.

'On the way back we might take a detour through Karrada, maybe stop off at a couple of shops and pick up some stuff for dinner.'

I fixed the major landmarks in my head, two sections of river running east–west. The boundaries would be the highway to the south and the refinery to the east.

'Dora is a bloody great oil refinery and an excellent landmark,' Seamus told us, pointing at a spot to the south of the city. 'It has a tall tower with a massive flame at the top, which is bloody useful at night.'

We headed out to the parking lot and mounted up. We were off to see one of the most beautiful cities in the world.

EIGHT

Seamus and Cobus took Les in the lead car, an Opel. I mounted up with Hendriks and Etienne in a Nissan 4 × 4. That way we would have at least two people in each vehicle who knew their way around the city. The South Africans could track through the bush. Baghdad was a piece of cake.

Etienne was behind the wheel and I sat in the passenger seat next to him. We cocked our weapons as we drove out of the gate.

'Hello, Sierra Zero, this is Sierra Five Zero leaving your location now, over.'

Seamus's voice boomed out of a radio handset clipped to the sun shade under the roof.

'Sierra Zero, Roger out.' Angus's voice came through loud and clear.

'Ash, this is Les, radio check, over.'

'You're good to me, over.'

'Roger, good to me, out.'

Our new radios worked. That was one worry off my mind. They seemed quite small though, and I wondered about their range.

'These work through rebroadcast stations, right?'

'Ja,' said Hendriks from the back.

The most common threat at the moment was being shot up from behind by another vehicle, so Hendriks was facing to the

rear of the 4×4 with an RPD resting over the back seat. I
would be in the passenger seat for as long as it took me to get
used to the city and its landmarks.

'Sometimes the comms are *kak*,' he added. 'You can be
standing next to someone and not get him on the radio because
the signal do not go straight to him, it go out to the tower and
then come back. If the tower is out of range, or you are in a
dead spot, then it is *kak*, man.'

'Channel one, is that direct line of sight radio to radio?'

'*Ja. Ja.* If we lose comms you must switch to channel one.'

Hendriks was clearly the spokesman. Etienne kept his eyes
on the road and a faint smile on his lips.

I learned from Angus later when we sat down to catch up
on old times that we were hiring network time from another
company that had had the foresight to set up rebro towers all
over the city. In the meantime, Spartan planned to fit all the
vehicles for high-frequency radio, which would give us greater
range than our VHF handsets. HF could be difficult in desert
conditions, especially with the atmospheric differences between night and day. I wondered if comms training would be
included. In the meantime I buckled my seat belt.

Etienne was driving like a lunatic.

Literally. Like. A lunatic. He made Mohammed, who had
driven us from the border, look like a Sunday driver on the
way to the mosque.

The roads and traffic through the city were indescribably
chaotic. But whatever gap Les managed to put the car through
in front of us, Etienne was right on his rear bumper. I thought
at one stage he was going to park us in the Opel's boot, but it
was obvious Etienne knew his stuff and like a good Close
Protection (CP) driver he never let another car separate the two
of us. Which for Baghdad was amazing.

We had our safety catches off and sat there scrutinising every
car we passed in the mayhem. Added to the general insanity
and the general impatience of Iraqi drivers, the electricity grid
was still iffy so there was not a single working traffic light.
There wasn't a single working policeman, either. There were
cars shoving into every available gap in the road and
kamikazes coming back down the wrong way in our lane.

Etienne out-brazened them. If they were playing chicken they didn't know who they were dealing with. One driver Etienne simply shunted off the road and I watched the car spinning round in circles behind us in the side mirror. The high kerbs in Baghdad were useful in the seasonal flooding but they also served to prevent traffic from spreading out and driving across the desert to cut the bends.

Seamus on the radio kept up a steady commentary of potential threats. I appreciated his style. Knowing we were all experienced he was not wasting time mentioning everything he saw. Instead he focused on potential threats further afield, and at the same time identified anything near us he regarded as a serious threat. I had been in some vehicles where the commentary from the lead vehicle was just mindless drivel so totally useless to the vehicles behind that the occupants would end up tuning it out.

Seamus's voice became urgent.

'*Coalition dead ahead coming this way, weapons down, weapons down.*'

A CF patrol of four Humvees ploughed its way through the traffic. We were still in the honeymoon period before suicide bombers arrived so the CF had yet to adopt the drill of keeping all civilian traffic at least 50 metres away from each patrol. A good defence against the current attacks by small arms and RPG was to have lots of local traffic around you, but this strategy would have to adapt as time went by.

We lowered our weapons while the patrol passed. American soldiers were still not used to seeing security contractors and we didn't want to startle some young machine-gunner with the sight of armed men in civilian vehicles not wearing friendly uniforms.

Unlike the Brits mounting occupation and peacekeeping duties, the US troops in Iraq, especially Baghdad in late 2003 and through 2004, were the same guys who fought their way in. The poor sods in the 3rd Infantry Division had a combat mindset not in any sense conducive to peacekeeping. As for their anti-ambush drills, they had to be seen to be believed. Every weapon in the convoy unloaded in a 360° arc into anything that moved . . . dogs, donkeys, taxis, children, buses, private contractors, you name it, it got some. They would be leaving this country without making a single friend. A pity because, as I was to learn, the Iraqis are the friendliest Arabs in the world.

The highest scoring killer of private security contractors up until then was, of course, the United States Army, seconded by terrorists, but only when catching stray terrorist fire because they were driving along in traffic mingled with a US patrol.

As long as one kept away from the Yanks it was 'pretty *gut*', Hendriks informed me.

The patrol passed and we continued on our way. I gawped like a tourist at horse- and donkey-drawn carts. The animals were emaciated and you could count every rib and knob on their spines. Their drivers beat them viciously with long sticks. It was a sad and hopeless sight that ranked up there with crippled children begging. You saw that too, sometimes.

We turned on to the six-lane highway and I relaxed somewhat. We were moving at speed now, the cars around us spaced out, Seamus still scripting the way ahead. In a mixed packet, with two different types of vehicle, it was considered less likely that the enemy would spot us. But Etienne was blonder than me, a blue-eyed Boer, and everyone in our two cars – except me – was wearing a fancy pair of shades. As far as I could see we stuck out like tits on a bull.

I started to look towards the relatively distant tree lines and rooftops for threats. In the middle of the city, I had been keeping my eye on the nearest cars and doorways, AK held left-handed as I was sitting in the right-hand seat, ready to shoot without hesitation. It is the first few seconds that matter in close-quarter contact and I was comforted to see that the others all seemed to be always and instantly ready to return fire.

I noticed the burning flame on top of a tower in what had to be Dora refinery to our left and fixed the landmark in my mind.

Within minutes we arrived at the All American range set up by the 82nd Airborne – known as the All Americans – and unloaded the ordnance from the vehicles. The first order of business had been to zero our own weapons, but we decided instead to test-fire the entire batch so that we could then select the best ones for our own and return the rest to the armoury. We laid out some cardboard boxes at 50 metres as targets and then some Coke cans for rough zeroing.

'I'll give it a go,' said Les, stepping up to the mark.

He loaded the first rifle, checked the safety selector was all the way down to single shot, cocked it and shouldered the weapon. I already had my ear defenders on, as did Seamus; the South Africans had popped a couple of 9mm rounds out of the top of their pistol mags and jammed them into their ears. That's how they did it in Africa.

Les pulled the trigger. Nothing happened. He cocked it again, ejecting the first round, and pulled the trigger. Again we could hear the hammer clicking forward but the rifle didn't fire.

'For fuck's sake.' Les cocked the weapon again and the third round fired.

He worked his way through another ten rounds, of which less than half fired.

'What is this shit?' Les said.

Hendriks and I checked the ejected, unfired rounds. All of them had strong strike marks into the primers at the base of the cartridges, so it was not a fault with the firing pin.

'You see this at home,' Hendriks said. He pointed at the line of marks where the bullet itself was crimped into the top of the brass cartridge. 'They just clamp the rounds in and they do not fokken seal it. If the ammunition is stored for a long time, moisture gets in the holes and the powder. Then the round is fokken useless. Sometime even worse, the round fire but it only goes halfway up the barrel, then when you fire the next bullet, faaark, you are in trouble *boet*, yisss!'

The Yaapies all had this bizarre habit of hissing an excited 'Yissss', when something awful happened. Someone would crash in front of us on the road and they would all chorus, 'Yissss, yisss,' like a bunch of snakes.

Anyway this did not help our ammunition problem. We squatted around the boxes of ammo, picking out the rounds that had successfully fired. They had either Cyrillic script, indicating Russian or Yugoslav origin, or had Arabic numbers

with a thick red sealant on the case. We divided the Eastern
Bloc ammo into one tin and the red-sealed Arabic stuff into
another. Everything else, we dumped on the ground. Many of
the useless rounds had been Iraqi. Next we started testing the
weapons we had brought and quickly discovered that half of
them were just AK-47-shaped junk. Once we'd identified the
decent weapons it was time to zero.

We would fire a couple of rounds at a Coke can with a
partner spotting the bullet strike in the sand bank, apply
safeties, bang the sight left or right or screw it up and down as
appropriate, then fire another couple of rounds.

This was *not* like zeroing in the army. But it was fast.

In five minutes of furious firing we were all hitting the cans
from 50 metres. Seamus called a halt. I was sweaty and quite
pleased with myself. Less than 48 hours ago I'd been on the
road to Heathrow. Now I was in the countryside in the most
dangerous place on earth firing an AK-47 at Coke cans. The
sun was a washed out blur behind the fumes and dust and, in
spite of our target practice, a swarm of small bright-green birds
the size of wrens were wheeling above the range. The gunfire
drives the insects higher and the birds were feasting.

While the South Africans loaded the vehicles, Seamus
produced a couple of phones from his daysack to show Les and
me. The first was a small grey and white mobile, an MCI
phone, he explained. They used American mobile numbers,
which meant if someone wanted to call from the UK, it would
only cost them the same as an international call to the USA.
'And you can get some pretty cheap rates these days,' Seamus
added.

That would be good. Krista and I had wondered how I
would be able to keep in touch. There was only a three-hour
time difference so we would be able to talk in the evening.

'However,' Seamus carried on, 'coverage is shit and limited
to the city boundaries. As you can see there is no coverage out
here.' He pointed to the screen where we should have been able
to see the bars indicating reception. There was nothing.

Then Seamus pulled out a Thuraya, a hand-held satellite
phone. A chunkier piece of equipment, this was a lot more
useful.

'It works best if you are out in the open with a clear view of the sky, but it may just about work from vehicles and to a limited extent from within buildings if you have a big window. But it usually doesn't, so get outside if you need to use it.'

He showed us how to switch it on, how to get the phone menu and also how to use it as a GPS. I was impressed but I supposed it was obvious that a satellite phone would have a global positioning capability.

'That's the good thing about it because if you come under contact and you are immobilised you can send an exact grid reference to the cavalry. But don't get anyone to call you on this number, it's bloody expensive. We get one of these per team and we are each allowed to make two phone calls home a week on it.'

The South Africans had finished loading and we strolled over to the vehicles.

'I'll ask Jacky to get some MCIs for you. They are CF issue only, or for contractors working for the CF, but we have a pet US colonel who can get them for us,' said Seamus. 'That's not a friendly gesture, by the way. He has plans for us and he wants to keep us sweet.'

'What route home?' asked Etienne.

'I know I said Karrada,' Seamus replied, glancing at his watch, 'and we finished earlier than I thought, but we need to get these weapons sorted out at the armoury and I can't be fucked sitting in rush-hour traffic today. It will take a while to do these tonight, so let's just go home up the highway the way we came and go shopping tomorrow.'

We mounted up and called into Sierra Zero to inform them we were leaving the range and that we were coming back along the highway.

It had been a useful exercise. Had we not tested the weapons we might have been driving around Baghdad with pieces of junk in our hands. I wondered how many security companies were as efficient, and how many guys were driving around out there with useless ammo. At least any enemy we came across were likely to be carrying weapons loaded with Iraqi rubbish and, on a brighter note, we were now carrying decent weapons with live rounds. We would sorely need them both before the month was out.

Spartan had scored one of the contracts to escort journalists and my first PSD tasking with the gang was to collect the AP journalist Lori Wyatt from Baghdad International Airport.

NINE

After surviving insurgent bullets and friendly fire to bring reporter Lori Wyatt safely into the Green Zone, our boss assigned another Spartan unit to act as her dedicated team in Iraq.

After Les and she had exchanged numbers, they would meet up at the Al Hamra hotel, where she and many other journalists were staying. The Al Hamra was an ugly concrete ten-storey building 200 metres from the CPA gate in a protected street with guards at each end, but it had that feeling of being outside the safety zone and when the Palestine Hotel was full, this was where the journalists wanted to be. In the lobby there was a sign saying: 'Please check your weapons at the desk', which made you think you were in the Wild West and, like gunslingers, we ignored it. The great thing about the Al Hamra was that it had a really nice pool and on Thursday evenings there was a pool party.

Adam Pascoe had developed a relationship with an ambitious US Army colonel who was after his one-star promotion to general and was working on a deal for Spartan to get the task of safeguarding the water purification infrastructure, one of the major utility contracts for the reconstruction. Adam had told all the teams to keep our eyes peeled for water facilities, make a note of the terrain, fencing, vulnerable points, the current security, and bring it back to HQ with photographs. With this material, when Spartan went for the water contract, Pascoe would support it with a dossier of intelligence.

Next day we were tasked to pick up a French reporter from the CPA building and take her out to do some interviews. Her name was Michelle Delacroix.

'You know I speak pretty good French,' I told Seamus.

'That's what they teach you up at the Factory, do they?'

'I was just wondering –'

'All right, Rupert, you can have this one.'

We were in the chow hall eating scrambled eggs and crispy bacon flown in from Kansas. Hendriks, bladder of steel, downed his seventh coffee and we were set for the day.

Michelle was waiting for us dressed for clubbing in an Armani jacket, blue jeans and a red bandana. Apart from the three-day stubble, he wore one of those skimpy French moustaches and it wasn't Michelle. It was Michel. A man! If any of our team had been hoping to meet an attractive Frenchwoman they had been sorely let down.

'Tasty,' Les murmured, and Monsieur Delacroix couldn't understand why the rest of the team were roaring with laughter as I introduced myself as his personal bodyguard.

We marched Monsieur Delacroix from the Presidential Palace back to the car park. Having trashed the Opel we now had a Peugeot saloon, again without armour plating. It was almost new; new, as such, didn't appear to exist in Iraq. I thought all the vehicles probably came across the border from Kuwait when they were about ten years old and had long since had their day.

I gave Delacroix the same speech that Les had given Lori, that nothing was going to happen but if it did, he was to get down on the floor and I would protect him.

'*Oui. Oui.* You don't have to say nothing. I do this one million times.'

Michel had a three-man team of Iraqi fixers waiting outside the safety zone. Most Iraqis weren't allowed inside the CPA, naturally. The team had been engaged independently of Spartan by Michel's news agency and included a reasonably good interpreter, a cheerful, middle-aged man with a pot belly named Assam, whom we immediately nicknamed Sammy. He had fine pale hair lacquered and backcombed over his bald spot and blue eyes. I thought at the time that this was something of a rarity, but Alexander the Great had marched through Babylon and his soldiers had left their mix in the gene pool. Sammy was with two surly young guys with dilapidated AKs. Their main task seemed to be to stand next to the Frenchman while he posed for photos.

I pointed at their weapons. 'Just keep those out of sight. I'm sure you don't have permits, and if the Americans see you they won't leave a grease spot behind.'

'Grease spot?' asked Sammy.

I drew my finger in a line across my throat. He translated for his companions and reluctantly they slid their guns into the foot well.

Sammy pulled out an old dog-eared map and in his antiquated English stressed that we should avoid the highway and take the road through the desert. We were heading for the town of Fallujah, a hotbed of resistance and apparently too precarious for us to enter, even armed to the teeth. We were surprised since Spartan Ops had said the area was safe, but Sammy shook his head.

'This place very bad, Mister. Very dangerous.'

My first instinct was that he was overplaying the danger either to squeeze out more money, or to separate Michel from us in order to flog him to the highest bidder. For some reason, Seamus said nothing and I decided to let it go and trust the man.

The revised plan was that we would take our principal to the outskirts of Fallujah, then Sammy's team would escort him through the city walls. We were not entirely happy with the arrangement, but our job was to chaperone reporters and this is what reporters did when they were trying to make a name for themselves.

Delacroix lit a Gauloise and looked faintly bored as Sammy traced our route over the thin grey lines crisscrossing the vast featureless wilderness on the map. He knew the roads, he said, *like the back of my hand*, and told us proudly that as a pilot in Saddam's Air Force, he had been based at the air force base close to Lake Habbaniyah.

He stabbed the map with a stubby finger and Seamus's
eyebrows shot up. Lake Habbaniyah was in the heart of the
desert west of Baghdad in a place called al-Anbar Muhafazah
and was fed by floodwaters from the Euphrates. The lake
provided irrigation for crops and was the largest in Iraq, in fact
one of the largest inland seas in the world. If you happened to
be looking for a water pumping station, this wouldn't be a bad
place to start.

Seamus pulled out the new digital camera Adam Pascoe had
given the team and took a photo of Sammy looking over the
map. He grinned. Iraqis loved having their photos taken.

'For the family album?' Sammy asked.

'For the record,' Seamus replied.

If our principal was kidnapped a shot of Sammy might turn
out to be useful.

We didn't have a radio for Sammy's vehicle and went
through our set of prearranged signals in case there was an
incident; flashing lights and the horn-honking drills. We would
remain a single packet; if one vehicle pulled off the road, we
would all pull off.

'Is that clear?' Seamus asked.

'Like the crystal,' Sammy replied.

Sammy would lead the way, but if there was a roadblock or
an attack, he would pull over and let us overtake. Our
Coalition ID would allow us to speed through roadblocks; our
superior firepower was the best remedy if nastiness raised its
ugly head.

'Is that clear?' Seamus asked again.

Sammy saluted. 'A OK,' he replied.

I glanced at his decrepit yellow Toyota. 'Is that thing going
to make it?'

He looked mortified. 'I beg your pardon, Mister,' he said.
'But I have cared for this car for ten years and it has *never* let
me down. I love my car more than I love my women.'

'Women?'

He took a breath and threw up his plump hands. 'It is the
burden I must abide. The women, they love me too much.'

I wasn't interested in the old boy's love life. 'You have
enough benzene?' I asked.

He tapped the side of his nose. 'Yes, Mister. No problem.'

We set off with the Toyota leading. Les was driving the Peugeot, Seamus at his side, me in the back with Michel. The Yaapies were bringing up the rear in the 4 × 4. We steered a course through the morning rush hour, slipped out of the path of a kamikaze with about two dozen women cowering in hijabs in the back of his truck and left the city limits, heading in a southwesterly direction.

'Who are you going to interview?' I enquired.

I spoke in French and he answered in English. He turned to look at me. 'The other side,' he said.

Delacroix waved his finger like a baton as he told me he had been against the war, that *everyone* in France had been against the war, and he thought the Coalition Forces were doing a shitty job in the post-war reconstruction.

'The Americans came in with no plan to get out and you English follow like poodles. You should have been united with France and Germany and Russia. One man could have stopped the war and that one man wasn't Bush.' He paused to stab me in the chest. 'That man was Mr Blair.'

'I'm sure Mr Blair had his reasons,' I said, not that I could think of any. It was obvious to anyone who could find their own arse with both hands that the CF were not going to find any weapons of mass destruction, even though that autumn they were hopelessly still looking.

'This country is in chaos,' Michel resumed. 'Soldiers are dying every day. Iraqis are dying every day.'

'That's why we're here, to try and make it better.'

'You are an optimist,' he spat.

Maybe he had a point. But the Brits in the car all had mates serving in the armed forces in Basra and we didn't need a lecture. Delacroix told me he had excellent contacts among the insurgents in Fallujah and was going to tell their side of the story. Personally, I was worried that the next time we would see him was going to be on Al Jazeera in an orange jumpsuit; the terrorists had copied the Americans in Guantánamo and it was an effective PR coup when hostages appeared on TV dressed in that way.

We fell silent. The country roads were steeled in a thin layer of tar that blended into the landscape. The arid wasteland stretched to the horizon in every direction, not waves of sand in undulating dunes like you imagine from *Lawrence of Arabia*, but a dusty red rocky plain as old as time.

We zipped along at about 130kph for two hours without seeing another vehicle. When I caught my first glimpse of Lake Habbaniyah, I thought it was a mirage, a vast blue eye shimmering like a mirror. As we drew closer, I could see a flock of wading birds, their black wings draped over white bodies like capes; they had sharp elongated beaks and fragile pink legs. They turned their long necks to glance in the direction of the noise made by our vehicles. As they returned to their meditations, the tranquillity of this fleeting scene seemed almost surreal after the turmoil of Baghdad. I couldn't at that moment have imagined anything better than plunging in the lake for a swim.

I suggested as much to Seamus and he laughed it off.

Sammy stopped at a water pumping station and Seamus went to take some photographs for Adam.

Les wandered off with Sammy towards the guards from the Facilities Protection Service (FPS). They were sitting bored out of their skulls in the hut by the main gate. Behind them were breeze-block buildings with tin roofs housing pumps and purifying equipment. The entire compound was circled by a rusting mesh fence.

I sat on the hood of the car and watched Hendriks studying the desert like a hunter waiting for something to shoot. There was nothing. Nothing moved. Just the spirals of dust dancing over the plain.

The philosopher Cicero said as Rome's legions marched across Europe that in times of war the law falls silent. We didn't appear to have learned much in the last 2000 years. From the first $87 billion awarded by Congress for the reconstruction of Iraq, millions were already unaccounted for. Along with thousands of crooked Iraqi subcontractors, the FPS was one of the black holes that had consumed an abundant share of those millions.

When the Coalition chiefs set up the FPS, they went back to Saddam's old cronies with great bundles of dollar bills. The cronies duly re-employed all the people who had worked for

them before: their brothers and cousins, sons and son-in-laws.
There is a sense of Iraqi pride. Sunnis and Shias fought side by
side in the war with Iran. But their first loyalty is to their
family and the tribe.

Saddam's old security guards had been given new jackets
with navy blue brassards embroidered with the white FPS
insignia and the Iraqi flag. They were armed, equipped and
paid by the Americans and continued doing exactly the same
job they had always been doing, but with more money to buy
packs of Marlboro so they could smoke themselves into an
early grave.

Seamus got his pictures. We piled back into the cars and had
only been motoring along for ten minutes when we ran into a
storm of machine gun and small arms fire. An IED on the side
of the road exploded, probably a buried mortar or artillery
shell, not that hefty but with sufficient calibre to shred one of
the front tyres on the Peugeot. Les wrestled with the steering
like he was fighting a wild bear and we careened off the road.
I pushed Michel down into the foot well and disengaged the
safety on my rifle as the car shuddered to a halt. The South
Africans swerved straight into a protective position.

As for Sammy, our grinning guide, he put his foot down on
the gas and the Toyota disappeared in a cloud of dust. I
thought if I ever saw the little shit again I'd rip his head off.

Whether the gunmen had been smart enough to know that
the principal would be in the centre vehicle of our convoy, or
whether this was just a lucky hit, we had no way of knowing,
but it warned us that they were more likely to be fedayeen than
looters.

How they had come to be lying in wait in the middle of
nowhere would give us plenty of scope for debate, although the
most likely option to me was that it was Delacroix's alleged
contacts manning the assault. And if they knew we were on
this road, at this time, Sammy might have tipped them off for
a $20 backhander. He had insisted on taking the desert road.
He had been one of Saddam's officers. It made sense.

Of course the FPS guards could have been playing both sides
of the fence, but they would hardly have had time to set up an
ambush.

Right
Shiite village women starting the long walk home with gas canisters. It is 45 degrees centigrade!

Below
A map of Iraq.

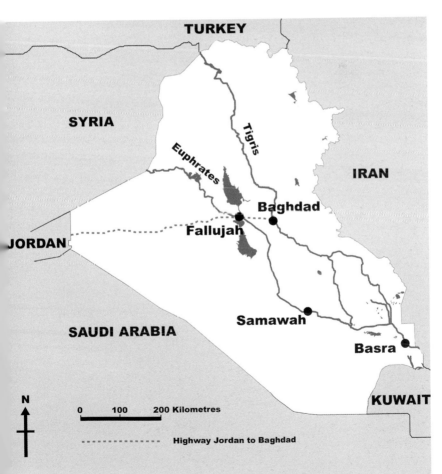

TURKEY

SYRIA

Tigris

Euphrates

IRAN

Baghdad

Fallujah

JORDAN

SAUDI ARABIA

Samawah

Basra

N

0   100   200 Kilometres

Highway Jordan to Baghdad

KUWAIT

Left
Money! Piles of US dollars for paying Iraqis and buying weapons and supplies – a sight to gladden the heart of any security contractor.

Below
Wayne in front of a crashed Iraqi jet near Fallujah.

Right
Riot in Samawah. I'm just left of centre in the foreground. This is taken about thirty seconds before the arrival of the CF convoy.

Right
A typical overt PSD Counter Assault Truck with spare tyre, towing strap instantly ready and rear-gunner with home-made armour. A sign warns locals to stay away from the convoy.

Right
One of our weekly timed running, driving and shooting competitions where we bet fiercely with the South Africans and huge amounts of dollars change hands. Wayne and Cobus are timed by Les with pistols at 20m.

Left
A selection of short weapons for car use brought in for sale from a black-marketeer. Clockwise from top; Beretta M12, shortened AK47, Tariq, Browning Hi Power with 20rd mag, Glock 19, Sig P226, HK MP5.

Below
Individual equipment for each contractor, including medical kit top left and comms kit on the right. Kevlar body armour and tactical load carrying vest are not shown (I was wearing them when I took the photo). Weapons are selected according to mission requirements.

Left
A destroyed Iraqi T-72 at one emplacement of the so called 'ring of steel' around Baghdad.

Left
'Al Qaeda Killer', one of the M1 tanks on guard at the Route Irish checkpoint in the CPA. A Stryker personnel carrier is visible in the background.

Below
A standard Spartan issue of weapons for a four man team. Four M4 carbines, M249 SAW, Remington 870 shotgun with solid slugs to stop enemy vehicle engines, spare AKM for guests and RPD LMG.

Left
A truly hideous bust of
Saddam removed from the
top of the Presidential Palace
after it was claimed by the
CPA.

Below
Tasteful décor in the palace,
gilt thrones and murals of
scuds.

Me with covert 'soft' car gear: short-barrelled G3, shotgun with solid slugs, Sig pistol and smoke grenade to cover any debussing in contact. Once we got armoured cars we all switched to long-barrelled rifles.

Left
Sammy on the left, disguised in tribal fashion, a true and loyal friend. I'm in the centre and a tribal guard with AK is on the right at a Task Force Fountain site near Habbaniyah.

Below
Bradley Infantry Fighting Vehicles, taken when I did two weeks patrol with the CF around Baghdad.

Les in those two seconds leapt from the car and was popping shots along the enemy firing position about 200 metres from us. The South Africans de-bussed and were quickly laying down withering fire. The explosion from the IED was still ringing in my ears although, even as I scrambled out of the car, I realised how lucky we had been. The bomb had been buried deep enough for us not to see it, but too deep to do any real damage. Most of the blast had gone vertically into the air, otherwise we would all have been shredded by shrapnel.

Seamus and I stoop-crawled to the front of the Peugeot. It had dug itself into the dusty grey sand. Enemy fire was getting closer. A line of bullets skittered along about a yard to my left. Seamus took a quick look around. There was no shelter as far as the eye could see. I calculated there were between twelve and twenty men out there. Seamus must have done the same arithmetic. He shouted to me to get Delacroix out of the car.

'We're going to bug out in the Nissan,' he said.

He shouted instructions to the South Africans. They nodded and carried on emptying their belts at the enemy position in measured bursts. Les started to slide backwards like a crab towards the 4 × 4. The rebel fire wasn't that accurate, but one of them at least was hitting the Peugeot and the rest were finding their range. As always happens, the explosion had deafened me at first, but I could now hear bullets snapping by my ears. Iraqis are a volatile lot and gunmen get very excited when they have a Western target. I knew if they ever calmed down and started aiming properly we were going to be in serious trouble.

As the designated bodyguard, I climbed back in the car to get Michel.

'Let's. Go. Let's go.'

He totally refused to move.

'Michel, *allez*! *allez*! Let's go, man.'

He had wedged himself like a foetus half under the front seats and was clinging on for all he was worth. I started screaming every Anglo-Saxon curse that came into my head, but threats and punches would not budge the man. I even chopped him across the back of the neck to try and stun him enough to drag him out bodily. It didn't work. Paralysed by fear, he was a tight little ball weeping and gibbering, but he was putting everybody's lives at risk.

'Get that cunt out of the car,' Seamus screamed.

'I can't move him,' I screamed back.

Seamus gave me a scornful NCO scowl as he came to take charge.

'Get out, you fucker,' he said, and ripped the sleeve off Delacroix's Armani jacket as he tried to haul him to his feet.

We both worked on him but the Frenchman had some animal sense of survival and for him survival was staying inside that Peugeot even while the gunmen were finding their range and scoring some fresh hits on the car bodywork.

I watched as Seamus, with scant regard for his safety, raced across to the South Africans and told them that we were going to have to tow the damaged vehicle out. Good soldiers that they were, they hawked up phlegm for a good spit and got on with it.

Etienne was quickly behind the wheel and edged across the firing zone in front of the Peugeot. Cobus climbed in the back and started unrolling the loose end of the tow strap. Hendriks carried on doing what he did best, spraying the enemy position with concentrated bursts so deadly accurate the ambushers could only fire back blindly without taking aim. Cordite fumes hung in the still air and I thought momentarily of the languorous calm of the wading birds back at the lake.

Cobus passed me the loose end of the tow strap and I looped it around the eye-ring on the undamaged side of the Peugeot.

'That's two fucking cars we've trashed in two days,' Seamus said, as if he was worried about the book-keeping all of a sudden.

He climbed into the driver's seat and gunned the engine. He tooted Etienne, who eased forward to tauten the tow straps, and both drivers put their foot down. The Peugeot had dug itself into the dust at high speed and edged out laboriously a grain at a time. Les and I put our weight behind the vehicle, while Cobus and Hendriks went through another couple of cartridge belts.

The damaged vehicle was still trying to shake itself free of the dust when to my complete and utter amazement Sammy's old Toyota appeared on the left flank like the cavalry in a cowboy film.

He must have made a circle through the desert and now raced into the killing zone with guns blazing at the enemy's unprotected left side. Sammy's men were firing ancient AKs and their accuracy was awful, but the shock on the enemy coming under fire from two sides was such that the gunmen started backing off. They retreated in good order, eight or nine guys laying down fire while eight or nine ran back. They were trained soldiers, almost certainly Saddam loyalists.

Sammy had parked up and his gang kept firing at the enemy until they retreated from view. Then they jumped back in their car and drove down to join us. Sammy was grinning from ear to ear.

'You took your time, what took you so long?' I asked him.

'Traffic,' he replied, without missing a beat.

Hendriks and Cobus had come to join us pushing the Peugeot. We were grey with dust from the spinning rear wheels as Seamus gunned the engine. Sammy joined in and eventually the car slithered on to the road.

Seamus got out of the car and took a look at Michel Delacroix, still in a vegetative state on the floor.

'Right, interview cancelled. Back to Baghdad,' he said.

If he was anticipating an argument from Delacroix, he didn't get one. He got back behind the wheel. Les and I climbed in the 4 × 4 with the Yaapies and, with Sammy leading the way again, we towed the Peugeot back towards the water plant, the rim of the damaged wheel gouging out great chunks of tarmacadam as we went.

We had only been going for about five minutes when Seamus gave the horn signal for us to stop.

'Fuck it,' he said.

He untied the tow straps. He then opened the rear door and gazed down at the Frenchman.

'All right, Sonny Jim, you're out of danger, let's go,' he said.

Delacroix would not budge.

'Did you hear me, we're abandoning the car. Get in the Nissan.'

No movement.

'What's wrong with this fucking bloke?' He looked at me. 'Get him out before I lose my temper.'

Les and I tried levering up the prostrate Frenchman with the barrels of our AKs. We dragged at his jacket and pulled off his boots. Still he clung on. Les had done the arrest and restraints course and brought those skills to bear: you take hold of the person by the thumb or little finger and bend it back. As their mouth falls open in a scream, you jab your finger like a fish hook in their mouth and haul them up. Delacroix against fifteen stone and six feet of angry Englishman. No contest.

As Les hooked Delacroix out of the car I told him if he didn't behave we were going to leave him behind in the desert. He had been traumatised by the bullets punching through the doors and window next to him. I was surprised by this – he was supposed to be a war reporter who knew the dangers. He had put all our lives at risk by refusing to get out of the car while we were under fire. Les poked the snub of his AK in the Frenchman's chest.

Sammy came back towards us.

'You have problem?'

'No problem.'

Delacroix was quivering but was at least trying to compose himself. Les manhandled him into the back seat of the Nissan and climbed in beside him.

'Ash, there's no room for you,' Seamus said. 'Hitch a lift with the Iraqis.'

TEN

We put the medical kit and ammo in the boot of Sammy's car, I grabbed a radio, and Etienne pulled up close behind us. Sammy wanted to siphon the gas from the Peugeot but it was time to get the hell out of Dodge.

It was difficult to remember that Iraqis did not live in a throwaway society like our own and every dollar had a lot of homes to go to. Old car tyres are cut up for sandals; they flatten oil drums for roofs and weave palm fronds into baskets; bricks are taken from bombed buildings to build new buildings; cartridge cases are saved for the brass and electrical cables are dug up at night by the ali-babas for the copper.

'That was quite a move, coming up behind the enemy like that,' I said as Sammy started the car and put his foot on the gas.

He turned to me. 'An old pilot's trick,' he answered. 'It was the only thing to do.'

'Well, it was bloody well done. I'm grateful,' I told him.

'Grateful! Why grateful? We are brothers.'

He had taken his eyes off the road and was still driving at top speed. I steadied the wheel.

'Steady on. You're not flying your Mig now.'

'Bandits at four o'clock,' he said and grinned as he turned to me again. 'You are an officer?'

'Infantry,' I replied.

'Sandhurst?'

'Is this a third degree?' I asked and he patted my leg paternally.

'You British are too reserved for your own good.'

We had a two-hour journey back to Baghdad and as we chatted I realised that Assam Mashooen was the first Iraqi with whom I had had a proper conversation. It turned out that his father had trained as an artillery officer at Sandhurst in the 1950s. Sammy followed his father's footsteps to England where he learned to fly with the RAF in Southampton. He had fond memories of the English and even fonder memories of English girls.

'You know Southampton?'

'I do a bit,' I said, thinking *not really*.

'Then you must know Joanna. Who can forget Joanna?'

'I hope your wife doesn't know about your sordid past,' I said and he laughed heartily.

He had risen to the rank of wing commander and had flown hundreds of sorties in the Iran–Iraq War. Saddam had personally presented him with a gold-plated Tariq, the Iraqi-licensed version of the Beretta. He pulled the pistol out of his waistband and, when he dropped it in my lap, I was in awe of a piece of history actually touched by the dictator himself.

Sammy waxed nostalgically. 'Sometimes we would see the Iranian jets coming over. We would ignore them and they would ignore us. We were all pilots together,' he said. 'They would go and drop their bombs, I would go and drop my bombs, and we would wave to each other on the way back. It was a stupid war.'

Sammy talked about the internal no-fly zones that had existed, even during the war. If a pilot strayed into the wrong space, like over one of Saddam's palaces, a convoy of black cars would be waiting at the airport to drive him off to some subterranean cell where he would be hung on meat hooks as a punishment.

'Saddam Hussein is very bad man. I am happy the Americans came and drove him out.'

'If you were so unhappy before, why didn't you just fly out and ask for exile?'

'They will rape your wives and daughters, they will kill all your sons. They will fuck you.'

He was still driving flat out and Hendriks's voice crackled over the radio.

'Wait up. This is *kak*, man,' he said.

'Take it easy,' I said.

He dropped down to 120.

I asked Sammy how he got the job translating for Michel Delacroix. He rubbed his thumb and finger together. 'I need dollars.'

'How much are you getting?'

'Trade secret,' he replied.

'Come on, Sammy, you know you're going to tell me.'

'You know how much I get as a pension from the Iraqi Air Force?'

'I've no idea.'

'Come on, guess. You English like puzzles.'

'I'm Scots,' I said and he laughed.

'I get two dollars each month. Two dollars,' he said. 'The French man, he pay me hundred dollars each month.'

'For?'

'I find the guards, I get them wine and special things you can't find in the CPA. I always charge a few dollars more.'

I thought about that for a moment and made a decision that wasn't really mine to make.

'Come and work for us. My outfit is paying interpreters three hundred dollars a month and some of them don't even speak English. The last guy got a job because he's the cook's cousin,' I said. 'Your English is as good as mine.'

It wasn't. Sammy's English was quaint and broken, but with his pale hair combed over his bald spot and his gold Beretta, I knew he would be helpless to flattery. I told him an officer whose father had gone to Sandhurst shouldn't have to make extra cash the way he was. Spartan was in Iraq for the duration and the job would be better paid and longer lasting.

He stuck out his hand. 'Thank you very much, Mr James. You are a good man.'

As we shook hands, he almost skidded into the desert and did a neat pilot's manoeuvre to swerve back on course.

'Now what about these two guys in the back?' I asked him.

'Nothing. They are rubbish.'

They were sitting their nursing their AKs and I glanced back with a smile. 'Do they speak English?'

'No. The agency wanted two guards so I asked these men. They are from my village, my wife's relatives. They are no use to you.'

At Spartan we would be building up a guard force if we got the elusive water contract and although the two young guys didn't have particularly good table manners, they had done their job: they had risked their lives that day with Sammy and shot at their own countrymen. I told Sammy this and he said that if we needed guards, he could find them. Wine. Weapons. Ice cream. Even girls. Sammy had his plump fingers on all the buttons.

One of the problems private security firms had was being overcharged by the locals. We were pumping more money into Iraq than the country had ever seen in its history: Sammy was getting $2 a month pension; doctors, lawyers and teachers probably earned no more than that; $300 was a fortune and I got him to agree to report to me when our Iraqi fixers at Spartan were ripping us off. We expected to pay over the top. We just didn't want to be made to look complete idiots. We shook hands again. I had my own mole.

We stopped just short of the CPA to drop Sammy and his guards off where we had picked them up. Sammy took me in an embrace and planted a slobbery wet kiss on both cheeks. He went to do the same to Les, who fought him off, ducking and weaving to avoid Sammy's attempts to kiss him.

'Not while I've still got strength in my body,' he said.

'You English, you are too reserved.'

Sammy glanced at Seamus and shrugged. They shook hands and Sammy touched his own hand to his heart. We told him to be back there at nine a.m. the next day when Seamus would have sorted out a temporary ID card for him. Then we drove back into the Green Zone and made our way to Spartan HQ.

Michel Delacroix was still shaky. He went to the office to complain to Adam Pascoe that not only had he not been able to reach Fallujah to conduct his interviews, but we had ruined his Armani jacket. He stuck his hairy wrist under Adam's nose and pointed at his Rolex. It was broken.

After a brief quarrel between Les and Delacroix, the Afrikaners escorted Delacroix out of the office and drove him back to the CPA car park.

Adam took it in his stride that I had employed Assam Mashooen; Sammy's heroics would be in the report, but now it was his turn to lose it when Seamus told him we had abandoned the Peugeot in the desert.

'How many cars are you going to get through?'

'As long as you send us out to shit holes in soft cars they are going to get shot up,' Seamus said. 'When are these B6s coming in? It's in my contract that we're supposed to have armoured vehicles.'

'They're in Kuwait . . .'

'In the Golden Container?'

'Waiting to be driven up,' Adam explained. He had the grace to look embarrassed.

'We'll fucking go and get them if you want,' Les added.

We headed off to the palace canteen for a pineapple pizza. For the first time I thought how unfair it was that Iraqis were barred from entering the CPA building itself. We may not have made it out of that contact without Sammy.

We remained as Michel Delacroix's PSD team during the following three weeks and it was the best job I had during eighteen months in Iraq. We did bugger all. I spent the days swimming in the Al Hamra pool. Then Seamus and I would train in the gym while Shagmeister Les Trevellick spent long afternoons pursuing Anglo-American relations.

While Lori Wyatt was with Les, her PSD team would be killing time like us at the CPA and we'd run into the guys regularly at lunch.

Jacko Jackson, the team leader of Lori's new PSD team, was an Irish charmer, a Colin Farrell lookalike, dark and handsome and at 5ft 7in a bit on the short side. He'd been an Irish Guards sergeant and was unusually well spoken. He had considered being an officer 'but had too much self-respect', he said over the Cajun chicken wings one lunchtime.

'That's what I'm going to do, give up this shit and go to Sandhurst to train as an officer,' he added.

First he had too much respect. Now he was going to Sandhurst! Seamus was shaking his head. 'You what?' he said. 'You don't have what it takes.'

This was a back-handed compliment and Seamus's mouth clamped shut when he noticed my satisfied smile. You don't compliment officers. I guess everyone forgot that I was just about the only British officer working the roads in Iraq. I know I certainly did.

Jacko's mate was Steve Campbell, a pale, skinny guy who wore glasses and had been in the Royal Logistics Corps (RLC), the biggest corps in the British Army and better known as the Really Large Corps.

Jacko, and Steve to a lesser extent, both thought they had a chance with Lori and we would sit listening as Jacko boasted how Lori made it 'so bloody obvious' that she fancied him.

'So when are you going to score one for the team, then?' asked Seamus.

'Tonight's the night. I just know she's gagging for it.'

We never let on that Les had got there before him.

The other Brit on their team was Rafael Fernandez, half Spanish and with the broadest Glasgow accent in the world. He was known as Badger; ex-Royal Military Police (RMP), he had done the Close Protection course conducted by the SAS, one of the best courses of its kind. RMP men with this course under their belt were among the most highly sought-after operatives in the security game. Badger was like Del Boy, a wheeler dealer who traded with the Americans just for the sport. He'd buy a crate of fifty 40mm grenades we didn't have the means to fire, then find a unit where the grenadiers were low on ammo and swap it for a box of med packs or spare Kevlar plates. If you wanted a French Brie or yesterday's *Daily Mail*, Badger was your man.

In Spartan tradition, the remainder of the team consisted of three South Africans, Johannes, Pieter and Jaki, friends with our Yaapies, in fact Etienne had brought Johannes and Pieter to Iraq. Just as the Africans were a little mafia, Marines chatted with Marines, Paras with Paras, SAS with SAS, and the topic of conversation was always the same: money.

How much are you getting? What's the leave package? How about expenses? What's the insurance if you get slotted?

Every time you walked into the CPA building you met operatives from all the other PSCs; the CPA was a good place to discuss contracts and to be offered new jobs.

Jacko, Campbell and the South Africans had all been with another company but they jumped ship and came over to Spartan as a team, an advantage to our company because they'd already been processed at Camp Victory and had their CPA passes. Spartan had a fair-pay policy and they were all paid $15,000 a month, as well as getting leave every nine weeks instead of twelve.

We spent a lot of time discussing money, and during those three weeks when Michel Delacroix was conducting his research from the safety of the Green Zone, when I wasn't swimming and gossiping I went off on my own to explore.

The Green Zone stood behind high walls with gates at every entrance, ten square kilometres of palaces and government buildings where the Coalition Provisional Authority had set up its administration. This is where Saddam had his palaces; there were numerous government and ministry buildings and private villas with pools. The buildings were connected by wide boulevards trimmed with tall palms and statues of Iraqi soldiers in heroic mode. It must have been peaceful and pleasant in Saddam's day, but now the logistics of maintaining 130,000 United States GIs meant parking lots overflowing with Abram tanks, Bradleys and Humvees, and dumps with hundreds of tons of rations, gasoline and war materiel.

Private companies, security firms (including Spartan), NGOs and the press had their offices in the Green Zone. Bizarrely, there was a residential area where the Iraqis who had been living there before the war had remained. They worked as cleaners, translators, and drivers and the Americans didn't appear to find anything unusual in this even though access for all other Iraqis was heavily restricted.

Saddam's palaces were not architectural jewels but fortified bunkers built to withstand bombardment. Ideal for the CPA. The buildings boasted a few arched windows and ornamental minarets, but the extravagance was saved for the interior where everything was made of marble, velvet and gilt. There were enormous carved eagles perched on tall columns and chandeliers from Paris. The bathroom fixtures were marble and gilded monstrosities. The palaces now billeted grunts from the 3rd Infantry. They were sleeping in cots in Saddam's bedroom and pissing in Saddam's golden urinal. The fleeing government officials and local looters had taken the Ming vases, the Picassos and Monets, the gold-leafed sofas, the gold-rimmed mirrors, and tasteful items would sometimes turn up in a breeze-block hut with a tin roof, like an installation by a conceptual artist.

Everyone would have liked to have taken a piece of treasure home but by the time I arrived the palaces had been picked clean. One lunchtime I came across a copy of the *Stars and Stripes* with a photo of three guys who had found $15 million in suitcases. They were all clean-cut American boys and they'd given the money back. I showed Sammy the newspaper. He knew where the Ba'athist officials had their villas outside the zone and we agreed when we had some free time we'd take a look.

We did find one big old villa, a shell, clean as bone, and I took photos of the garden from the roof to see if the ground had subsided over any hastily buried caches. We never discovered those telltale signs, but Sammy and I enjoyed the fantasy.

ELEVEN

In the last week of Delacroix's tour of Baghdad, his agency cancelled the PSD contract. Bearing in mind that Spartan's standard charge was $1,000 per day, per man in the guard team, Spartan had effectively lost $42,000.

Our boss, Adam Pascoe, therefore, made an effort to get Spartan more secure deals from the CPA. When he scored the contract to PSD Colonel John Hind it was like opening an untapped seam in a gold mine.

At first glance private security may have appeared expensive, but when the US Government calculated that it was spending $25,000 per soldier per month in Iraq, then using private contractors was in fact *more* cost effective. They are paid to carry out specific defined tasks, and once the contract is completed, the costs end immediately.

On 13 December 2003, three months after my arrival in Iraq and eight months after the end of the war, Saddam was found burrowed in an eight-foot hole in Tikrit, his old stamping ground in the heart of the treacherous Sunni Triangle. Some 600 soldiers of the 1st Brigade of the 4th Infantry Division with special operations forces of Task Force 121 had carried out the raid in Ad Dawr and had found Saddam's bunker near a group of ramshackle buildings. Saddam had a scruffy beard and a pistol. He didn't fire a shot and emerged from his hole a broken maniac suffering the shock and awe of having been drugged by his own bodyguards.

Most Iraqis had hated Saddam. They enjoyed seeing his humiliation on television, but it was a tipping point, a reminder that thousands of Iraqis had died in the bombing and during the occupation life wasn't getting better, it was growing worse. Electrical goods were flooding over the frontier, but there were now fewer hours of electricity in which to use them; there were shortages of food, gasoline and medical supplies. Every day that I had been in Baghdad the number of attacks on Coalition Forces had risen. The response by US troops was often heavy-handed and resentment from ordinary Iraqis resulted in a lack of co-operation at best, and at worst more volunteers for the uprising. Privatising security was clearly making a lot of sense in the White House. In December 2003, more than a thousand American soldiers had made use of the boxes piled up at Camp Victory and had gone home draped in the flag; more than 2,300 by April 2006. Americans didn't like that. It was upsetting when they tuned into the evening news. The Administration started bringing the boys home at night in secret, but their buddies got photographs and leaked them to the press. They had fought for the streets of Baghdad with these guys. They were heroes. By outsourcing security, the US could avoid unfavourable headlines in the press. Busy fighting the propaganda war, spokesmen were rebranding Shock and Awe as Operation Iraqi Freedom.

'I remember Operation Angola Freedom,' Etienne said over his roast lamb one night. 'I lost a lot of mates in that war.'

'When they say freedom, it means it's going to be a long battle,' added Cobus.

'*Gut. Gut.* I can pay off my bond,' said Hendriks, practical as always.

Colonel John Hind was in his late forties, a guy who had been fit but was now going to pot, with a ruddy face, fair hair that was almost white and eyes hidden by wraparound shades that could have belonged to Bono. He had been put in charge of Task Force Fountain and had come to *I-raq* with the objective of scoring his one-star: promotion to general. As the American boss of water resource protection he had moved into the CPA expecting to have a plush office and fifty Marines in support. What he got was a box room without so much as a gold-plated urinal and a sergeant to do the typing.

I felt sorry for Hind. I had seen a few officers in the Dukes who craved promotion and it's not a pretty sight. It's like trying to upstage other actors in the theatre; the kind of officers, as Krista had astutely observed, who speak louder than anyone else at dinner parties and then write thank-you notes that are all hype and no heart.

Hind had persuaded the general staff at the CPA that he needed to get out and see the water. Swinging the budget to get himself a PSD team had been a coup. Now we had that job, we were hoping to get Spartan more contracts with him as the project commanding officer. More kudos to John, more money for Spartan.

The military command at the CPA was under pressure to make the post-war reconstruction in Iraq a media success. Hind in his quest for promotion was working on getting a reputation as a can do guy and volunteered his expertise in situations where no one was sure what had to be done and who exactly was responsible.

His favourite task was taking us on a water inspection jaunt where, sometimes, we would run into a convoy of materials for the reconstruction coming in from Jordan or Kuwait. He would insist on accompanying the convoy and, as his PSD team, we would find ourselves acting as de facto convoy escorts.

I told him that it wasn't our job and if the trucks came under fire, we would whisk him off to safety and bugger the convoy.

Convoys brought in everything from sewer pipes to dumper trucks, from loo rolls to portaloos, from M&M's to sandbags. Convoys came in many sizes; a hundred trucks wasn't unusual. These were protected by the US military, often in conjunction with security firms that had scored those juicy escort contracts. Smaller convoys from lesser reconstruction outfits than KBR would take their chances with drivers from Egypt, Nepal and the Philippines who were risking their lives to make the sort of money they could never even dream of earning at home. These motley caravans were magnets to insurgents and looters alike. The Americans didn't like losing these vehicles and John Hind was trying to expand his influence by saying he could provide cover. By *he*, he meant *us*. I told him to bugger off.

'We're saving people's lives here, don't you see that?' he said.

'By risking our lives,' I replied. 'You get Spartan a convoy escort contract, and we'll bring in as many convoys as you can wave a stick at.'

'You think I'm Houdini? You think I can conjure contracts out of the air. There's a process.'

'Then get the ball rolling.'

Our policy at Spartan was to be only out on the street for the minimum amount of time required for our principal to carry out necessary site visits. Instead, we were rolling eight hours a day because the Colonel was constantly trying to impress any general or State Department official who might give him a favourable report.

'Listen, boy, this isn't about me,' he said, lowering his voice. 'I'm just trying to do what I can for the people of *I-raq*. We came to this *goddamn* country to bring democracy.'

'I thought it was to get rid of Saddam's WMD?'

'WMD. Democracy. You sound like the *New York Times*. There's no difference. That's what you people don't understand.'

'What I do understand is our contractual obligations, and that is to guard you and only you.'

Colonel Hind was the water man but I thought he had his own agenda. We would set out to inspect some irrigation facility and find ourselves in a lumber yard counting telephone poles. One time we went to a steel works and ended up escorting a fleet of trucks carrying gun towers for the American bases, vast welded monsters, just one fitting prostrate on a flat-bed truck. The convoy was so slow an old Iraqi man on a bicycle passed us without losing breath. If we had come under contact, we had the gun towers and no big guns.

It came as no surprise to me that when convoys of petrol tankers started being attacked, Hind began a campaign to get himself involved with security. He was the water man. But oil is the lifeblood of Iraq. No one went anywhere by foot except goat herders and women lugging Calor Gas canisters, the people too poor to be worth abducting or killing.

Oil is Iraq's saviour and its tragedy, its only source of income and the cause of all its problems. Sammy, though always spick and span, smelled faintly of petrol, and it wasn't his aftershave. Every time you saw him wander into the company car pool he was carrying a five-gallon jerry can with a length of rubber tubing around his neck. We could fill up in the CPA. Sammy was denied this luxury and siphoned gas from our vehicles whenever he was on a job for Spartan.

The problem getting gas into the gas stations in a land floating on oil was a major headache. When you have ten-mile tailbacks outside filling stations you get civil unrest. There was civil unrest anyway. What the Americans didn't need was the people rising up in a country where everyone is highly strung and armed with an AK-47. When the Coalition overthrew Saddam, Iraqis were promised freedom and so far we had delivered little more than satellite dishes and Internet porn. Now they were defeated we could entertain them to death. Cars were crossing the desert from Syria and Turkey carrying volunteers for the insurgency and gear for the black market: TVs, laptops, Game Boys and DVDs of movies that wouldn't be released in London for months. Where they got their petrol supply from was anyone's guess.

Queues at gas stations were a self-fulfilling prophecy. Drivers would see a line, realise the tank was half full and pull over just in case. For a taxi driver, it was more economical to line up for gas all day with his boot and back seat full of jerry cans and put his family on the side of the road selling gas at five times the regular price.

Filling station bosses ran their own jerry can fiddles and would keep their cousin on one of the pumps filling jerry cans for gangs who controlled the market in their own strip of Baghdad. When the station managers couldn't be bothered filling jerry cans, they'd announce that the station had 'run out' and close down, only to re-open after hours to sell the benzene at inflated prices. No one who lined up legitimately was going to make a fuss. The station managers were armed and protected by the local hard man for one thing, and for another, this was the custom, a way of life understood and practised by everyone. The schoolteacher who had to pay the jerry can boys five times the true rate for his gas charged parents to pass their children when they took their exams at college.

All this was very un-American and for the Americans it was so crucial to keep the gas stations filled and the prices fair. They were paying KBR a fortune to bring in convoys of benzene from Kuwait – taking coals to Newcastle, to quote the old adage, and were fighting bandits every inch of the way.

When the electricity was down, as it was practically every day, the petrol pumps didn't work. Petrol tankers would be sent in, but delivery from tankers is gravity not pump driven, the process is slow and the tailbacks would stretch back twice as far as usual. This made good footage for the Iraqi and international media, but it was essentially a false picture because many gas station managers would say adios to the security escorts accompanying the petrol tankers, then hop up with the driver and head for the backstreets to sell the gas like the jerry can boys at five times the normal rate. Either that or sell the entire tanker to a criminal gang.

There was a lively market in ripped off petrol tankers, as our team at Spartan would soon find out.

The oil infrastructure was next to useless. As fast as KBR could cut ditches and lay new pipelines, fedayeen planted bombs and blew them up again. Petrol stations were coming under attack. The second-biggest oil fields in the world, and across most of Iraq there were shortages at power stations resulting in electrical shutdowns and more angry confrontations between Coalition Forces and irate citizens. *It wasn't as bad as this under Saddam*, they'd say. And they were right.

The problem hit home to us when our guards started calling in to say they couldn't come into work because they had drained the gas from their cars to fill the tanks of vehicles belonging to family members who had an emergency. When their big families didn't have emergencies, the guards were sucking the benzene from their vehicles to power the generators bought on the black market with the $150 a month we

were paying them. They were staying cool with air conditioning, keeping up to date with the news from Al Jazeera and
picking up assault tips watching *Black Hawk Down*.

When there were shortages, people would come to me and
ask why we weren't doing anything about the situation. *Come
on, you're the white man, what's going on?* Sometimes it was
like living in a *Monty Python* sketch. They would spend the
night digging up the electricity cables to sell for the copper,
then the local headman would come to me to ask why their
new TV wasn't working.

'You are here to help us.'

'Yes, but you have to help yourselves.'

'We are helping ourselves.'

Iraqis have a sense of humour.

TWELVE

John Hind got his big break just before Christmas and must have dreamed of his one-star gleaming like the star over Bethlehem, which wasn't far from us. Just a Scud's flight from Baghdad.

He convinced the CPA that on his water inspection trips he had acquired good local knowledge and that he was the best man to liaise with the military escorts bringing in convoys of oil tankers. As the Water Man, he saw it as his duty to get oil to the refineries in Baghdad in order to keep the power stations going. Without power, his water purification plants would fail. If the Coalition Provisional Authority was worried about civil unrest when there were petrol shortages, he said, then just wait and see what happens when the local population runs out of water.

He got the job.

The test run for John Hind consisted of a convoy of 65 oil tankers coming in from Kuwait. Convoys usually crossed the desert in relative safety, and were then hit in the densely populated zone around Latifiyah, about 30 miles south of Baghdad, where we were going to join them. Colonel Hind planned to park the tankers overnight at the water plant south of Latifiyah, then race into the city before dawn with us riding shotgun.

When we were tasked to PSD the outing, it was hard to
know whether Adam Pascoe had taken his eye off the ball, or
whether he thought this would curry favour with the CPA and
win Spartan a regular convoy escort contract. In the field,
when you know there's a risk of being slotted, you make sure
everyone in the unit knows why they are there and what they
are trying to achieve. On this particular gig, he had not made
this clear.

Hind was happy. Pascoe was happy. Sammy was thrilled
because he had parleyed a bonus acting as an interpreter for
the Americans. The first three interpreters Colonel Hind had
tried had hung up the moment he mentioned the road to
Latifiyah.

We set off in a three-car packet before first light, the safest time
to travel. Most people weren't out of bed, and if there were
any bad guys waiting in ambush they would be fatigued from
having been up all night. Lose one per cent of your attention
and your shooting ability goes way off target.

John Hind was travelling in his own SUV with another
officer who wore gold-rimmed glasses like John Lennon.
Behind the wheel was a black sergeant named Harvey, a man
with the same ponderous calm as Sergeant Willows, the guy
who had led us into the Green Zone the first time we came
under contact. We led the parade, Les driving, Seamus, Sammy
and me. The Yaapies brought up the rear.

Latifiyah is in Al Qagaa province in the heart of bandit
country just over half an hour's drive from Baghdad. The town
had a chemical complex and a water-softening regeneration
plant. It was an ugly, earth-coloured place with narrow streets
and a skyline broken by the domes of mosques and tall
chimneys that were constantly pumping out fumes that gave
the clouds a yellow tinge. The air was dry and tasted of
chemicals. Seven Spanish intelligence agents had died on that
road and the local CF fought running battles there virtually
every day. Two private security guards from another company
had been killed in Latifiyah the previous week.

We reached the plant at Latifiyah at 6.00 a.m. and couldn't
get in the main gate. The depot had come under attack during

the night and unexploded rockets were strewn all over the highway.

We made a circle across the desert and entered the depot by the back door. 'Another fucking cake and arse party,' Les said as we turned into an enormous parking lot with the 65 tankers lined up with military exactitude.

A swarm of Iraqi and Egyptian drivers and the GIs from the infantry unit guarding the convoy were wandering around without any idea who was in charge. They had crossed the desert in the dark without any dramas, sat up all night in the water depot praying the rockets didn't hit any of the tankers and now had no idea how they were going to get the convoy moving again.

Hind stepped out of his SUV, threw out his chest and strode about like Colonel Kilgore, the guy who loved the smell of napalm in *Apocalypse Now*. The soldiers were happy to salute the Colonel, but didn't seem to recognise his authority to lead the convoy out of Latifiyah, although that was academic at this stage. Old, tarnished and clearly the property of Saddam Hussein, the unexploded rockets were everywhere: on the road, on the office roof, between the parked trucks.

While Colonel Hind strutted around showing everyone he was in charge, Seamus and Sergeant Harvey stood together watching the show like a pair of rugby props waiting to go into a scrum.

'So, what are we waiting for?' said Colonel Hind. 'Let's get the show on the road.'

'We'd like to do that, sir, but we do have something of a problem,' said the sergeant in charge of the infantry unit.

As he spoke, Les Trevellick started dealing with that problem using the stock tactic employed by the RUC (Royal Ulster Constabulary).

In Northern Ireland if the coppers can't be bothered to wait for a bomb disposal officer to come and examine a suspicious item, they just give it a good boot. If it doesn't go off, the patrol carries on. Les kicked the rocket lying across the main exit gate and it echoed back across the depot with a hollow ring. I went to join him.

'Yes, that one's clear,' I announced.

We lifted it out of the way and continued along the highway repeating the process. Les doing the kicking, the pair of us doing the schlepping. We looked like heroes or nutters to the American GIs. As far as we could see, the rockets were just the propellant tubes and were missing their warheads. Seamus and Sergeant Harvey came to join us and together we cleared the road and the depot.

Les finally climbed up on the office roof to check the unexploded rocket wedged in the guttering. He called and I went to join him.

'This one's got its warhead on,' he confided.

'Let's leave it, then,' I replied, whispering.

We gave the all clear.

Seamus spoke to Sammy who in turn told the Arab drivers to saddle up.

Colonel Hind signed for the 65 tankers. When Hind told the American soldiers to return to their vehicles, they looked for Seamus's nod of the head before they did so. Seamus told them they should deploy the ten Humvees evenly among the trucks in packets of two. We would remain a separate packet of three vehicles travelling up and down the length of the convoy.

The Arab truckers, *jundhis* they were called, were now jostling to be first through the main gate: the further back in the line the more dust you ate. They kept a wide berth around the rockets littering the rocks along the side of the road, the dust spiralling in the air and coating everything in grit. When the first thirty trucks had exited the depot we joined the caravan. As was all too often the case, we had no comms with the Humvee drivers. They had radios on their own secure frequencies and no spare handsets for us.

It was now getting on for 0700 hours. So much for our pre-dawn dash. There were a few private cars on the road but no sign of fedayeen. They had been hammering at the plant all night. It was gruelling work getting Saddam's dead rockets to fire; we'd been in the same predicament on the range with his bullets. I imagined the bad guys were still at home sleeping. The tankers had arrived late and after the long drive across the desert, the insurgents would have expected the drivers to sit out the day drinking *chai* and smoking. A day on, a day off, was the normal work rate.

Les weaved around the tankers, turned and motored back again. We were 78 vehicles in all and covered two kilometres of road. We moved in our own dust storm, the wipers not clearing the windscreen but smearing a shit-brown arc over the glass. It was cold out there with a brisk wind. I was glad of my fleece and Kevlar vest. I was nursing my long, thumb flicking mechanically over the safety. We were twenty minutes into the journey and were just reaching the outskirts of Mahmudiya, a town about the same size as Latifiyah and just as dangerous.

'Looks like Colonel Hind's going to make his delivery without a drama,' I said. 'A nice quiet run.'

'Shut the fuck up,' said Seamus sourly. 'I don't believe you've just said the "Q" word.'

He had turned in his seat. As he was still speaking, there was an enormous explosion and a fireball like something out of the *Bible* rose into the air.

It was difficult with the dust obscuring our vision to see exactly what had happened but there was nothing wrong with our hearing. One of the tankers ahead of us went up like an atom bomb, like a sonic boom magnified a thousand times, and the sound reverberated to the rear of the convoy almost bursting my eardrums. The tanker had probably been hit by an RPG and a massive column of flames and smoke rose into the sky. The driver was toast.

The drivers behind the explosion slammed on their brakes and were zigzagging across the road as they piled into the back of each other.

Les instinctively pulled straight off the road and cut across the desert towards the ball of flames. There was small-arms fire thundering into the ground and little fireballs of petrol were raining down, splattering on the car roof and cleaning the windscreen. It was like Guy Fawkes night. The Arab drivers were jumping out of the cabs and fleeing in the opposite direction of the rifle fire, which was sensible: they were driving 50,000-gallon bombs.

Two of the Humvees were close to the explosion. They had been lucky not to be engulfed by the blast and the men inside were putting down return fire by the time we got there. Had there been more American soldiers we would have let them get on with it, but there were just half a dozen guys and we weren't going to leave them to take on an army of insurgents if that was what was out there dug into the desert.

Colonel Hind was following in his vehicle, yelling instructions over the radio, although we couldn't be sure if he was telling us to stay away or join in the battle.

We remained about 100 metres south of the Humvees. Seamus, Les and I took up fire positions and started putting a few rounds back at the enemy. Sammy slipped into the driver's seat and kept the engine running. I estimated there were about a dozen bad guys. They had two or three belt-fed weapons, at least one RPG, and five or six more were firing small arms.

The South Africans cleared the Nissan with their belt-fed guns and began spraying 7.62 at the main fire coming from the cluster of buildings off to our right. In spite of not having radio comms with the American soldiers, they could see what we were doing.

The gunner on the nearest Humvee let loose at the house where most of the enemy fire appeared to be coming from in a long burst from his Mk19, a fearsome weapon with a short, stumpy barrel that throws out 40mm high-explosive grenades. I had never seen one fired in anger before. Holy shit!

Hind, his driver and the guy in glasses didn't budge from their SUV throughout the contact. Remaining inside a vehicle in this way seemed to make people feel safe; the French journalist Michel Delacroix certainly gave that impression on the road back from Fallujah, but these were military men and should have known better. The SUV was a plumb target for an RPG and what they were doing sitting there was a complete mystery to me.

The exchange of fire was going nowhere. The insurgents were melting away surprisingly quickly and what fire they did return could have been coming from any of the hundreds of windows in the apartment buildings overlooking the highway.

Our priority was getting the remainder of the convoy moving, not going on a wild-goose chase across the desert. Firing from the enemy position became sporadic: the terrorists were learning that when there was superior fire power it was best to draw back and try another tactic.

The dust had settled during the firefight and we only now became aware that the front half of the convoy had vanished over the horizon. The drivers from the abandoned trucks were chasing about like headless chickens but didn't need much persuasion to climb back in their own vehicles. Sure, they were driving 50,000-gallon bombs, but better that than getting left outside Mahmudiya among tribesmen who knew they had been working for the Yankee Zionist Crusaders.

The drivers pulled themselves up into their cabs babbling prayers. The Americans in the two Humvees seemed pleased to have seen some decent action without taking any hits and took up positions at the front of our half of the convoy.

We took off at 140 *klicks* to catch up with the other half. It was like trying to put the two halves of a pantomime horse back together. The front half of the convoy was lumbering along in a huge cloud of dust and we spotted the Humvee at the back in about ten minutes. The Mk19 grenade launcher was aimed at our windscreen, but we had the Stars and Stripes stuck on the glass and we moved by without any hassle. We got to the front, slowed the pace to allow the back half of the convoy to play catch up and wound our way to the big oil depot beside the main railway station in Baghdad.

Colonel Hind strutted around pressing flesh and telling the guys they'd done a great job. He had proved, at least in his own mind, that his presence had saved the day. We had lost one tanker, but what the hell, they had fought off a brigade of foreign fighters and they could have lost the lot.

'Good job, Corporal, where you from?' asked Colonel Hind.

'Ohio, sir.'

'Well, you can write home to the folks in Ohio and tell them you're a hero.'

He shook hands with the Arab driver who had led the convoy.

'I am from Alexandria,' said the driver. 'Very beautiful.'

'I'm sure it is, son.' He grinned at all the soldiers. 'Good job, everyone.'

The officer with the gold-rimmed glasses had one of those clickers and was counting in the trucks. Les Trevellick, an engineer, a good maths man, was counting on his fingers. The tankers were coming in sporadically like marathon runners.

'That's ten,' said Les.

The guy in gold glasses nodded.

Two more, then another one. Then three together.

Colonel Hind spotted me hiding behind the Yaapie wagon and marched over. He stuck his hand out. 'That's the way to do it, Captain Ashcroft,' he said. 'We make a great team.'

'If you say so, Colonel Hind.'

'I do, son, I do. We're going to whip this country into shape, you wait and see. We knocked those terrorists six days from Sunday.'

I heard Les shout 'ten' as another truck turned through the gate and brought the total so far to twenty.

It seemed to take an hour before all the trucks were in the depot, but it was probably no more than twenty minutes. Les and the American officer counted in 43 trucks. Behind the last one was the pair of American Humvees that had taken the tail position when we left Latifiyah.

'That's forty-three,' said Les.

The American translated for Colonel Hind. 'Forty-three, sir,' he said. We were way short of the 65 we had started with.

'That can't be right. Check again.' The winning smile faltered.

Sergeant Harvey stood at the gate looking down the road. It was empty. Les and the officer in gold specs counted the trucks together. There were 43.

We all took a look up the road. And we all counted the trucks.

One tanker had been blown up.

Twenty-one had vanished into thin air.

Well, not in the strictest sense of the word. Twenty-one drivers had driven off into the dust never to be seen again. We discovered on questioning the Egyptian drivers of the 43 trucks who had made it into the depot that all the missing vehicles had been driven, as far as we could gather, by Iraqis. The local drivers knew the desert tracks between Mahmudiya and Latifiyah and, we assumed, they knew where they could shift $21 \times 50,000$ gallons of petrol on the black market.

Colonel Hind would write up in his report that we had lost the tankers in a firefight with fedayeen terrorists, but a lot of acts attributed to the insurgency were just plain banditry and for me the barefaced theft of 21 trucks of petrol bore the hallmarks of a well-organised criminal gang. First the bombardment with dud rockets overnight. Then the explosion of one truck to create mayhem. The gunmen took a few pot shots then fled. I had thought we were lucky to lose just one tanker. Now I understood that they had only needed to destroy one as a diversion. They had not melted away in fear of the spectacular hail of grenades from the Mk19, but because their job was done.

We would have been able to establish the facts more clearly had we had more men to go forward after the contact and search for enemy bodies and other evidence. It didn't happen. It wasn't going to happen. Mahmudiya and Latifiyah were two towns notorious for their violent inhabitants. Iraqis avoided them. They were more likely to be kidnapped and killed than we were; we were better trained and more heavily armed.

It was doubly disappointing for Colonel Hind. It had been his strategy to park the trucks in the water depot and race them at daybreak into Baghdad under the radar of the insurgents. The fact that a third of those tankers disappeared meant that there was something fundamentally wrong with the plan.

Hind had created the package, all hush-hush. But it didn't matter how top secret it was; it was doomed to failure because any Iraqi employed as a driver was likely to be in the pay of the black market or the insurgency. When you employed locals you were either hiring the enemy or giving information to the enemy. The only way to prevent trucks hot-wheeling off from the convoys was to employ American drivers. Or turn the job over to private security.

John Hind had wanted to present a clear-cut success story at the CPA and, rather than acknowledging that we had lost 21 tankers, he described a full-on battle where we had managed to salvage 43. He described how the drivers had fled from their vehicles in fear after the initial explosion and bandits had taken over the trucks and driven off in them. The missing drivers never turned up to refute his story and as Spartan received credit at various meetings in the CPA, Adam was delighted by the positive publicity.

I did wonder when it was all over how many of those 43 tankers that we had successfully escorted to Baghdad would simply be driven into the city to disappear into the black market anyway.

THIRTEEN

Angus McGrath was going on leave and promised to email me photos of his sexual conquests back home.

'With a woman this time, right?' I joked.

He made a gun from his fingers and shot me.

I stuck my empty plate back in the kitchen and eyed up the fruit bowl. I was looking in vain for an apple that had no obvious maggot holes to stick in my daysack for later. Apples were a treat.

Seamus had only just left the dining room and ran back in with all his kit, strapping on his vest.

'Jacko's team's been hit in Karrada. Wheels up now.'

'I'll be in Ops,' Angus said, and went running out.

I was wearing my vest. I snatched my rifle from where I'd left it in the hallway and ran for the door. Les was already behind the wheel in the lead vehicle. I jumped up with Seamus and Sammy. He'd started out as an asset. He was now one of the team. I caught a glimpse of Etienne in the beaten-up Nissan. He was ashen, all the blood had drained from his face. Etienne had recruited two of his best friends into Spartan. Both were in Jacko's gang. Cobus was driving with Hendriks manning the rear window and Dai in the back seat. He'd just got in from leave.

We accelerated at high speed through the morning rush in

two 4 × 4s, ignoring traffic lights and mounting the pavement if the traffic was blocked.

'Left here, Mr Les.' Sammy leaned forward between the two front seats and indicated the road. He returned to speaking on the phone in Arabic, his voice tense and rapid.

Jacko's team had been hit by an IED close to the supermarket on one of the main streets in Karrada. They had not sent a contact report but Hayder, Angus's Iraqi assistant in Ops, had recognised them on his way into work. Hayder was now on the phone to Sammy from Spartan, directing us to the hospital. The guys had been taken in an Iraqi ambulance, along with the Iraqi casualties. This came as a surprise, given the growing tension those last weeks, and the only explanation for it was that Jacko's team had Union Jacks in their windscreens, showing they weren't American. We usually went without markings. They flew the flag. There was no rule, but the choice made that day by Jacko and his team might well have led to the attack in the first place.

The Spartan casualties had already been in the hospital for forty minutes. FPS and Iraqi Police casualties were often followed into hospitals and finished off by the fanatics. We wanted to make sure that if they tried it on with us they'd have a nasty surprise.

Sammy handed the MCI forward. Seamus listened for a few moments, acknowledging with the occasional 'Yes.'

'OK, listen in, here's the situation,' he said, handing the phone back to Sammy and speaking at the same time on the radio handset so that the guys in the back vehicle could hear as well. 'The Brit wagon took the main hit. At least one dead and one VSI. The South Africans are OK, just minor injuries from broken glass.'

VSI (very seriously injured) was bad news. It meant that you had suffered a life-threatening injury.

I could almost hear the sigh of relief from the vehicle behind. Etienne must have been wondering how he was going to break the news to their families. No one wishes ill to members of other teams, but you can't help being grateful when it is someone else that's caught it and not your friends.

'We're about two minutes from the hospital,' Seamus continued. 'As soon as we get in I'll speak to the surgeon and see how bad the VSI is. Ash and Hendriks, do a check on hospital security. Cobus, set up the RPD and stay with the vehicle. Les, Dai and Etienne, be ready to drive straight out with the remainder of Jacko's team to the Cash.'

The Combat Support Hospital in the CPA, or CSH aka 'The Cash', was a state-of-the-art American military hospital capable of dealing with every type of battlefield trauma.

'Les, soon as you get to the Cash, establish comms with Sierra Zero, give them a full casualty report,' Seamus added. 'I'll try and get HQ to organise a casevac for our casualty now.'

'Roger that,' said Les.

Sammy was leaning over again indicating and Les swung left across the oncoming traffic into a walled compound containing the hospital. Johannes and Pieter were standing beside their 4 × 4, rifles at the shoulder, scanning in all directions. They were Etienne's friends. Both had blood smeared across their faces and looked less shaken than bloody angry. Badger was in the car giving Jaki basic first aid, but Jaki needed to get moving to the Cash to get proper medical attention.

We pulled in next to them and de-bussed, ready for action. Seamus asked the South Africans for a report. Etienne could not speak but the way he hugged his mates said it all. Cobus set up an RPD on the hood of our car facing the entrance gates on to the main road. Seamus looked grim when he returned from speaking to the South Africans.

'Jacko's dead. Steve Campbell's in a shit state. The others have cuts from broken glass but can self-evac to the Cash and get stitched up. Les and Dai, you lead the way. I also want you to try and reach Mad Dog and get the CF out here to collect Jacko's body and casevac Steve. I'll try and find out from the medics whether Steve can be moved or not.'

Colonel Hind had done so well saving all those oil tankers he now had two assistants, Sergeant Harvey and another full colonel, Steve 'Mad Dog' McQueen. While Hind was growing his empire within the CPA, he had tasked Mad Dog to liaise with us directly and do the dirty work out in the Red Zone; i.e. outside the steel barriers at the CPA.

I remembered that day when Jacko had said he was going to quit being a hired gun and try and get into Sandhurst. I'd heard other soldiers say the same. It was a dream that would never come true for Jacko Jackson.

Seamus dragged at his moustache, and turned to Sammy. 'Sammy, can you try and get the full score from the doctors? I'll wait here with Cobus until you get back.'

'I am ready.'

Sammy marched off and Seamus called after him.

'Thanks, man,' he said, and the old wing commander saluted.

Patients took their guns into hospital with them, but Sammy could enter in safety. Seamus in his kit stood out like the flame above the Dora oil refinery at night.

I glanced at Hendriks. 'Ready?'

'*Ja, kom uns gaan*,' he replied, indicating that we should go.

It wasn't that likely that insurgents were going to make a raid on the hospital, but our job was to make sure that if they did we were ready for them. We set off anticlockwise, weapons held with the butt just touching the shoulder, ready to be brought up into the aim position in an instant.

I watched as Les led the surviving vehicle from Jacko's team out of the gateway. He tooted his horn and then they were gone, swept away in the mid-morning traffic. Officer training teaches you to be thinking about everyone's safety, every eventuality. I was wondering if Les had thought about the route he was going to take to the CPA. With a bomb going off in Karrada there was a good chance that the road we had just driven down had now been blocked off by Coalition Forces and all the streets in the area would be choked with angry Iraqi drivers. Les would need to head northeast and come in from the Assassin's Gate at the northern entrance to the CPA. He'd work that out for sure.

The wall around the hospital complex wasn't that high and a platoon from the Dukes would have gone over it in full kit without breaking sweat. From what we had seen of Iraqis they were astonishingly lazy. There was a good chance that if the bad guys were coming they would go for the obvious entrances to the compound, the front and rear gates.

We passed an Iraqi guard sitting at the side door with an AK across his lap. With the equipment and drugs in the hospital they needed guards to prevent the local community from looting it into an empty shell. They would have robbed the building in an orgy of greed and destruction and then the next day they would have complained bitterly that the Coalition Government wasn't providing them with the medical care they needed. It was the same with the electricity supply, the same with many things. The people seemed to be able to live with this paradox and it startled me every time I came across this maddening concoction of the familiar interspersed with episodes of totally alien reasoning.

We reached the rear gates. They were chained and padlocked. Good. One less thing to worry about. On the far side of the hospital, the wall belonged to the neighbouring block of apartments that stretched back to the main road. There were a few narrow windows, but no one was going to be coming from that angle unless they rappelled down from the roof.

The sound of voices grew louder as we approached a ring of dusty trees halfway back up towards the front gate. Crows circled high above where the voices were coming from.

'Fok, YISS!' hissed Hendriks.

We had stumbled across what was serving as the hospital morgue, a bare patch of concrete behind the administration offices. According to Muslim tradition the dead should be buried within 24 hours. A dozen bodies were laid out in a row below the shade cast by the trees. Nothing much in Iraq was neat. Nothing was put straight, tidied up, kept in order. Except the bodies. They were always in precise rows. Here there were weeping relatives wailing and howling over them.

The dead bodies were undoubtedly the civilians killed in the bomb attack on the Spartan convoy. We could see that the wall was clear all the way back up to the front of the hospital and I didn't want to intrude and make their misery worse.

'Let's pop in here.'

We said *salaam alaikum* to the armed guard sitting at the entrance to another door and he seemed pleased that we paused long enough to show him our ID cards. He probably thought we were just going to barge in and this moment of courtesy demonstrated that he wasn't beneath our notice but actually had some authority. It was good PR. It made him look good in front of the Iraqi office workers smoking in the corridor behind him.

I looked back at the women in black, kneeling and screaming over the bodies of their men and children. The crows continued circling high above. I followed Hendriks inside.

The hospital was filthy. Not just dirty. This was ancient filth. This was biblical. The germs in that hospital would survive nuclear fallout. The corridor leading to the front of the building was packed with Iraqis squatting on the floor smoking. I couldn't tell whether they were visitors, staff or patients. There were no smiles here. Sullen stares followed us all the way to the main door. I smiled politely, looking for hostile intent in the body language of the people we passed. Hendriks had his expressionless killing face on. His icy eyes flicked across clothing and bodies, looking for concealed weapons.

As we reached the entrance, I saw a woman with blood oozing through her bandaged head being pushed in a wheelchair down another hallway. The crowd made way for her with far more animation than they did for us.

We followed behind and saw Seamus and Sammy talking with a bunch of Iraqis, two of them wearing white coats. To my surprise one of them was a woman; female Iraqi doctors – this one was a surgeon – were a rarity.

'The place is clear,' I said to Seamus. 'There are four local guards with AKs on all the doors coming into the building. As long as we stick together I think we'll be OK.'

'OK. Hendriks, if you stay with Cobus out here. We'll go and see how Steve's getting on.' Seamus pointed at Cobus and the 4 × 4.

Hendriks nodded and left. I watched Hendriks speak to Cobus before sitting on a low wall, rifle ready, in a position where he could see the exposed side of the hospital building. Cobus stood relaxed behind the bonnet of the Nissan watching the passing traffic over the front sights of his RPD.

Seamus and I followed Sammy and the doctors into the hospital.

'Did the Yaapies recover all the weapons and radios?' I enquired.

'Yeah, they've got them in their wagon,' Seamus replied.

These questions need to be asked and these things have to be done, even when colleagues have been killed and wounded. More so. You've got to stay cool, keep a clear head, work the drills. You don't want to add losses to your losses by making errors.

'How did they catch it up?' I asked Seamus.

'They were in the usual order of march, Brit wagon in front, South Africans behind. The Yaapies saw them swerve around a car in the street, obviously a setup. The device detonated under them. The shrapnel got Steve and Jacko in front, but didn't touch Badger. It went off under the engine block and most of the blast was deflected sideways into the crowd. That's why they've got a dozen civvies dead.'

'We need armoured vehicles in this environment,' I said.

'Damn right we do. I'm going to give Adam an ultimatum on it, mate.' Seamus handed me his MCI phone. 'I gave HQ a sitrep on the Thuraya but we haven't been able to get hold of Mad Dog,' he added. 'Try him again while I speak to the surgeon.'

A sitrep is a situation report. They had the report at Spartan, but it was more urgent to get the information to Colonel Hind or Colonel McQueen at the CPA so that they could organise a casevac.

We'd reached the operating theatre. A rusty assortment of unidentifiable medical equipment from the 1950s sat around the place like a museum of junk. The room was cramped, hot and full of flies. Swarms of flies. Small ones that bit and big ones that aimed for your eyes. The power was out. What lighting there was came from a lamp with wires trailing from the window out to a generator that throbbed like an old metal fan. The air from the window shifted the cigarette smoke in swirling clouds and a crowd of people stood around the room like spectators at a show watching us as if we were part of the performance – two doctors, two white guys, Sammy with a gold Beretta in his belt. The people carried on smoking, dropping their ash on the floor, watching, always watching.

'What the fuck is this?' said Seamus. I could see a tic vibrating in his neck.

Sammy put a hand on his pistol butt. He shouted at the spectators and they reluctantly shuffled out to watch from the doorway.

Steve Campbell was on the operating table at the centre of the room. Both his arms were bandaged stumps just below his shoulders and one of his legs was missing.

The female surgeon spoke good English. She told Seamus that Steve's genitals had been traumatically amputated by the blast. He would make a good recovery but would be incontinent. It was an odd thing to think, I know, but I wondered how he was going to wipe himself with no arms and only one foot. He didn't have a loving wife waiting for him at home. And it wasn't as if he was going to be attracting anyone soon. His nose was a mess and his face was pockmarked with shrapnel.

I was suddenly aware of the smell of shit. When someone is killed they always shit themselves. Always. It is an aroma I will forever associate with violent death. If someone dies next to you, you smell the shit as well as the thick, metallic scent of blood. If you are unlucky enough to see them dying slowly, the other telltale sign is that just before they go off they get goose bumps and all the hairs stand up on their skin. Steve's skin had no goose bumps. He was breathing.

The smell of shit was obviously coming from the corner of the room where a child-sized shape wrapped in a plastic sheet lay on a trolley.

I had the MCI to my ear. No one was answering. Mad Dog McQueen was probably running around clearing up after Colonel Hind. I stuck the phone in my chest pouch.

'Is that the other Englishman?' I asked the surgeon, pointing at the plastic sheet.

'Yes. He died in the ambulance. We brought him here in case some of the people in the hospital became angry and mistreated the body.'

'Thank you.'

The woman smiled. It was nice to see that smile in that room.

Seamus looked at me. I was standing closest to the body.

'Shall I check him?'

The South Africans had probably already done so but the

professional thing to do to was to get his operational kit and personal effects.

'Yes, if you would, mate,' said Seamus.

I gave Sammy my rifle and gingerly pulled back the plastic. Jacko was dead all right. No legs, no arms and no face; the lower jaw had been ripped away and the rest of the face and scalp was flayed off. His torso lay in a thick pool of blood and shit. I surmised that the ambulance crew must have slung him straight on to the plastic sheet at the scene of the explosion to avoid messing up the interior of the ambulance.

There were no personal effects to recover. The blast had ripped off his clothes as well as all the ammo pouches from the front of his body armour. They were gone too, along with his radio, ID cards and his arms and legs. I waved the flies away and put the sheet back over him. I knew that I would never be able to smell shit again without thinking of Piers Jackson. He'd been a good-looking bloke, but when we sent him back I'd recommend adding fifty pounds of sand to the body bag and telling the family to keep a closed casket.

'Anything worth keeping?' Seamus asked.

'No, mate. It's all been blown away.' I retrieved my rifle from Sammy.

'What about his body armour?'

'It's the only thing holding him together.' I tapped the plastic shrouded form in the area of Jacko's chest. Soft. No hard plates in the Kevlar vest. Pity, they might have been useful.

The female surgeon confirmed that Steve was stable enough to be transported. 'He should be moved to the CPA hospital,' she advised.

The other doctor had melted away and now a richly dressed man in a Western-style suit appeared and drew us to one side. The woman watched with a sour expression, then shrugged and went over to wash the blood from her hands and arms.

'I am the Surgical Director. Come. I must show you our intensive care unit.' The Director grabbed Seamus by the arm and led him into the corridor. I shoved through the crowd of spectators and followed.

'It does not matter to me what religion your friend is, Muslim, Christian, even Jewish,' he confided, his free hand clicking through a little loop of prayer beads. 'I am a doctor and I treat all patients.'

His clothes were immaculate and he smelled of aftershave. He didn't look like he had treated any patients that day.

'But I must warn you that this woman, she is a liar woman,' he hissed, his face twisting in fury as he glanced back at the doctor. 'And,' he added meaningfully, 'she is a *Christian*.' He raised his eyebrows and waggled his prayer beads at us.

Seamus made appropriate noises of commiseration.

We were led into a room full of beds and rusty oxygen tanks. Green metal machines with dials and blinking light bulbs that looked like Soviet military surplus were piled around the walls. Like everywhere in the hospital the walls were bare concrete under peeling paint. Unlike the other wards we had passed there was a couple of nurses and a man at the door who served the dual function of keeping out random spectators and waving a newspaper at the flies. I realised that this must be intensive care. Those patients who were conscious were moaning in pain, and I thought to myself that there was probably not a lot in the way of analgesic medical supplies in the hospital.

'Here you see,' the Surgical Director declared jubilantly, 'we have bed for him right here. Your man, he must stay in my ICU.'

He indicated the only free bed. It had filthy crumpled sheets stained with unidentifiable fluids from its previous occupant. I wondered if it had been the woman I had seen being wheeled through the hospital. The only reason that I had thought that she might have still been alive was that they had not been wheeling her in the direction of the car park out back where the rest of the dead had been dumped.

Seamus took a deep breath as he looked round the ICU. 'That's very kind of you, but we really do want to move him to the CPA,' he said.

'Why is that?' Our host suddenly turned belligerent and started shouting angrily. 'Iraqi hospitals are the best in the world. He will get better care here than any hospital in England or America.'

Seamus stared at him. He was diplomatically controlling his anger, but the tic on his neck was dancing.

I stepped between them. 'It is not that at all,' I said. 'It is just that you may have many Iraqi people here needing this specialist care and we do not want to take one of your valuable beds.'

'This woman, she is a liar woman. He cannot be moved. He is too sick.'

I was still shocked by the gory spectacle of Jacko's corpse and really could not think of a single reason why this man would want a Westerner in his hospital.

The female surgeon turned up and a massive argument ensued between the two of them.

I moved Seamus to one side. 'It's hard to tell whether Steve's stable enough to travel,' I said. 'I don't know if they are giving us their professional opinions or using him to argue with each other. Personally I trust the woman, and she says he can go.'

'Too right, mate. Quite apart from the security, I wouldn't leave an Iraqi in that bed, let alone Steve.'

We slipped out and made our way to the front again. Seamus briefed the others on the situation.

Finally the phone started ringing. I retrieved the MCI from my pouch. It was Les reporting to say that they had arrived at the Cash. I handed it over to Seamus.

'Vot's it like in there?' Cobus asked.

'Almost as primitive as the witch doctors you lot use in South Africa,' I said.

Hendriks smiled. It was rare to get a smile out of Hendriks.

Seamus pocketed the phone. He told us he'd given Les the grid for the front of the hospital and that the American casevac team was en route to collect Steve.

Someone from HQ had managed to get hold of Mad Dog. He had been waiting for Les when they arrived at the Cash. The medevac team had been standing by waiting in their wagons for a grid from us.

'Any news on the others?' I asked Seamus.

'Minor injuries. They're tough fuckers.'

Twenty minutes later a gaggle of Humvees turned up with a US military ambulance containing more medical equipment and drugs than I imagine was on the shelves inside the hospital. The paramedics leapt out and we watched open-mouthed as they took photos of each other with their guns in front of the hospital entrance. They held up their fists and pistols, then ran a trolley through the double doors like we were in an episode of *ER*.

The American ambulance driver stood next to his vehicle and looked us up and down as we stood there in our shades and mercenary gear. I noticed that he had picked up a Beretta SMG from somewhere. A lot of Americans in the CPA were gun fanatics and had armed themselves with fancy weapons that would look exotic to their buddies back home. I wondered where he got his 9 mil ammo from. Phil, our procurement officer, was still having problems getting hold of it.

I wandered out on to the road where the Humvee escorts were waiting and spoke to the commander and gunner in the rear vehicle. They were infantry and looked tired.

'Morning, men.' I smiled cheerily.

'Morning, sir.'

'When you lot move off we're going to follow you back into the Green Zone. We just have the one vehicle, a white SUV. I thought I'd better just warn you off.' I didn't want him to shoot us by accident.

'Roger that, sir, we'll keep an eye out for you.'

'Thanks.'

It always helps to keep friendly with the Coalition rear gunner.

'What happened here, sir?'

'IED in Karrada. Killed one of our men. And one VSI.'

'Hurt bad?' asked the gunner.

'He won't be holding a gun again, that's for sure.'

'That's a real shame.' He glanced at the crowd of Iraqis around the gate, the usual band of men smoking and stroking their moustaches, you seemed to see them on every street corner; men in mismatched suits, boys in jeans and T-shirts. There was a herder with a dozen goats and an old woman in the colourful rags I recognised from a tribe in the south of Iraq. The air was hot and dusty and smelled old and sick. 'This whole country sucks, if you don't mind my saying, sir,' the gunner added.

'Just get home safe.'

'I intend to, sir. And I'm getting out the day I get back.'

I returned to the hospital driveway in time to see Steve being wheeled out and loaded into the back of the ambulance. There was a cluster of medics all talking at the same time; an oxygen mask covered most of his ruined face and there was a reassuring number of tubes and drips stuffed into him. A smaller, covered lump on a second stretcher was loaded into the ambulance behind him.

We piled into the 4 × 4, Seamus and Hendriks in front, me behind with Sammy, and Cobus in the boot with his RPD facing out of the rear window.

FOURTEEN

You could always move at speed through Baghdad when you were part of a military convoy. The tightly packed cars and trucks pulled over and a wall of eyes watched from every side as you barged through traffic. The gunners facing left and right stared back over the front sights of their weapons and the Iraqis stayed low in their seats in case the patrol came under attack and they got caught in the crossfire of insurgent Kalashnikovs and Mk19 grenade launchers.

Fifteen minutes later we were pulling into the Cash.

The escorts had peeled away after we entered the Assassin's Gate. We followed the ambulance and parked up near the entrance to the ER. Seamus followed the stretcher into the Cash. The South Africans from Jacko's team were still inside being treated. Badger was standing outside with Etienne. I was pleased to see that the stocky Jock seemed to have survived unscathed.

'Hello mate, weren't you in the front wagon with Steve and Jacko?'

He told me that he had been knocked unconscious by the blast, but as the rear gunner, he'd been sitting in the nest of spare bulletproof vests behind the rear seats. He was suffering from nothing more than mild concussion and ringing ears. He had been lucky, that was for sure. The South Africans, particularly Jaki, had suffered more since much of the blast had been directed out from underneath the front car. Both the Brits and the South Africans had been travelling in 4 × 4s. Our 4 × 4s carried the spare tyre winched on a chain under the vehicle, just behind the rear axle, and the Brit spare tyre had been blown out horizontally into their front bumper, totally destroying it. They had been fortunate to only receive cuts from the shattered windscreen. They had all been wearing shades so no one had been blinded.

I walked into the hospital. It was beautiful.

It was like walking into the reception lobby in a hospital in Los Angeles. A place fit for the stars. It was brightly lit, freshly painted, as clean as a new pin. Immaculately dressed administrators looked up from their computers with gleaming white American smiles. Theatre nurses and surgeons in fresh scrubs strode purposefully along the long hallways discussing medical charts. I looked around, lost, and then saw Steve 'Mad Dog' McQueen approaching along the corridor.

'Ash, sorry man, it hasn't been a good day.'

We shook hands and he led me back up the corridor into the ward where Steve Campbell was already in an adjustable bed with starched white sheets and half a dozen 21st-century monitors all pumping and dripping and beeping reassuringly. The ambulance team had been amazingly fast.

A nurse turned towards me when she finished telling Seamus and Les that Steve was stable, that the Iraqi surgeon had done a good job and that they were not going to open him up again right now, but just keep him under observation before shipping him home.

'That's very reassuring, thank you.' I put on my most charming smile but she got the wrong end of the stick.

'You're too late,' she said and jerked her thumb at Seamus. 'I already agreed to meet up with your buddy here in the chow hall for dinner.'

'I can assure you, I didn't mean –' I began and ran out of words.

'Sure. Right.' She gave me a no-nonsense look, tempered with a smile. 'Look, pal, I'm an army nurse and I ain't got tickets on myself but I'm one of about a dozen hot girls in the

CPA and probably the only one you've seen in *I-raq*. If you weren't going to come on to me with some line like the other ten thousand guys on this post then you're either gay or dead.'

I thought it was no use arguing with her but curiosity got the better of me.

'So what did he say that won you over?' I could always do with a tip.

'That's for me to know and you to die wondering.' She tapped her nose, then winked at Seamus. 'Besides, he's hot.'

'Hot! You're kidding. With that moustache?'

'Especially with that moustache. Oh yeah, baby.'

She disappeared out of the doorway.

I turned back. The rest of the gang was smirking. Seamus carefully groomed his bandit moustache.

The nurse was right. There were about 10,000 guys for every decent-looking woman in Baghdad, and even those that you wouldn't wave a pole at when you arrived started looking fit after three months, whether you were attached or not. Dai had once calculated that in the CPA alone there was 100 metres of cock for every available woman. Even with the odds stacked against them, Les had scored with Lori and now it looked like Seamus was going to score with the nurse.

'I suppose I'll be training by myself in the gym every night while you two get laid.'

I walked out and Mad Dog followed to commiserate, saying that he wasn't getting any either. As we walked down the corridor I took another look at the bustling modern hallways and the clipped efficient medical staff going about their duties. Of course, this was *I-raq*, so all the surgeons were packing M9 pistols in thigh holsters.

FIFTEEN

Colonel Hind had gone on leave in November and returned with the patronage of a one-star general in the Pentagon. With the general's support, he had convinced the Project Management Office in the CPA that he was the man to run Task Force Fountain, the protection of Iraq's water infrastructure, and to head a team to train a private guard force.

Hind now had an office in one of the plush palaces in the CPA and a staff comprising Colonel Steve 'Mad Dog' McQueen, who had come in as Hind's assistant a month before, Sergeant Harvey, Hind's driver that day when we managed to lose 21 oil tankers outside Mahmudiya, and two First Sergeants, equivalent to the rank of sergeant majors in the British Army.

When Spartan got the contract to train the guard force, plastic-wrapped blocks of $500,000 with seals from the CPA began to arrive at HQ like it was Christmas. It was just before I went home on my first leave, and I couldn't help visualising ways of slipping one of those sealed bundles of loot in my bag to take home to Krista as a surprise.

Here darling, I couldn't think what to get you . . .

It was an idle fantasy, like finding the hidden suitcase of cash in some Ba'ath Party back garden. It transpired that Mad Dog's brother worked at the Federal Reserve, tracing stolen notes. He told me that when money vanished it was always traceable and that his brother's department was more vigorous than the Canadian Mounties, 'They always get their man.' When a bill with the serial numbers from missing money turned up anywhere in the world, teams of agents would swing into action like a well-oiled machine. I wanted to know what they were doing about those lost millions from Pentagon contracts in Iraq.

'Legal theft,' he said. 'Another department.'

Spartan would continue to be based in HQ in the Green Zone, where it was both more secure and easier for Adam and Angus to follow up potential PSD contracts within the CPA.

Our team, however, reporting to Task Force Fountain, would be tasked to begin training and managing a guard force that would eventually rise to 1,500 Iraqi nationals. It would be impossible to get Green Zone passes for all of them, let alone carry out any small-arms training, so we decided to set up a secure satellite location where we could live and work out in Baghdad – the Red Zone.

We informed Sammy of our requirements and he went off as thick as thieves with Ibrahim, our black-market arms fixer, to scout the area. They came back with a potential location in Aradisa Idah, an area in the southeast of the city between the CPA and the water plants we were going to be responsible for. The people in the district were anti-Saddam, pro-Westerners, which meant they hated Americans, but tolerated Europeans. Like all Iraqis, they appreciated the new money rolling in.

Ibrahim was a former air force officer like Sammy and spoke excellent English. He was a dark-skinned Shia with thick black eyebrows and the usual Saddam moustache. With the CF tightening security and restricting access into the Green Zone for Iraqis, Ibrahim, most of the guards and a number of the Iraqi administrative staff from HQ had volunteered to transfer to our water-management team. Ibrahim was diligent, highly motivated and, while he assured us that we were 'his brothers', it didn't have quite the same ring as when those words were said by Sammy.

Sammy was at the wheel of his old Toyota when we went to take a look at the property. With the leave structure, nine weeks on, three weeks off, it was unusual that we were all there at the same time: Seamus, Les, Dai and me, the Brits; Cobus, Hendriks, Etienne and Wayne, the Yaapies. Wayne had just got in from Cape Town. He was as wide as he was tall, with dark eyes sharpened by the sun on the veldt, a shiny, bald head and a beard. Like Etienne, Wayne didn't say much; like Hendriks, he had 20/20 vision when he looked down the sights of anything that shot bullets.

We met Shakir Ahmad, the owner of the property, and a group of local elders. Ibrahim was from the area and would be able to vet the local guards we were going to hire for our immediate security. It was important that the men we hired were either related by blood or tribal links, since that would guarantee more loyalty than the Yankee dollar. I would have preferred to live in a neighbourhood where Sammy had similar influence, but Sammy's house was in the middle of bandit country. We scored a lot of points announcing that we were there to keep the water flowing not rob the country of its oil.

'And they are British,' added Sammy, standing to attention.

The old men nodded wisely like magistrates and Ibrahim had a slight look of distaste as Sammy spoke. This was a mixed area, but there were more Shia, like Ibrahim, than Sunni. Yet all of the sheikhs in the room were Sunni.

I am not sure why being British always helped. Hadn't we and the French raped and pillaged Iraq before the Americans got in on the act? Whatever the reason, as Iraqis moved into administrative posts to prepare for the handover from the Coalition Authority to an elected Iraqi government, there were many officials who refused outright to deal with Americans. As soon as we identified ourselves as Brits, the tea was laid on and we'd discuss the pros and cons of Manchester United versus Liverpool and the chill weather before getting down to business.

The Iraqi obsession with courtesies was impressive. Even when trying to obtain information from a site under attack, I would always have to earnestly answer that I was fine, that my family's health was fine, that all of us expats were very well indeed; then I'd have to ask the guard commander how he was, and how his wife and children were, before slipping in, 'By the way, I hear that you are currently under attack, how many men are shooting at you?' It could be trying at times, but these exchanges were fundamental to the Iraqi character and, when they weren't trying to kill you, the people were friendly and good-natured.

The daily pleasantries occupied a lot of time, particularly first thing in the morning, and this drove Americans crazy. *Hey, what the hell is this? Can we cut to the chase?* They wanted to do things the American way.

For decades the entire Arab world had been warned by their media and their imams that the United States was spreading its own moral decadence through film, television and now the Internet in order to destroy the Muslim way of life. They saw on their TV sets Israelis armed with American M16 rifles and Apache helicopters and F16 jets killing and oppressing the Palestinians. Closer to home in Iraq they had spent ten years watching their old, their sick and especially their children dying as a result of UN embargos; deaths ordered, as far as they were concerned, directly by the White House.

Now they watched Humvees patrolling their cities, and American soldiers searching their houses; they watched steel walls with Hesco barriers going up around the CPA and now instead of Saddam and the Ba'athists, Americans were living in the marble palaces and putting their young men into the same filthy prisons; they watched boys of eighteen from Florida and New Jersey spitting chewing tobacco at their feet disrespecting both them and their women in front of everyone on the street. Over cups of morning *chai* in every tea shop they swapped rumours of Americans massacring civilians during firefights across the country. Shoot off a loose round in the UK and there's an inquiry. Shoot a few ragheads in the streets of Baghdad and it just didn't seem to matter.

Now if a man wanted to survive and feed his family he had to beg for a living working for the only people with money – the hated Crusader occupiers who watched without helping after they had turned their neighbourhoods into blacked-out, sewage-ridden playgrounds for gangs of murderers, kidnappers and rapists. The vast majority of the Iraqi people hated the Americans with a passion that would never be understood by those who had come to liberate them from Saddam.

The end result was that Iraqis put in charge of the handover refused to deal with Americans and TF Fountain commander Colonel Hind couldn't get a meeting with officials at the Ministry of Water. Decisions costing tens of millions of dollars – which should have been made jointly by the CPA and the Ministry – involving water purification, pipe-laying and security, were negotiated over hot sweet tea in tiny glasses by Seamus Hayes and me, two guys off the street with no authority whatsoever.

The property Sammy and Ibrahim had found was an abandoned bus depot with a block of offices and an administration building. There was a gate at the entrance and enough space for several vehicles. Shakir Ahmad, the owner, was about my age, mid-thirties, with short-cropped hair circling a bald spot and a moustache. He had the typical Iraqi build, portly and pear-shaped, with heavy lips that swelled into the deep satisfaction of someone who would now have a dollar income every month of the year. The fact that we would be looking to hire guards from the local area was another boost to the local economy and had brought the village elders on side.

Aradisa Idah was a crisscross of streets like many streets in Baghdad, with two-storey buildings with flat roofs. The windows were always shuttered, the exteriors giving no clue to the lives going on within. Sometimes you would hear Arabic music or televisions, but mostly the houses would be eerily silent. Many of the buildings contained shops on the ground floor. There were market stalls along the pavement selling lengths of rope, flattened oil drums, old books and odd bits of unidentifiable produce grown on the surrounding smallholdings. Beyond the cluster of streets were fields with a few buildings, shacks for the most part with palm-frond or corrugated-iron roofs.

The faces of the candidates running in the upcoming elections stared from posters plastered on the mud-coloured walls, each seat being contested by scores of new parties. The ballot paper was like a telephone directory. People would only vote for those they were related to or who were members of the same tribe. By the next full elections there would be over seven thousand candidates. It was a kind of democracy.

This was an area of hard-working people, policemen, small businessmen, government workers. They didn't feel under threat from insurgents, but from the criminal gangs that had mushroomed since the fall of Saddam. We set out to make friends with the local people. We reminded them that we would be employing at least one male member from every family in the area as well as supplying purified water. We discreetly gave them bribes, and in return they indiscreetly reported when there were bombs and bad guys in town. The streets looked safe enough but it wasn't wise for Westerners to walk around. The word would go out and some bad news would come looking for us.

From a military standpoint, we had to look at the property in terms of how we could extricate ourselves from it if the need arose. Was it defendable? How many potential firing points on to it were there? Were there any obvious landmarks on the skyline at night which would allow rebels to mortar us? Was there satisfactory ingress and egress for our vehicles? More importantly, was there easy ingress for a suicide bomber to ram the gates with a car bomb?

The answer was that 'the villa' would do very nicely.

The property comprised two single-storey, bare concrete buildings in a compound behind eight-foot walls. The main building was twenty feet from our next-door neighbour, a residential house where a family lived. All the other properties in the immediate vicinity were also occupied, which we considered an advantage. Like us, our neighbours wanted to avoid mortars, bombers and badness. The road network around the complex was far from perfect, but the addition of a few strategically placed barriers would be the ideal compromise between allowing us easy exit routes but denying easy entry to any potential car bomb, or vehicle-borne IEDs (VBIEDs).

The two buildings were in a state of total disrepair and the owner nodded contentedly as we outlined what changes we intended to make. We planned to rewire the complex, put in plumbing and bathrooms, paint the walls, put in windows, furniture, phone points, computer jacks and a satellite dish. This was going to be our home and it would all belong to Shakir Ahmad when we left.

'*Shukran jazeeran*, Mister. Thank you very much.'

Ahmad touched his palms to his chest and the village elders watched as eight burly white men chased through the derelict building, each one of us intent on grabbing the best room for ourselves. There were four rooms that we'd convert into bedrooms and I ended up with Dai, a smoker.

We told Sammy we wanted to get moving straight away and a gang of workmen were waiting to start first thing the following day. They wanted to get in, get the job done and get out with their dollars. Carpenters wielding biblical tools started putting in windows, electricians ran a cable from the mains up walls and across ceilings. I don't think we ever got an electricity bill. *Fucking cowboys*, Les kept saying, but the house was being transformed a damn sight quicker than you'd ever get it done in London.

The rooms were cleaned and painted, sometimes just painted. We built an extension on the front of the main house and the plumber installed a shower block; he was the same guy who had cut six inches off some of the AKs, the pipe and tube man.

We sent Sammy off to buy some furniture. Bought from a warehouse, it was cheap and nasty, very cheap, in fact: each room was furnished for about $40, a price that included everyone putting their cut on top.

The warehouse owner probably didn't sell cookers, fridges, microwaves, cutlery, crockery, saucepans and all the little comforts you expect in a modern kitchen, but someone from the tribe probably did and all these things were found and ferried out to the villa in the coming days. It's surprising what you can achieve in the developing world with a few hundred thousand dollars in your pocket.

We had saved so much money from our original budget that Les, Seamus, Dai and I sat down to think of what else we needed.

'How about a projector and a surround sound system?' suggested Les. 'We could watch TV on that big wall. Don't forget, the Olympics are coming.'

'Mate, I don't fall out with that idea,' replied Seamus enthusiastically.

'Hey, what about us, don't we have a vote?' piped up Cobus from the doorway.

'Fuck me, here we go.' Dai pulled his fag out of his mouth. 'As if you Seth Efrrikaan cunts know about electricity and televisions.' He pointed out the window where the rest of the South Africans were standing around their *braii*, barbecuing dinner. 'When you lot have finished inventing fire, I'll teach you how to use flushing toilets.'

'Yer Fokken Welsh rabbit,' Cobus said and slapped the Glock in the holster on his thigh.

We took the piss out of the Yaapies and they took $50 off each of us every time there was a shooting competition.

Seamus immediately tasked Ibrahim to go and find us the projector and surround sound system. He had no idea what we were talking about but once the concept was described to him he was delighted and zoomed off into town.

'I fokken bet he's getting two sets now, man,' said Cobus. 'Fokken one for us and one for him.'

Dai stubbed out his fag. 'What are you cunts cooking for dinner tonight?' he asked.

'We have a nice piece of lamb,' said Cobus.

The walls around the flat roof were four feet high and above the walls we erected a four-foot black canvas cover-from-view screen so snipers couldn't pick us off. As the infantry man, I was occupied for several days arranging great piles of sandbags into sangars.

I went up there early one morning and caught Seamus and Les standing there brooding on something. Snipers? A mortar?

'Problem?' I asked.

'Big fucking problem,' Seamus said.

'A job for Sammy?' Les suggested.

'Right!'

He stormed off with Les behind him and I carried on shifting sandbags.

Next day, a weights bench, a punch bag and a rowing machine appeared. Is a home really complete without them? Seamus and Les were like a couple of kids. Where Sammy found these objects I've no idea. It was hard enough to get Iraqis to work. They certainly didn't work out.

While my mates lifted weights, I carried on lifting sandbags. Mad Dog had organised the delivery of 10,000 empty bags and a couple of tons of grey sand. A team of local farmers was filling them for ten dollars a day, carrying them up to the roof two at a time, and I was constructing six sangars, one on each corner and one at the centre of each wall at the front and the back. I ran two low walls of sandbags across the middle of the roof in case anyone got close enough to lob a grenade over the cover-from-view screen. Les built a cement battle box and stashed half a dozen AK-47s, a belt-fed PKM, a shitload of ammo, a medical pack and bottles of water. This was our covert armoury, secret from the guards. If we ever needed a last-ditch stand in the event of an emergency, we would get to the roof and fight from there until help arrived.

We didn't want the villa to resemble the typical Coalition stronghold with their fortified sangars, gun towers, barbed wire and blast walls. On the other hand we were not suicidal. The UN and Red Cross buildings had both been blown up – a lack of blocking structures meant that the bombers had been able to deploy VBIEDs close enough to inflict major damage on the buildings.

Our compromise was to line all windows and doors with sandbags and to reinforce the outer walls of the complex on the inside with double-stacked Hesco blast barriers. The house was now protected against VBIEDs, mortars and direct small-arms fire. Two rolls of razor wire camouflaged by palm leaves in the alleyway to the back and another two rolls on the inside of the wall would stop any intruders creeping in from there. On the roof I attached one end of another roll of razor wire to the top of the stairs and the other end to a 10kg weight disc. If we did have to retreat to the roof the last man up could just throw the weight down the stairwell and fill it with razor wire to slow down attackers.

At the front of the house, inside the wall, we built a guard room for the administration of the Iraqi guards. From the outside the property looked the same as the rest of the street, especially since once the neighbours saw our cover-from-view screen they started erecting their own; keeping up with the bin Joneses. We placed a sentry box beside the gates where our guards could sit protected from the elements but still see up and down the street. This was the only external sign that the property was unlike the others.

We had just about finished when it was time for my first leave. I was dying to get home.

SIXTEEN

The Chinese philosopher Chuang Tzu once dreamed he was a butterfly. When he awoke, he couldn't be sure if he was a man who had dreamed he was a butterfly or a butterfly now dreaming he was a man.

As I wandered down Regent Street among the Christmas shoppers, that was exactly how I felt. It was early December 2003. I had been back in London for three weeks and Baghdad was a vague memory a million miles away. I could barely believe that I had spent nearly three months there.

I was holding Natalie in my arms as we pressed through the crowds, Krista behind us weighed down with bags. Those three weeks had flashed by like a shooting star. I was leaving again for Iraq in the morning and that last day in mid December we had celebrated Christmas early with a turkey lunch followed by the entire afternoon at Hamleys, the giant toy store in the West End.

Natalie was exhausted and had fallen asleep. I looked back at Krista and blew her a kiss. She smiled. We had agreed that I would slip away next day and go to the airport by myself. Krista was the bravest woman I had ever met, but the last thing I wanted was to have my emotions put through the wringer with Krista's tears and Natalie's little body clutching at my legs while she begged me not to go. It was hard enough knowing that I couldn't spend Christmas with them.

First thing I'd have to do in Baghdad was get back in the gym. The last three weeks had been a whirlwind of visiting friends and nonstop eating. After 97 plates of lamb and rice – yes I counted them – I had been so desperate for variety we had hit a different restaurant every night.

I had been away with the army many times, but Baghdad had been so intense, so chaotic, London during the first few days of my leave had seemed dazzling and extraordinary. I was like a tourist. The streets were bustling and busy, but remained orderly and safe. I drove Krista crazy insisting that she must have had the flat painted, everything was just so *clean*. The first afternoon, we had gone to the supermarket and I spent an hour walking up and down the aisles goggling at the immense variety of goods on display.

Later that first evening, after an emotional family dinner and an exhibition of a very proud three-year-old's paintings, it was as if I had never been away.

We talked about money. The good news was that my first three months' pay from Spartan had cleared our credit cards and one of our loans; it would have taken two or three years had I remained in my last job. Another tour in Iraq would clear all our debts and buy a decent car for Krista. After that I could just pile up the money until we retired to our own private island in the Caymans.

The bad news of course was that Baghdad was hell. I told Krista about Jacko and Steve. I hadn't meant to. It just slipped out after an extra glass of wine late one evening. Up until that moment, although there were dangers every day, we had felt invulnerable. British Army-trained soldiers. We were superior and we felt superior. The death of our mates made us take a good hard look at reality and gave us all a sense of our own mortality.

Krista knew I was never going back into a law office. This job was me. I wanted to climb the security ladder, but I was only on the first rung and Iraq was the place to set down your marker and show what you could do. Krista said that she trusted my judgement and we made an agreement which was probably typical among the married men working in Iraq. I set up an imaginary bar in my mind and if the violence and

bloodshed rose above the level of the bar, I would resign and
come home. There was no point earning all that money if I
wasn't going to live to spend it.

I assured her that we were taking all the necessary precautions to avoid IEDs, and that the threat of a firefight would
be manageable. Bandits were content to shoot up moving
convoys, or groups pinned down in the open, but only when
they had the upper hand or overwhelming numbers. Our own
experience and evidence from PSD teams up and down the
country showed that as soon as heavy and accurate fire was put
back, smaller enemy forces quickly withdrew. I never managed
to tell Krista that I had already been in contact three times. The
right moment just never seemed to come up.

I slipped away while Krista was still sleeping, caught the Tube
to Heathrow and flew to Amman. I went through my own little
ritual, dinner in the Library, a few drinks at the Sports Bar,
then an early morning drive across twelve hours of desert back
to Baghdad.

The office block and training classrooms that had been
under construction before I left had been completed in my
absence. As the last one in, I found that I had the least amount
of space and was sharing my office with Sammy, which meant
he had the pick of all the cheap gifts that I had bought for our
Iraqi staff. The first evening back I handed out these Christmas
presents.

'No point waiting for the day, is there? One of you lot might
be dead by then.'

I had also brought back a stack of running and cycling
magazines for Seamus and Les and 200 cigarettes for Dai. By
the time I'd unpacked my kit, adjusted my pistol holster and
popped out to the kitchen for a plate of roast lamb, London
was just a vague memory. This was real life again.

It is common in areas where there are embassies or rich
officials to have guard posts at the end of the street, perfect for
keeping alibabas from digging up the electricity cables and
preventing the kidnapping and criminal activities of rival
tribes. We ran the idea by the elders and they nodded
perceptively as they saw the value of their properties increasing

as we took the neighbourhood upmarket in this way. We constructed two posts with concrete barriers, one at each end of the street. The guards knew everyone and the local people passed in and out without hindrance.

We then contacted the nearest Coalition unit to inform them that we were in their area employing local guards, a vital precaution or they would drive by on patrol at night, see our guys sitting about with AKs, assume they were terrorists and zap them. Although our guards were not members of the FPS (Facilities Protection Service), the FPS brassards with Iraqi flags were the most widely recognised by the CF and we enlisted Ibrahim's special skills to acquire some similar-looking ones for us.

Working on the house in this way was satisfying and occasionally tedious. We really did begin to feel like members of the community and exchanged pleasantries when our neighbours dropped by to report 'bad men up to mischief', or to complain that the power had failed in the middle of the latest episode of *Baywatch*.

The CPA (i.e. the American taxpayer) had paid for us to set up the house and was paying our salaries and expenses, which relieved Adam and Angus of the burden of seeking tasks for us. As part of the contract, the CPA would be supplying transport and weapons for an initial manning requirement of 300 men. We had put in an order for fifty vehicles, of which thirty would need to be 4×4s to visit pumping stations in the desert. The other twenty runarounds were for the city.

The cost of 50 vehicles at a modest price of $20,000 each is a simple sum: $50 \times 20,000$. That is $1 million. We would need to buy 300 weapons at $400 each ($120,000), plus ammo and uniforms ($100,000) and pay the guards $150 a month each – $45,000 every month and rising. And don't even get me started on fuel for the vehicles, spare tyres, air filters and other consumables. Office equipment, computers, air conditioners and office staff would also take out a huge chunk of cash. For our professional services, Spartan charged the CPA $1,000 a day per man: about $1.3 million a month.

If you multiplied our team of eight by the several teams at Spartan, then multiply that by the 50 or more private companies comprising the 25,000 private security contractors – that's not counting the 100,000 civil contractors with KBR, who were earning even more than us – it was hardly surprising that the first $87 billion for the reconstruction of Iraq granted by Congress was running out and Mr Bush was asking for more. He'd get it, too.

The Brits knew how to manage a budget and we knew we'd be doing our own legs if we didn't spend every penny that came into the villa. If we gave money back to Phil Rhoden, the accountant, when we didn't need it, it would be a devil of a job getting it back again when we did.

I thought about Krista as Seamus said: 'One thing we do have to do and that's spend, spend, spend.'

We clinked cans and tore off lamb from the *braii*.

Every morning we held what we called morning prayers, a team meeting to decide the day's order of business. We each gave an update on our tasks and status to Seamus. Seamus decided to acquire new Western weapons and duly sent Ibrahim out to Sadr City to find them. It would have been better to have gone ourselves – you wouldn't buy a pair of shoes without trying them on – but Sadr City was a no-go area where American patrols came under attack every day of the week.

Although we were living in Aradisa Idah, Karrada was known by some (don't ask who) as the Fifth Avenue of Baghdad and that was our destination as we pulled out of the courtyard in a two-car packet with a shopping list as long as your arm. We needed to stock up and spend that reconstruction money.

We took the main Karrada high road towards the 14th of July Bridge, which crossed into the Green Zone, turned off halfway along the road, and parked on the street outside what was generally considered the best supermarket on the block, a place that had been frequented by aid workers, the press and the Japanese before the spate of bombings including the one that killed Jacko.

Two men stayed with the cars. Etienne sat with the engine running, Les stood guard. It was arranged this way so if anything happened we could bug out in one set of wheels. Seamus and Wayne stayed outside the entrance, watching the street, weapons ready to put down a shitload of fire if the need arose. With our longs in the car and our pistols inconspicuously in our belts, Hendriks and I pushed three trolleys up and down the four short aisles like a pair of housewives.

You could get just about anything, sometimes brands you were familiar with but packaged in strange ways, made under licence or just made in the Middle East with phoney labels. There was recognisable toothpaste and corn flakes, Gillette razors of the type that were going out of date at about the time I was learning to shave in the eighties. We bought toiletries, shower gel, some lacquer for Sammy so he could keep his hair glued over his bald spot. I found Orange Pekoe and Earl Grey tea. Les had on the list 'Irish Breakfast Tea' and was distraught when they didn't have any. We gathered up armfuls of chocolate; Mars, KitKat and Twix, all the same names, all slightly different like something seen in a distorting mirror. I was thrilled to find frozen chicken after all that bloody lamb. Frozen and tinned vegetables. Cases of tinned fruit.

The off-licence further down on another road was signposted by a stack of crates in the street outside. You could buy any brand of spirits and most beers. You pointed to what you wanted, the 'licensee' would load up the vehicle and we'd remain seated, engine running with weapons pointing in every direction. Pity the poor alibaba who tried to take Dai's bottle of Jack Daniels.

At each stop a swarm of kids would appear selling cigarettes and old AK bayonets *LaLaLa* . . . no, thank you, we'd say, and we'd toss them our dinars. We paid for everything in dollars, but received change in the Iraqi dinar. There had been inflation before the war and since the invasion it had begun to spiral out of control. Local people paid for everything in bricks of money held by elastic bands. In the supermarket there was a money-counting machine, but most traders didn't count the money, they'd just feel the thickness of a block of currency and shove it under their dish-dash.

The dollar bills that came to us were always in fifties. If we spent $203 at the supermarket, we'd hand over five bills and receive a supermarket bag full of blocks of dinars in change. The rate of exchange ranged from about 1,000 to 3,000 dinars and was finally fixed at something like 1,450 dinars to the dollar. All this meant that, like private security guards, every Iraqi with a new satellite dish tuned in to CNN to check the international currency rates and the price of a barrel of oil.

In the supermarket, even at the off-licence, we asked for a receipt and they'd scribble something in Arabic (*bollocks*, probably). We accounted for every penny we spent. Personal integrity prevented us robbing Spartan blind but we made sure the company paid for every chicken breast and can of Stella, every spark plug, 9mm bullet and bribe, of which there were many. You couldn't get receipts for the bribes, but they were logged and signed off by the accountant.

The problems with currency would continue. As we started to build the guard force, the guards were happy to be paid in dollars, but then found they had problems paying for the family groceries. If local people had too many dollars, the insurgents considered them collaborators and they'd catch a bullet in the back of the head.

We had that to look forward to but, before Christmas, we were able to go shopping and mingle with the locals. Sort of. I went out with Sammy to look at some Mesopotamian artefacts some crook was trying to sell, but I didn't have the exorbitant price nor the desire to rob Iraq of what remained of its heritage. Many of the antiquities looted from the museum had already been smuggled across the border and sold to private collections.

That evening with Seamus and Les, I had the rare pleasure of being invited to Sammy's home to dinner with his wife and two children, the first time I had been inside an Iraqi house, at least as a guest. His wife was slender, cultivated and spoke French, which Sammy did not. I told her in French that I considered her husband a hero. She replied that she did, too, but we must never let him know that because to be a good Muslim you must avoid the sin of pride.

Next day, I went with the South Africans to the famous leather street to order a jacket. I chose a stylish blazer in black glove leather and took the piss out of the Yaapies as they drew pictures of biker jackets and impractical long coats like costumes from *The Matrix*. Hendriks designed a jacket and waistcoat combination with a mass of inner holsters and straps for knives, magazines and grenades. I laughed myself silly, but the last laugh was on me when we returned to the shop for the finished items. Hendriks's creation was the ultimate in cool. It fit to perfection and when he opened the jacket, there were all the secret slings and zips to carry his implements of death. It cost him $40.

That was our last shopping trip before the Christmas festivities broke out with a chain of IEDs, firefights and mortar attacks across the city. The streets became a no-go area for the white-eyes. I had promised Krista that I would leave if the violence became worse. I'd been back a week and I was already raising that bar in my mind. I thought about this alone at night while I stood on the roof watching streams of tracer cross the sky and couldn't decide if I was only staying on for the money or if, like some of the old mercenaries I'd met at the CPA, I was getting too used to the danger.

The sky was alight for three consecutive nights while the US pounded the city from a Spectre AC-130. The Spectre is a modified Hercules that acts as an airborne artillery firebase and is quaintly known as 'Puff the Magic Dragon'. The plane flies around in a huge circle with its 105mm and 40mm automatic cannons thumping away with horrifying accuracy at targets on the ground. It also has a couple of large Gatling guns that sound like the world unzipping. Every bout of firing is echoed even louder as the shells hit the ground and explode seconds later. Boom, boom, boom ... BOOM, BOOM, BOOM. *Brrrrrrt* ... BRRRRRT.

During the early hours of 23 December 2003 the battle came closer to home with the Spectre directing its fire just west of us, between Aradisa Idah and the Dora refinery. The Yaapies spent the evening on the roof watching the assault like it was a fireworks display, but I preferred to lie in bed blocking out the noise listening to Teach Yourself Arabic tapes on the headphones. The Americans malleted the insurgent bases by night and by day the insurgents brushed off the dust and set up their mortars. It was like ping pong.

I got up bleary eyed and carried on my job as an infantryman building a four-sided range out on the farmland to the south. This was where our new recruits in the guard service would be training and for now I was supervising an Iraqi bulldozer, a 'shovel', the locals called it, into completing twenty-foot-high sand berms. Hendriks and Etienne were tasked with security, but seemed to have different ideas on strategy. Etienne was standing on top of the berm like a tourist.

'Why are you fokken standing up there silhouetting yourself?' demanded Hendriks.

'I am trying to draw fire so I can shoot the bastards. Why are you hiding down there?'

'Man, I'm waiting for you to draw fire so I can shoot someone.'

We got back at lunchtime to find the office block drilled with bullet holes. Ali, the new armourer, had accidentally discharged 50 rounds from a PKM belt-fed machine gun inside the office block as he tried to unload it. He was mortified when he told me what had happened.

It was Christmas Eve. We were bored being stuck out in the suburbs and in the afternoon decided to make a dash for the CPA and find a party. With this fresh wave of violence, there was less traffic on the road, which meant there were less cars to hide among but at least we could move faster.

We picked up Del Waghorn from HQ, an ex-marine commando who had been on the Circuit for years; the 24th was also his birthday and he was one guy who didn't need an excuse to get out of it. We then went to Hind's office to collect Mad Dog and Gareth, one of the sergeants. They appeared carrying a huge chest of booze which they slung into the back of the Nissan. Mad Dog McQueen liked to hang out with the Brits and was one of the few American officers with whom you could discuss the war without being accused of being a commie or a traitor or an ignorant son of a bitch incapable of grasping the intricacies of America's obligations.

It was a warm afternoon, the sky was almost blue and we decided to go sightseeing. We popped into one of the palaces, bribed a guard and strolled along Saddam's famous carpet of dollar bills. They looked real, but we discovered sadly they were fake. We shot some snaps, posed in front of the crossed swords on Victory Parade. The giant fists holding the swords were modelled from Saddam's hands and suspended from them were nets containing hundreds of Iranian helmets. There were more helmets concreted into the ground so that the parading soldiers would be marching over what in Saddam's mind was the defeated enemy. We had a suspicion that the original owners were still wearing those helmets and the guards had to stop the Yaapies from trying to dig one up to find out. Dai dropped some baksheesh on the same guards and they looked the other way while we climbed up inside one of the fists to get some photos of us hanging out of the top.

When it began to get dark, we decided to have a drink at the Al Rasheed Hotel. It was closed due to the elevated threat level and a group of weary Iraqi guards stood outside wondering if they'd find more job satisfaction in the insurgency. Money was pouring into Iraq from the US Treasury and more money was coming from fundamentalist groups all over the Arab world. Now that the insurgents were better organised, they had a pay structure slightly better than the wages for those joining the security forces. We had been told that the families of suicide bombers received $25,000 and there was even a suggestion of families receiving a pension. I could see the time coming when a broker would find a way to make money selling suicide bomber insurance.

We set off for the Sheraton, but the hotel was in the process of being mortared. We headed instead for the British compound back in the CPA where we had a decent sing-song and headed back to the villa at midnight with the Spectre AC-130 circling above with its automatic cannons picking out targets. Fortunately, we were not one of them.

What happened next is hard to remember, but I had the best night's sleep I'd had in a long time and spent the morning sunbathing on the roof with a hangover. Mad Dog and Gareth had spent the night, too drunk to drive, and came out to the range full of enthusiasm for our Christmas shooting competition. They both considered themselves crack shots and were astonished when they had to dig into their wallets and hand over $150 apiece to the Yaapies.

'Anyone would think it was Christmas,' said Mad Dog.

'In Seth Efrrika it's always Christmas,' said Hendriks.

I called Krista to wish her Merry Christmas while Les cooked Christmas lunch. We had three-quarters of a turkey; stray cats had got the other quarter while it was defrosting. Nothing else. No potatoes, Brussels, stuffing, trimmings or gravy, not even a piece of bread – just turkey. Ho Ho Ho. At least it was a day without lamb.

SEVENTEEN

The true wealth of Iraq is its vast collection of archaeological sites. It had always been my intention to pay some of them a visit and take some photos to send to my ex-girlfriend at Oxford who'd told me Baghdad was the most beautiful city in the world.

Present-day Iraq is situated in what was called Mesopotamia and deserves its reputation as the cradle of civilisation. The fertile plains watered by the Tigris and the Euphrates rivers supported the empires of Akkad, Babylon, Sumer, Assyria, the Hittites and Persia for thousands of years before the birth of the Romans. Scholars recorded the exploits of King Gilgamesh in what is one of mankind's first written texts. It was the site of the Hanging Gardens of Babylon and legend has it that this was where Eve tempted Adam in the Garden of Eden.

In September 2003 when I'd first arrived in Iraq it would have been possible to visit a few sites, but there had been too much going on at Spartan. We were now interviewing and training guards for TF Fountain, but while this left quite a lot of free time, the hostilities in the opening weeks of 2004 made it far too dangerous to cruise around the country with my camera.

Every day after morning prayers we practised our car drills and actions on. In the afternoon we hit the CPA; it was more treacherous in the streets, but we could report our progress directly to Mad Dog and enjoy the delights of pineapple pizza at the same time.

I went to the gym and trained on the running and rowing machines, while Seamus and Les went shagging, then we all returned to the villa for roast lamb dinners cooked on the *braii*. I'd email mates at home to tell them what a great life I was having, then stretch out with the latest stack of pirate DVDs we'd bought from the roadside stalls in the Green Zone. Once Les got our wall projector and surround-sound system set up, we celebrated by getting Sammy and Colonel Faisal over to watch *Black Hawk Down*. Again.

Faisal was an old air force buddy of Sammy's and had been working with Phil Rhoden procuring supplies. We needed a 'Colonel' to head up our guard force and used that old army technique of nicking the best one you could find. Faisal held the equivalent rank of brigadier and had studied at the Iraqi staff college. He was dark-skinned like Ibrahim, but a Sunni like Sammy. He wasn't so bouncy and gregarious, but a quietly spoken natural leader who kept his opinions to himself and commanded the absolute respect and loyalty of all the Sunni and most of the Shia guards we recruited.

Our two old pilots watched *Black Hawk Down* as if it were live footage from a war zone and went home nodding thoughtfully, Sammy in synch with Faisal's temperament and keeping for once his own counsel. I went to bed and was dreaming about Mogadishu when at three in the morning I found Seamus shaking me awake with instructions to pack for a PSD task.

'Get kit for four days including food, maps and sleeping bags. Wheels up at five. That's two hours, mate.'

'Fuck, it's a bit short notice, isn't it?'

'Dai's been ready all afternoon. He told me you wanted to go instead.'

'You jack Welsh wanker,' I said to the lump under the duvet on the other side of the room. 'There's no "I" in TEAM but there's a "U" in CUNT.'

'Hey, fuck off. You've been moaning for weeks about wanting to go to Samarra, now's your big chance.' It was odd, but when he was tired or drunk his Welsh accent started to come through.

'Samarra?' Damn right I would jump at the chance.

'That's what I said.'

'All right, but don't fucking smoke in the room while I'm away.'

This was unbelievable good luck. Samarra had been occupied for nearly 8,000 years, but the building I particularly wanted to see was a more modern piece of Islamic architecture: the spiral tower called the *melwiyeh* built on top of the town's mosque in the ninth century. It is one of the best known and most enduring images of Iraq and is represented on carvings, paintings and banknotes. Thousands of Westerners had probably bought Iraqi souvenirs with the *melwiyeh* on them and not even known what it was.

I had resigned myself to not seeing it. Now that it was practically within reach the night's fatigue slipped away. Shame there were insurgent attacks in Samarra on a daily basis. I packed some extra magazines in case we ended up pinned down by an angry mob and checked the battery in my camera.

An hour after being awoken I went into the living room with my bags to find Wayne and Cobus waiting. We loaded the 4 x 4 and then went back in to make some breakfast. Our job was to act as bodyguards for the Middle East correspondent of a Japanese national TV channel while he covered the arrival of the Japanese Military Contingent (JMC), 550 non-combat soldiers making up the first deployment of Japanese troops since the Second World War.

The Japanese public had been vehemently against sending their military forces overseas for any reason and the questionable ethics of the invasion of Iraq had polarised public opinion against Prime Minister Junichiro Koizumi. There was such a furore over the decision it was thought that it might topple the Japanese government, especially if the JMC ran into dramas. The international press, especially the Japanese, would be covering the deployment closely.

Personally, I was surprised they were sending them to such a dangerous area.

'Why didn't they find a peaceful sector for them?' I said. 'Any Japanese casualties and there'll be a shitstorm back home.'

'What the fok you talk about?' asked Wayne.

'It's open season in the Sunni Triangle,' I said. 'To be honest, I'm not that happy just the three of us are going.'

The two South Africans looked at each other, then back at me.

'*Moenie kak praat nie, man*,' laughed Cobus. Don't talk shit. 'We are going to fokken SAMAWAH, three hundret Ks south near Nasiriyah. It's the fokken safest place in Iraq.'

'Sa – ma – wah,' I repeated with a sinking feeling. Not Samarra. That little Welsh shit.

'*Ja*, Samawah. Stop acting crazy, Ash, and have some breakfast.'

Wayne put a great dollop of scrambled eggs on my plate and pushed a mug of coffee across the table. I went for the pot of salt. Its shape reminded me that I was not going to be seeing the *melwiyeh* any time soon.

We set out before first light for the Palestine Hotel, passing through a dodgy part of town where a car bomb had killed twenty people the previous day. We wanted to be on the road to Samawah before the morning rush hour, not only to get an early start on the long journey but also because the rush hour was prime time for the suicide car-bombers.

We arrived at the hotel to find our Japanese principal, Tanaka-san, waiting behind the wall of sandbags at the Palestine entrance. Unfortunately his Iraqi press team was still fast asleep. We eventually left the hotel at the height of the Baghdad rush hour and Cobus scared the shit out of Tanaka-san as he ploughed through the traffic like a knife blade going through silk.

We thought we could make up time on Route TAMPA, taking a chance that we would get turned back on the section of highway at a major military refuelling depot restricted to CF use only. At the checkpoint I showed a hassled sergeant our IDs.

'The two vehicles behind are with us,' I said.

'Any Iraqi nationals in those vehicles?' the sergeant asked.

I glanced at his name tag and then looked him straight in the eye.

'It's the Japanese press team, Sergeant Greves,' I replied.

Half of them were Iraqis but the sergeant took a long look at the vehicle behind us where four Arab faces were pressed up to the window with their droopy Saddam moustaches and *shemaghs* around their heads. Sergeant Greves started another question and then decided he couldn't be bothered to argue. He glanced again at my pass.

'OK, sir, you have a nice day.'

Samawah was 300 kilometres south, a busy town with purposeful, friendly people in the streets and no beggars, a nice change from Baghdad.

There was no insurgent activity in Samawah, but when we arrived we still had our Baghdad heads on and de-bussed in full armour with weapons ready, scanning all the buildings and vehicles around us. The locals looked on bemusedly before going about their daily business.

We were staying in a four-storey house, surrounded by a walled garden. It was heavily ornate and gaudy in typical Arab style and I had no doubt that Tanaka-san's company was being charged a king's ransom in rent. I imagined the former occupants had been well-placed in the Ba'athist hierarchy to afford such a palatial residence and wondered what had happened to them. Our principal waited with the camera crew while we checked the location was secure.

'Wait here for one minute,' I said.

'Thank you. Thank you,' Tanaka-san replied with a little bow. He was a charming man in his thirties with swept back, jet-black hair and a natural smile.

Wayne checked the interior while Cobus and I scouted around the outside of the building. When we returned, Tanaka-san and the film crew had vanished. We assumed the Iraqis had parked the two cars and Tanaka-san was inside. We went in to look and found no one but a man sitting on a stool smoking with tears in his eyes as he chopped onions.

'Hey, where is everyone? Hello, do you speak English?' I asked the cook. Cobus ran up the stairs to check the first floor while I mimed the question again.

I was rewarded with a torrent of Arabic and waving. I caught one word that I recognised.

'*Sayara?*' I mimed driving to the cook. 'Car?'

'*Sayara, na'am*, Mister,' said the cook. He pointed down the road leading into town.

Wayne was looking out the window.

'Fok.'

Tanaka-san had gone off into town with the Iraqis without his PSD team. I went to join Wayne. At least our car hadn't been stolen or booby-trapped. Cobus was first out, fired the engine and we burned rubber into town. I wondered how we were going to explain to Adam that we had lost the principal and his camera crew on the first day.

'*Bliksem!* There he is,' screamed Cobus triumphantly as we reached the main shopping street.

'That's not him,' I said. The two South Africans assured me it was.

'No, wait, there he is.' Wayne pointed at another Japanese man rooting around at a roadside jewellery stall across the street.

I watched from the rear as both their heads swivelled left and right in furious disbelief. Then they saw a third Japanese man way up in front of us.

'Faaaaark,' roared Cobus, 'there's fokken hundreds of them.'

The arrival of Japanese soldiers in Iraq was such a big story, there were at least two dozen Japanese news teams in town covering the event and it fell to me to identify Tanaka-san. I remembered that he'd mentioned getting an aerial view of Samawah and after about ten minutes scanning the rooftops we saw Tanaka-san's camera team on top of an abandoned tower block.

I left the Yaapies outside and ran up the dilapidated staircase. Tanaka-san bowed. I bowed. I asked him not to go off again without us. He bowed again. I bowed again. There was a lot more bowing during the next four days while we accompanied our principal to meetings between the Japanese advance party and local dignitaries. Tanaka-san persisted in dashing off with his crew and we usually found him in the scrum of Japanese paparazzi. The Yaapies were only able to identify Tanaka-san by his clothing, and removing his jacket while among the rest of the press caused Afrikaner hysterics.

* * *

The word must have gone out that Samawah was safe and we saw only one other Japanese TV crew with a security team. It was the first time we had observed foreigners mingling freely on the street, bartering for souvenirs and sitting in the carpet shops with little glasses of tea. As well as being the most peaceful town in Iraq, the locals, according to Tanaka-san, genuinely welcomed the arrival of the JMC. The Japanese had built the hospital ten years earlier, and in addition to the PR campaign directed at the local sheikhs and imams, the word on the street was that the Japanese were going to invest a lot more money in the town.

The effect on us was that rather than driving around looking at everyone over the front sight of a rifle, we drove around making a note of decent shops and nice-looking restaurants. We kept vests and longs locked in the car, stuffed pistols down the back of our belts and covered them with a shirt. As far as the locals could see we were armed with nothing more than walkie-talkies. I worried that we were losing our edge. If we relaxed any more we wouldn't survive our first five minutes back in Baghdad.

The house was spacious but once behind the façade, everything was depressingly primitive. A tiny petrol generator provided only enough electricity for Tanaka-san's laptop and lighting for two rooms. We showered in cold water in the dark, the ten of us used the one working toilet and we ate what the locals ate, i.e. the food was appalling. Breakfast was the only edible meal: flat bread, boiled eggs, cheese and yoghurt.

Most of our evenings were free and, after starving ourselves since the hard-boiled egg at breakfast, we would check out the good restaurants we'd noted while Tanaka-san was busy on his laptop editing the footage taken during the day. Then each night around midnight we would escort him to the pool satellite van for his ten-minute slot where he uploaded his story to his Japanese office for the morning news.

The JMC had flown into Kuwait, crossed the border and, when they finally set out for Samawah, we drove to the joint Dutch-Japanese base to film the historic footage of Japanese troops deploying for the first time in fifty years. Every Japanese TV crew, journalist and photographer with their horde of Iraqi fixers set up cameras around the entrance to the base, each team frantic to be the first to confirm the Japanese arrival. Tanaka-san told us that the first correspondent to report seeing the JMC would gain kudos for his channel. In the press world, breaking the news even thirty seconds earlier than a rival could make a career.

'It is of the utmost importance to get the scoop,' he informed me with his usual calm. Only the way his eyes flickered to the satellite van hinted at his inner turmoil.

As the hunger for a scoop grew, the camera teams began to edge further and further up the road away from the camp. This was Iraq, so the JMC was two hours late.

The cameramen grew bored by late afternoon and started filming each other. Eight TV cameras covered the scramble around the tea urn delivered by the Dutch media liaison officer. I was impressed at how some of the reporters had dressed for the occasion. Several stepped out of air-conditioned SUVs wearing Indiana Jones outfits with safari vests and water canteens on their belts.

Even though Samawah was safe, after dark in the desert there were armed gangs of looters and the Japanese crews were afraid to stray beyond the protection of the Dutch soldiers. As the crews that had wandered furthest from the base started to edge back again, my own nose for a story perked up and I saw a way to give Tanaka-san a stab at his scoop. I liked the guy and, judging from the amount of time he was spending on the satellite phone back to Japan, he was being put under a lot of pressure.

'Don't go away,' I told the Yaapies.

'Fokkin Engelsman,' said Wayne, shaking his head.

I took three Iraqis from Tanaka-san's camera team and we set off with the sat-phone to the edge of the desert just within the city limits. We parked where we had a clear view down the highway so we could spot the JMC's arrival. The interpreter reported to Tanaka-san that we were in place and I sent a radio check to Cobus. There were no rebro towers down here but in the flat landscape we had excellent comms. Now that night was falling, Samawah didn't seem quite so safe and the Iraqis with me suddenly had a spot of second thoughts. They were

all for driving back and I told them that if they did, they were
definitely not getting paid for the whole trip. They shook their
heads, lit cigarettes and pondered the lunacy of the white-eyes.

I checked my rifle and pistol and went and made myself
comfortable behind some scrub 20 metres away, leaving them
all puffing and glowing in the dark. I made sure that I was well
hidden from both bandits and Coalition Forces alike. The last
thing I wanted was for some sharp-eyed turret gunner with
night vision sights to see me armed and crouching near the side
of the road. There was a pale crescent moon low in the sky and
absolute silence. After several false alarms, the silence was
broken by the sound of the convoy thundering down the road
towards us.

The JMC had arrived and I said a quick prayer that none of
the Iraqis would take photos. In noisy armoured vehicles, the
gunners rarely hear shots when contacted by the enemy. They
react to the visual stimuli that might indicate where the enemy
is firing from. A flurry of camera flashes on an isolated desert
road at night might elicit a spectacular if fatal response.
Which, I mused, might prove interesting when they reached the
Japanese paparazzi.

I called Tanaka-san, he called Tokyo and his channel
broadcast 'breaking news' that the JMC convoy was arriving
a full five minutes before any other reporter saw them. A
friendly Dutch captain at the camp later told me that five
minutes before the arrival, all the reporters' phones were going
off with furious producers back in Japan watching Tanaka-
san's channel reporting 'breaking news' that the convoy was
entering Samawah and asking why the hell their own people
had not reported it earlier.

The main excitement next day was following Japanese units as
they drove around familiarising themselves with the area. We
had a good look at their equipment, noting their rifles, which
were unfamiliar to us, and their body armour, which seemed
comprehensive. I was impressed by their armoured cars, which
superficially resembled up-armoured Humvees. But the hull
armour and gunner's turret was a far better design than the
crude, home-made armour I had seen welded on to many

American vehicles in Baghdad. Unlike the heavy American Humvees, the Japanese cars also went like shit off a shovel with impressive acceleration.

The JMC were covered in Japanese flags, on their chests, helmets, backs and on each shoulder, identifying them as benefactors, not another delivery of American-Jewish Crusaders. With 24-hour TV coverage broadcasting their every move, every handshake and every wrong turn in Samawah's busy streets, the soldiers were under enormous pressure. I was impressed to see them go about their business in a very professional manner. When interacting with locals they behaved with such courtesy and consideration it was obvious that they understood the principles and the point of winning hearts and minds in Iraq.

Next day, the press lined up outside another Dutch base on the main street to film a JMC unit driving into and out of the gates. Thrilling stuff. Twenty minutes later while this was still going on, two donkey carts crashed in painful slow motion, blocking the traffic. The motorists got out of their cars waving fists and yelling while the two maddened donkeys continued braying and kicking. At that moment, like the approach of a tsunami, marchers from a peaceful demonstration demanding free elections began to arrive; by peaceful I mean a howling mob, but no guns. CNN later reported that there were 10,000 demonstrators and that seemed about right to me at ground level. The passion was remarkable, even stirring, wave after wave of young men wailing, waving banners and battering their own heads on large portraits of ayatollahs.

This made good footage, although the braying donkeys and screaming hordes were all drowned out when, by unhappy coincidence, a convoy of thirty oil tankers and a platoon of escorting American military police appeared at the end of the street. They stopped, scanned the scene with binoculars, then stepped down from the vehicles and charged the crowd screaming *what the fuck* and waving weapons in a bizarre attempt to restore calm and clear the road for their tankers.

The crowd thought that the Americans were there to deny them the right of free elections and the American MPs had the impression that the crowd was there to block the convoy. Two

MPs started diplomatically beating the crowd's spokesman and the officer in charge fired shots into the air. The mob reacted with predictable fury and things got so rowdy I almost missed seeing the Dutch riot platoon deploying out from the gates behind me.

It was complete pandemonium. The Japanese press kept filming, while the South Africans and I stood to one side enjoying the chaos until Tanaka-san grabbed his cameraman, dumped his jacket and ran into the middle of the crowd to do a 'live-from-the-riot' broadcast. We piled into the horde, stamping on feet and shoving with elbows and knees. I had never realised how useful a public-school education could be.

The Americans carried on swinging the butts of their rifles and forcing the jammed cars off the road at gunpoint. The mob howled and surged forwards, although once they realised that we were press, in the very heart of the riot we found ourselves left alone in a small circle of peace. The Iraqis love publicity and cameras.

I was still wondering how the disturbance was going to get resolved, when two road workers further up the street put out their fags, picked up their shovels and wandered over to the mountain of sand on the side of the road. Bearing in mind that they were upwind in a gale throwing sand into the back of a high lorry, the first two shovelfuls took to the air and whipped straight across the crowd in a fine gritty mist.

Angry howling at the Americans changed into screams of pain as the distraught Iraqis clutched their eyes. The road workers carried on plying their shovels like lunatics, creating a dust storm, working like no men I had ever seen in Iraq before or since. The Yaapies and I were protected by shades, the same as the Dutch soldiers. Everyone else ran off with their hands over their eyes. Cool. Seizing the moment, the two donkeys stopped braying and began munching on the rubbish piled up on the side of the road.

With the riot over, the American convoy passed through town leaving behind resentment, confusion and an anger that would linger far longer than the dust settling in their wake.

The riot in Samawah was the perfect example of what was going wrong with the occupation of Iraq by Coalition Forces.

The American MPs that day had thought they were dealing
with a disturbance that required a forceful solution and had
treated the people with condescension and incomprehension.
The convoy escort officer had terrified the crowd by firing
shots in the air and had probably left Samawah believing that
he had effected a rapid and successful outcome to a minor
outbreak of disorder. Mission accomplished. End of story.

The soldiers had completely ignored the spiritual element so
important to people with little in their lives other than a fierce
pride and a sense of devotion to their religion. The demonstrators were carrying pictures of their leaders, they were unarmed
and they were demanding elections, the very aim of the
Coalition. The lack of respect, the violence and the lack of
effort or interest in listening to the crowd were a lethal insult.
If this had been a town garrisoned by US troops, the Iraqis
would have been out that same night shooting up their patrols.
In a tribal area they would not have waited five minutes.

EIGHTEEN

U S Secretary of Defense Donald Rumsfeld's man, Ambassador Paul Bremer, arrived in May 2003 and one of his first acts was the issuing of two orders that, in my opinion, may have had a significant impact on post-war reconstruction and may have been one of the contributory factors that took the country to the brink of civil war. He formally disbanded all existing Iraqi security forces, including the army, and also instigated a process of de-Ba'athification, which translated into the sacking of almost every senior administrator in central and local government across Iraq. This might have worked in a country in which other political parties existed, or in which it was not compulsory to be a member of the ruling clique to hold office of any kind including the administration of hospitals and universities. This was not the case in Iraq.

The Iraqi army and police had been the last visible remnants of Iraqi governmental control in the country. Now an American had ordered them gone and an American had placed American soldiers in charge. In the middle of a worsening situation Paul Bremer, by disbanding the only recognised Iraqi security infrastructure had succeeded in two things at the stroke of a pen. Firstly, establishing in the minds of the Iraqis that America was not a liberator but a conqueror, and secondly, putting nearly a million armed men on the streets with no employment options except organised crime or to join the insurgency.

This was an ill-conceived and fatal miscalculation. I doubted that there was a single military officer in the Coalition Forces who was not appalled by Bremer's decision. There was undoubtedly good reasoning behind it – to ensure that the human rights abuses and corruption committed against the Iraqi people by the Ba'athists under Saddam's regime could not continue – but to me, it was still a fundamentally flawed policy because there was nothing to replace those institutions. Those officers understood the ramifications immediately because they were out on the streets. With that start, things would go from bad to worse in the first few weeks of the occupation. I have no idea what the three men responsible for planning the post-war occupation, General Tommy Franks, US Deputy Secretary of Defense Paul Wolfowitz and Donald Rumsfeld came up with, but having seen an immaculately planned and successful invasion turn into the resulting chaos both in the CPA and on the streets, I took this to be the result of a poorly thought-out occupation strategy. Over a dozen US and British Colonels that I met in the CPA confirmed that no briefings had been given out regarding Phase IV, the occupation.

With combat missions completed, American units dug in and with few exceptions watched the looting around them with no orders to stop it. The crime rate spiralled out of control as gangs roamed with impunity, killing, raping and looting. The Arabic criminal tradition of kidnap for ransom was flourishing and ordinary Iraqis were afraid to walk the streets. Petty grudges dating back for years were settled every night with AK-47s.

Every single government building, not just palaces and villas, but schools and hospitals, was looted down to the bare concrete with furnishings, toilets, window panes, wiring, pipes and even the doors being taken. Shops and businesses suffered as well as government properties. Only a few survived, guarded by courageous owners with strong sons and an armoury of AKs. When I drove around Baghdad it was a poster advertisement for American precision bombing, with bombed government headquarters turned into rubble next to untouched apartment blocks. But the Iraqis themselves, liberated from Saddam, had done far more damage to their own city than the war itself. Shocking, largely unreported and true.

The American administration, CPA officials and local CF commanders were horrified by the cost of the destruction and realised that a permanent blow had been struck at the reconstruction budget. But they totally missed the far more insidious and spiritual message they had sent out which would cause far more damage in the long run.

For the vast majority of Iraqis, this was their introduction to 'freedom' and 'democracy'. Kidnap. Rape. Murder. Sewage running in the streets. No water and no electricity. Hospitals and schools burned. Rampant criminal gangs and terror. The only authority was that taken by criminals, the most ruthless and violent gaining the most power. The one exception was in the Shi'ite districts where religious leaders and Shia militias took over their own neighbourhoods, imposing not just order but strict Islamic laws. Once again women were forced back indoors and under the headscarf. Allowing the Shia to achieve armed control and increased influence across the south and centre of the country worried many Kurds and terrified Sunnis. It would take time, but I believed that the seeds of civil war had been sown by Paul Bremer in the first weeks of his tenure.

This was also the Iraqis' introduction first-hand to America and Americans. The initial message that they took on board was one of incompetence and, both ironically and more importantly, one of weakness. It is impossible to over-emphasise the encouragement this gave to any Iraqi considering joining the insurgents. Saddam may have been a brutal tyrant but he had kept order.

To further illustrate America's impotence and incompetence in the eyes of the Iraqis, in August 2003 a warrant was issued for the arrest of Moqtada al-Sadr, leader of the Mahdi Army, a dangerous Shia militia with support all over the country, yet he was still moving around with impunity in January 2004. A few months later he would launch a country-wide revolt that would bring the Coalition almost to its knees. He would only be brought to the bargaining table by Coalition Forces having to cooperate with Al Dawa and the SCIRI, two other major

Shia militias. Moqtada al-Sadr was never arrested and would later be invited to join the Iraqi Governing Council.

Replying to complaints about anarchy and looting, Donald Rumsfeld on 11 April 2003 uttered the immortal line that 'Free people are free to make mistakes and commit crimes and do bad things.' He got a lot of flak for that comment, but however irresponsible, arrogant and fatuous his remark, he was telling the truth. And it seemed the Iraqis were in complete agreement with him.

The Pentagon's refusal to allow CF Commanding Officer General Tommy Franks any more men severely hampered not just military operations but the Coalition Provisional Authority in its attempts to rebuild the country. In just a few weeks after the iconic toppling of the Saddam statue on 9 April 2003, Baghdad had become so dangerous that CPA officials were simply unable to leave the Green Zone to meet with Iraqi counterparts, where any remained after de-Ba'athification, or Iraqi subcontractors once work had been commissioned. The Military Escort Service, or 'Steel Dragon', operating from the 'Wolfpack' car park opposite the palace, was always fully booked. Higher priority bookings would bump civilian administrators off the list and some never managed to leave the CPA at all.

Coalition Forces mounted operations against insurgents where they could, but with such low manning levels the priority was on 'force protection', the military term for self-defence, rather than implementing a full peacekeeping strategy, which still seemed not to exist since no coherent civil order missions were being co-ordinated from the CPA.

As I met more and more State Department officials and CF commanders over the course of the coming year, what would disappoint me the most was the lack of willingness by senior management to pass bad news upwards. Even Paul Bremer had read the RAND report suggesting that at least 500,000 troops would be required for peacekeeping operations in Iraq but, as far as I could see, his requests for more men seemed not to get anywhere. In the same way, I heard senior officers in the CPA arguing that they needed thousands more troops but that no one was willing to put their career on the line to really push the point. They made requests and then accepted the refusals without a fuss. If Donald Rumsfeld was on Fox News saying that no more troops were needed and that he was looking forward to an imminent withdrawal of American forces from Iraq, it was a poor career move to tell him that you could not do your job without more troops.

I saw one task force go through six full colonels in twelve months. Each man arrived, took stock of the situation and reported that they would not be able to achieve target objectives without more personnel and funding. They would be 're-assigned' back to the USA and we would wait to see if his replacement came up with a plan either to achieve his missions or simply retain his career. Even in May 2003, Mr Rumsfeld was still considering a US withdrawal by the end of the summer. It was not until September 2003, when President Bush got his $87 billion from Congress, that the American people realised a much longer-term commitment was needed. By then it was already too late in the minds of the educated Iraqis, who saw the CPA as ineffectual and their country sliding into chaos.

At the time of writing, in April 2006, President Bush was asked when he thought American troops would finally leave Iraq and he replied that that would be a decision for future presidents.

Later in 2004, during the 'Iraqification' phase of the occupation, I would meet State Department administrators who freely admitted that they were just in Iraq to 'get their ticket punched'. They would hand back infrastructure authority to Iraqi organisations knowing that there was either a lack of funding or trained personnel, or both, and would do so in order not to rock the boat. If Washington said do something by a certain date and cut the budget, the only wise response was to say, 'Yes sir, no problem.' After their short stay in Baghdad, they had better things to do and none but the brave would let the truth get in the way of future career prospects.

In this climate, the CPA laboured in isolation from reality behind miles of concrete barriers in the Green Zone, working towards project goals set by Washington and the Pentagon, where, as far as we could see out in Baghdad, Bush and Rumsfeld's aides ignored any reports that did not fit into their perceived version of events and were totally divorced from the true situation on the ground.

NINETEEN

Les was arm wrestling across his desk with a big Iraqi lad we called Obi-Wan Kenobi.

A lot of the young guards we had employed challenged Les in these arm-wrestling duels and although Les always won, he made it look a lot harder than it was. The Iraqis are a proud, emotional people and are easily insulted. Tell a man his shooting is crap and you offend his family, his tribe, his religion.

'Only Allah is perfect!'

It was a useful catch-all but bloody useless if you come under fire and your guards don't know what end of the rifle they're holding.

Les let Obi-Wan almost pin his arm to the table and then slowly levered his way to victory. Everyone cheered.

'Next time I win, Mr Les,' the boy said in English. He was deadly serious.

Obi-Wan Kenobi had got the nickname from his complicated name which none of us could pronounce, but he bore no resemblance to the diminutive mystic in *Star Wars*. He was strong, a quick learner, with sharp eyes and a vigorous Saddam Hussein moustache. Obi-Wan was one of the best shift supervisors and good at his job.

The cheering died down. Seamus was telling people to get out of his office so that he could get on with some work when the door burst open and a runner appeared breathlessly from the Ops room.

The guards on shooting practice out on the range had been shot at from the wall of the date plantation west of Aradisa Idah between our training area and the river. The land had belonged to Saddam's family and among the trees were some spectacular mansions, now bombed flat or looted. The area had since become occupied by squatters, ali-babas and bad guys who occasionally took pot shots at the guard towers around the purification plant. They had never hit anyone because the wall was 500 metres away across ground devoid of cover. Iraqis in general tend to be poor shots, but it still scared the guards. None of them liked being posted closest to the wall on towers 2 or 3, their equivalent of being sent to the Eastern Front for a quick death.

The enemy had already shot up the towers at night twice that week – cue frantic calls to the villa asking for help. Our Iraqi quick reaction force, or QRF, had refused to respond as it was 'too dangerous'. We had a policy of not responding ourselves since one day it would be used to lure the white-eyes into a trap. We had yawned, told them to lie low until first light, then rolled over and gone back to sleep. We were training a guard force to take over security of the water infrastructure and it was essential that they learn to deal with these sort of incidents without our running out every time to help them.

We arrived the following morning to replenish their ammo. Judging by the piles of cigarette butts on the floor, the enemy would have had no problem aiming at them the previous night. In typical Iraqi fashion, upon being contacted by the enemy, in blatant disregard of the training I had given them, each guard had emptied his three magazines on automatic fire into the night as quickly as he could change mags, run out of bullets in twenty seconds and then laid down and gibbered with fear. I was seriously thinking of getting the armourer to alter the AKs so that they could only fire single shot, or even issuing SKS rifles, which could not fire on automatic.

We fired the QRF commander, and replaced him with Senior Lieutenant Usama, who was built like an outside lavatory, had a handshake like a car-crushing device and spoke in an incoherent whispering growl, the result of having been either shot or stabbed in the throat at one point. He had been a paratrooper major in the former regime's special forces, fought against the Iranians, Kurds and Americans and had been with the fedayeen until he saw the light. Usama that night had immediately left the water plant, jumped over the wall and mounted a solo patrol one kilometre into the plantation looking for bad guys to hand-shake to death. He had found nothing, but his action had been impressive. I had been tempted to give him a raise on the spot, but had told him that that would be dependent on actual bodies being dragged back.

The training at the range was a slow process and teaching the guards how to shoot had been a valuable lesson in just how dangerous people can be with firearms. In a proud, macho society like this one, not a single Iraqi man would admit in front of the others that he had never fired an AK except maybe at weddings. Sammy and I conducted dozens of dry weapons lessons with empty magazines and everyone would carry out impeccable British Army loading, firing and unloading drills. As soon as you issued live ammunition, it was like a tea party at a chimpanzee lunatic asylum – but with machine guns. Guards would fire at each other's targets, shoot straight over the top of the berm, fire from the hip with eyes closed, click and fire on automatic despite Sammy and I walking down the line before the shoot and checking that each selector was set to single shot, and then turn around to clear jammed weapons while pointing at each other and at me.

Months earlier, when we had started shooting drills, I had suggested to Sammy that the next group of men to shoot should come inside the protective berm, stand behind the firing detail to get used to the noise and to see what they were doing right or wrong, and then they would shoot afterwards. Sammy had looked at me in complete shock that I would even consider having an extra ten men inside the range.

'No, Mister James. Too many people will die,' he said simply.

He had been right. Every time we finished a range exercise we both thanked Allah that we had not been killed nor lost any of the guards. Having said that, there would always be about one in twenty of our recruits who was a crack shot, nailing all his rounds into a tight grouping. They would deny ever having been in the army but I knew better.

What this meant was that the guards waiting to shoot had to wait out in the open ground where they would invariably ignore instructions to wait behind the berm, and would crowd around the entrance to watch what was going on. They were then in line of sight from the plantation wall where the bad guys set up to do their own target practice.

Sammy had taken on conducting range practices on his own when I was busy and had earned his pay after a similar contact a week or so before. Bandits had shot up the range and the new guards had instantly dropped their rifles and bolted. I didn't for one minute believe the enemy were after the weapons, since they were cheap and easy to buy on the black market in Sadr City. The shots had probably been a warning to the new boys that the insurgents knew who they were and were dishing out punishment for taking dirty money from the American Zionist Conspiracy.

When the guards fled on that occasion, Sammy collected every AK he could find while still under fire, stacked them in the company pick-up truck and returned to HQ. Personally, I would have fired the whole bunch of young recruits, but they were hard to come by, even at a starting salary of $150 a month. I had to make do with giving Sammy a bollocking for risking his life. He just saluted and grinned.

'It is my duty,' he said. 'They will not steal the Spartan rifles, Mister James.'

'Sammy, how many times have I asked you to call me Ash?'

'So many times I have lost count.'

I shook my head. 'Sammy, Spartan can buy some more fucking rifles for a few hundred dollars. Rifles you can get anywhere. Remember you have children, Sammy, we can't afford to lose you.'

He flushed bright red. 'Thank you very much, Mister James. You are very good man. You are my brother.'

This morning's contact was different though. As the runner translated the Arabic cascading from channel one on the radio,

Seamus's IRAQNA phone rang. It was Gus Gazzard, a US Lieutenant from 82nd Airborne, the CF unit closest to us. He was a good officer and I got to know him well.

It appeared that the insurgents had simultaneously opened fire on our guards at the range and on the US unit opposite the plantation across the Tigris. Sammy and one guard, no doubt one of those ex-soldiers who knew how to hit the target, returned a lot of rounds and the enemy disappeared while the rest of the trainees had dropped rifles and run.

Four US Kiowa Warrior helicopters – small but heavily armed observation helicopters – had arrived five minutes later to kick ass and the only Iraqis they could find were my thirty trainees being herded together by Sammy. The arrival of the Kiowas spooked the guards again and resulted in further weapons-dropping-and-running-away activity, this time including the guards manning towers 2 and 3 at the water plant.

Fortunately the pilots had recognised our uniforms and did not open fire. The guards were dressed in the standard FPS kit of black trousers, grey shirts and navy blue brassards. We had added the refinement of black baseball caps to give them a distinctive silhouette, especially at night. Insurgents wore balaclavas or *shemaghs* and wouldn't be caught dead in American baseball caps.

Before Christmas there would have been a very strong probability of the Kiowa Warriors strafing the area and killing a bunch of guards. The fact that they didn't meant Coalition Forces and Iraqi security were working in harmony and that, in the long run, was to everyone's benefit.

The same alarm call that had brought the helicopters had also alerted the CF ground units on this side of the river and Gus Gazzard's platoon had been on shift to react to incidents. He was at the range now, telling Seamus over the phone that everything was under control but could one of us expats come and calm the Spartan guards. I nodded to Seamus, grabbed my Kevlar vest and rifle and slipped on my shades. My Browning was already holstered in my thigh rig.

It was only a short drive to the range but there was no point in taking any chances. I took the armourer, Ali, and Abeer, one of the guards, with me. Now that Ibrahim was a colonel it was

not appropriate for him to be stacking and degreasing the
guard force weapons and Ali had taken over a lot of his duties.
Ali was a tiny, lean man but as wiry and hard as beef jerky.
His close-cropped hair and moustache were silver and he was
a weapons expert after twenty years as a paratrooper in the
Iraqi army. He always had a Browning stuffed down the back
of his belt, sometimes two, and the week before had shot two
of the three men who had carjacked him. When he reported
the loss of a company vehicle he had expected to be sacked and
was stunned that we rewarded him for killing the two
insurgents.

'But, Mister, I kill just one,' he had protested. His English
wasn't that good and he mimed how he had shot one man in
the head, '*Th'nyeen talkat*', two bullets, and the other in the
stomach, '*Arba talkat*', four bullets, before the second guy
staggered off and was driven away in the vehicle by the third
carjacker. So he had double-tapped one guy and filled the other
full of lead. I had seen Iraqi hospitals, the second man was
definitely a goner. I looked at Les who opened the box of petty
cash and gave Ali $200, one hundred for each man. He was
thrilled and went out fingering his pistol, looking left and right
for more enemy. That was a month's pay he had just earned.

We took one of the guard pick-up trucks and headed out
towards the fields.

'We go range, shooting?' asked Ali, smiling.

'*La, Ali baba,*' I replied, miming shooting with one hand.
'*Sah'b aksam.*' Cock weapons. Ali and Abeer lost their smiles,
made ready and pointed their AKs out left and right.

As we approached the range, I slowed to make sure the
Americans could identify us and wave us in. Sammy was
already talking animatedly with Gus. I drove the last 20 metres
at crawling speed so as not to deluge them in a cloud of dust
from my truck.

'Hey Ash, good to see you,' Gus said and we shook hands
as I stepped out of the vehicle.

On Gus's wrist was a pewter cuff with the name, rank and
date of one of his former sergeants. When I had asked him
what it was he had mumbled that it was a memory thing for a

friend killed in Afghanistan. Many of the guys in his platoon
wore similar bracelets. Whatever the press or US Government
may have said were the reasons for invading Iraq, the guys in
that platoon were there to avenge the deaths of dead comrades.

Sammy was clutching his AK. I touched my hand to my
chest. Lieutenant Usama, the handcrusher, was hanging
around trying, in front of his men, to appear as if he had
something to contribute despite not speaking a word of
English. Usama would have been the guard who had stood his
ground with Sammy and held off the enemy. I greeted him
warmly, shaking hands and touching my chest.

'*Shlonek, zeeyen?*' How are you, good?

'*Kullish zeeyen, alham dul'illah.*' Very good, thanks be to
God. He beamed with pride and saluted.

I told Sammy to instruct the guards to clean weapons before
letting them go for the day. They had two pick-up trucks. I let
them have my vehicle after checking with Gus that he could
give me a ride back to the office. Ali looked crestfallen that
there would be no opportunities to earn another $100. The
thirty recruits with their guard officers piled on to the trucks
and bounced off over the fields, raising a huge cloud of fine
dust.

I called Seamus on my IRAQNA.

'Hello, mate, I have sent our guards back to the office. I'm
with Gus giving him a brief on the plantation. They'll drop me
off later.'

'OK, mate, roger that.'

Gus wanted to take a look at the area and see if he could
find any useful evidence, cartridge cases, vehicle tracks, anything that might spice up his report or lead him to the bad
guys. I could have gone back with Sammy, but it was a nice
afternoon, brisk not cold. I had been cooped up in the office
and I needed some fresh air.

Gus was looking at the trees in the distance through
binoculars. It was a wide area that ran along the banks of the
Tigris and stretched back two or three Ks. Between the
plantations there was a disorderly scattering of fields and
smallholdings where squatters scratched out a living with a
vegetable patch and a few chickens. They had moved into the

area since the end of the war and were not part of the local community or our early warning network of informants and farmers. It was an area where the insurgents had regularly cached arms and launched mortar attacks on the Green Zone.

Gus gave me the binoculars. There was nothing to see, just the wall and the tops of the trees. I told Gus what Sammy had told me, that the date palm was the symbol of life in the desert. When the Prophet Mohammed was in the wilderness, he had survived solely on a diet of dates and the palm was considered sacred by Arabs. Saddam's plantation was sacrosanct and Iraqis got quite shitty if anyone damaged the trees.

'That's a good guy you've found.'

'Yes, Gus, and he's our good guy.'

He smiled. I had read his mind. Gus Gazzard had an interpreter from Titan with him, a young Iraqi in blue jeans, a button-down shirt and American body armour. His English, I would discover, was terrible and I couldn't help wondering if he was playing both sides of the fence. I had no worries about Sammy disappearing. Although Titan Security was paying their interpreters a hell of a lot more than we were even paying our officers, they had the social stigma of working for the Americans.

I was pointing out the boundaries of the Ministry of Water property when two enemy popped up at different points on the plantation wall and opened fire. Bullets snapped by my ears and ploughed up explosions of dust around us. I threw myself on to the ground in the firing position, making my body as small a target as possible. I couldn't believe this was happening. We were a full platoon with six Humvees carrying a variety of belt-fed weapons. If we needed more guns, two Kiowa Warriors remained overhead.

Most of the shots coming in thudded in the dirt just in front of us. I saw one guy go down with a *whomph*, hit in the chest, and his buddies answered with a barrage of withering fire that pockmarked the wall; fragments spouted from the wall in explosive gouts of dust and I could barely hear Gus shouting orders over the fusillade of shots.

I sent, 'Contact, wait, out,' over the radio, before realising that none of the guys was likely to have their handsets switched on. I didn't bother with the phone. With all the firing it would have been impossible to hear anything. All of a sudden my earpiece crackled into life.

'Ash, Seamus, send sitrep, over.' Obviously they could hear the firefight at the office and he must have switched on his radio immediately.

'Ash, roger, contact, contact. Two enemy with AKs 300 metres east of range, Charlie Foxtrot is returning rounds, wait, out.'

Returning rounds was an understatement. The wall had been filled with holes where the enemy firing positions had been. After five seconds the platoon ceased fire under the shouted orders of Gus and their sergeants. They were all lying or kneeling down, cheeks welded to stocks and eyes looking through sights at the wall. Three men were around the soldier who had been hit. He was gasping and writhing on the ground.

The rebels were outnumbered, outgunned and in no position to take on a platoon. Was this insanity, religious fervour, financial? We had heard on the Karrada grapevine that insurgents who took out an American and could verify the kill would get $1,000. Where there's turmoil there's always plenty of money. Saddam in his day would send thousands of dollars to the families of Palestinian suicide bombers. He'd gone, but in Saudi Arabia there were banks brimming with blood money and the silent majority wanted the white-eyes out of the sacred holy lands. This war was never going to end. Like the South Africans, I wanted to pay off my mortgage and get the hell out of there.

I kept my eye on the plantation wall and was pleased to observe at the same time that the two Humvee gunners who had been facing away from the direction of the shots were still watching their arcs.

When the barrage from the Americans stopped, one of the insurgents put his AK back over the top of the wall and fired an unaimed burst that went miles into the sky above us. Every single soldier snapped off a single shot at that section of parapet except for a .50 cal gunner who tried to drill through the wall.

The Kiowas were doing passes over the plantation and I was surprised that Gus Gazzard was not in direct communication with the helicopters. He was on his company net talking back to his Brigade HQ. They spoke to the pilots and passed the reply back down the line to Gus. It seemed as if Rumsfeld's transformational military strategy had not yet filtered all the way through to the front line. Later on Gus would tell me that they were lucky to have such a quick link with only one relay. Some frontline units had to go through a chain of four or five relays to communicate with air assets. Some units had direct communications while others had no comms at all.

The guy who had taken a hit was OK, saved by the ceramic plates in his vest. He was bruised but revved up and ready to go and track down our attackers.

'Let's do it,' Gus said. ' I can't leave you here, Ash, you're going to have to come with us.'

Contractors were not allowed to accompany CF units on missions but this was different. I happened to be with them when they came under contact. My only other option was to walk home.

'No problem, but if anything happens, take my body back to Spartan and throw it over the fence,' I told him.

'I wouldn't do that, Ash.'

'You'd better, or Krista won't get the insurance money.'

We were under strict instructions that no expat was to leave company locations except with other members of the team. If I got slotted, I was only covered if I was working in a Spartan team. Lieutenant Gazzard twigged.

'Hey, nothing's going to happen.'

'I know that. But that's only because I've just told you.' I was wondering why the insurgents were taking on such a superior force. I waved at the wall. 'You know this is likely a come-on for a trap in there.'

'Yeah, but we're still going to go get them.'

I stepped up into the back of the Humvee and we set off bouncing over the sand berms with the Kiowas sweeping low overhead.

There are at least seventeen official variants of the Humvee in use with the US Army. Gus's platoon had the lightest and least armoured. There were two with enclosed passenger

compartments and turret rings mounting a .50 cal and a
Mk19. All the others, including the one Gus and I were in,
were load-carrying transports with unarmoured cabs and an
open load bay at the back. His company had welded steel
plates across the doors and down the sides of the load bay to
have some basic protection against shrapnel. The floor was
lined with sandbags and spare flak vests.

I knelt in the back with the paratroopers, our weapons
pointing out over the sides, while the SAW gunner stood,
resting his M249 on the roof of the cab pointing forward. The
gunner in the vehicle behind us had a 7.62mm M240, which
is basically the same as the British GPMG. One of the other
load-carrying Humvees had a steel post and pivot mounting a
second .50 cal.

I had heard many gripes from US soldiers about Humvees,
but that afternoon out on the range I was impressed. Much like
the Land Rovers I was more familiar with, the cross-country
performance was surprisingly good. Carrying very little armour and therefore weight we were soon flying across the
ground. Dust was billowing up around us from the vehicle in
front and for once I was glad of my sensible shades.

We skidded to a halt at the tall metal gates in the pulverised
wall. Potter, one of the soldiers from our vehicle, de-bussed
and checked for booby traps; I jumped down to go with him.
It wasn't my job but, with Northern Ireland and Bosnia on my
CV, I probably had more experience of IEDs and booby traps
than this entire platoon. I didn't want to see any of these guys
get blown up, but there was a selfish motive: I was going to be
driven through this gate in a few moments.

I gave Potter the nod. The gates were clean. The lead
Humvee crashed its way through as we doubled back to our
wagon and followed in the dust storm as the platoon wove a
path along the dirt tracks used by the cultivation crews. The
Kiowas were circling a few hundred metres in front of us and,
over the slight comms delay, we got the message that they had
found the terrorists, two or perhaps three guys. We took a road
off to the side and started a detour to circle around to their
position. I was glad that Gus was using his head. A less
cautious officer might have ordered his platoon straight down

the most direct track towards the fleeing enemy. That's how you find mines and IEDs the hard way.

I took advantage of the lull to dig out my IRAQNA and called Seamus.

'Hello, mate, how are you doing?' he asked immediately. I knew by the sound of slurping he was busy getting down his tea and biscuits.

'Good, mate. Only two or three enemy who have broken contact and withdrawn. Gus's lot are in pursuit. We've got six Humvees and two helicopters. I'll give you a call when I'm on my way back.'

I tried to sound as nonchalant as possible. After all I didn't want these Americans to think I was excited or stressed.

'OK, cheers, see you in a bit.'

As we approached the last sighted enemy position, Gus divided his vehicles in two groups, three circling one way and three the other.

Further ahead there was a complex of villas. The Kiowas were swooping in wider circles like disturbed hornets and confirmed to Gus that the bad guys had gone to ground there. A couple of the villas were piles of charred masonry, there was one with the roof in place, and another had been sliced cleanly in two like a doll's house with the front open, some scraps of furniture clinging to the concrete floors suspended precariously into space.

The three Humvees circled the space before pulling up, engines running. We sat there for a moment as Gus considered the ground to his front. It's important never to hurry these things. To take time, take stock, wait for the enemy to make a mistake rather than rush in and make one yourself. Gus de-bussed, making hand signals and delivering clear orders into his radio handset. The drivers and roof gunners remained in position, the rest scrambled out.

As soon as I jumped down from the vehicle, I took cover behind the engine block in a firing position on one knee. The Americans who had already de-bussed were standing around as if they were waiting for a train. When they saw my action, they sheepishly did the same. Their sergeants spread them out ready to go.

The other three Humvees by this time had turned up on our left, flanking the complex and Gus gave the order over the radio for them to de-bus. He had established his platoon HQ behind a low wall and had a good view of the complex. He had two machine guns for fire support and a radio operator with him. He wanted to clear the area but was aware of the possibility that squatters might be living in the ruined villas. We couldn't just strafe the buildings and grenade each room.

We were now facing south with the river running along our right-hand side, acting as a boundary that he could anchor his flank on. Three squads were in all-round defence with the other group of Humvees over on the left securing the left flank and also providing fire support to the front. Gus gave the order and his three squads moved forward, leapfrogging one another, going down and covering the next one to move forward.

This was bandit country and the enemy could have been anywhere around us. I had three choices: scramble over to the wall and hang out with Gus; climb back in the Humvee and watch the action from a higher vantage point; or join in with one of the squads which I had noticed was a man short.

Top & bottom
The other end of the scale. Unarmoured
Humvees were very exposed to any small arms
or IED attack. I was in one like this when
insurgents nearly blew us up at a junction
with an IED.

Above
Gus's lead squad of 82nd Airborne paratroopers deploying for
assault south east of Baghdad with two Kiowas overhead
observing enemy positions.

Below
A map of Baghdad showing
the Route Irish and CPA.

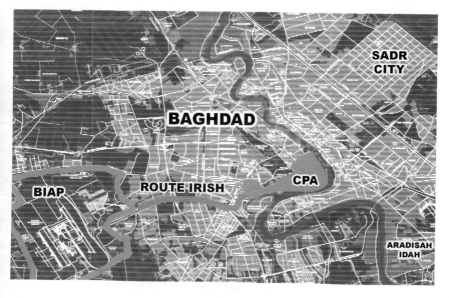

Above
Me with PKM machine gun, AK rifle and Sig pistol. I have 100 rounds ready to go and a spare 200 in the box underneath.

Below
Gus's platoon HQ and fire support position as the squads push forward into the villas.

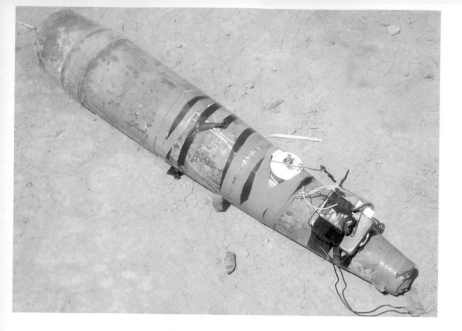

Above
An insurgent IED made from an artillery shell. This can then be disguised, buried near a road or hidden in a car and driven to its target.

Left
Out shopping for dinner Iraqi style. Lamb again!

Above
Innocent victims of a bombing in Baghdad who never knew what hit them. The taxi driver behind was seriously injured.

Right
New owners – Saddam's gilt and marble bathrooms used as storage by CF.

Above
A Dragunov SVD, an excellent medium range sniper rifle for rapid fire up to 600m.

Below
The result of insurgent sabotage; a blown oil pipeline blocking the road to Site Delta.

Above
The main pool at the palace and centre of social life at the CPA, a good place to meet up with other contractors and swap intelligence, tactics and news of other jobs – and the only place to see women in bikinis in the country.

Below
The team.

Above
Blackhawks at dawn east of Aradisah Idah.

Below
Colonel Mad Dog McQueen presenting me with one of my certificates in front of the 9/11 mural in the palace.

TWENTY

I attached myself to Potter and the squad from our Humvee. They were now moving forward along a fold of ground near the river. At least this way I would still be performing the valuable task of guiding the CF through an area of which I had local knowledge and would be able to point out to the forward squads any farms that I knew had 'friendly' civilians. Any farmers would also probably be more willing to talk to me as the local Spartan representative than to the Amerikeeyeh.

As I passed one of the gun trucks I paused by the gunner. He had a .50 cal pointed at the villa and an M4A1 carbine with a 40mm grenade launcher sitting on the roof next to him for snap shooting. He also had an M249 SAW sitting on the roof behind him. In the British Army soldiers call them Minimis.

'I don't want to be too cheeky, mate, but are you using that right now?' I pointed at the light machine gun.

'Naw, buddy. You take it and go kick some doors.' He grinned back and handed me down the SAW.

I slung my rifle on my back, tightening the strap so that it was tight against my body. I took the SAW, pointed it into the plantation away from the rest of the platoon, cocked the weapon and popped on the safety catch. Then I crouched down and doubled forward to catch up with the squad.

We were five men, Potter, two specialists, as the Americans call privates, Sergeant Navarro, a guy no more than 5ft 2in who looked like a head waiter, and myself. They all looked happy to see me, especially with the extra firepower. We were calling out to the squads left and right of us, ducking down every few yards as we approached the main building. The roof was in place and the windows had been blown out.

In thirty seconds we were up against the wall, weapons pointing forwards, backwards and out to the side. No one seemed to be looking up so I covered the windows above us. In street-fighting you stick as close to walls as possible. That way if an enemy wants to shoot you he has to lean out, and that's when you give him the good news. We waited while another squad secured the entrance. I noticed the eyes of the specialist next to me glaze over slightly. He was stressed and totally focused to the point of tunnel vision down the sight of his weapon. He was panting rapidly. I checked his name tag.

'Hey, Moss,' I hissed. 'Moss. Hey, how does my hair look?'

'Huh?' He looked at me blankly, still taking quick, shallow breaths.

'How does my hair look?' I gave my hair a quick pat down. 'Might be some ladies in there and I want to impress them.'

Suddenly he smiled, the tension broken.

'You're looking good, sir.'

'I know, mate, but I never get tired of hearing it.'

His smile broadened as he returned to scanning the plantation over the top of his weapon. His breathing was back to normal and his face was relaxed although still concentrated.

The squad ahead of us inside the front door of the villa called us forward. We slipped one at a time into the villa and paused in the lobby with its wide staircase and numerous doors. Everyone had their weapons into the shoulder, scanning through their red-dot sights. The houses all across Baghdad were squat and square, mud-coloured outside, drab inside, featureless and serviceable. The place we'd entered was a palace, or it had been before the looters got in, with high ceilings and tall arched windows looking out on the military ranks of palms on parade.

I moved to the side and knelt down where I could cover the hallways and stairs. My machine gun was a para model with a short barrel and I telescoped in the butt so that it was even shorter than the M4s the other guys were using. If we got into a fight inside the buildings every advantage counted and the smaller profile would buy me a fraction of a second. Despite the half-size 100-round belt on it I could still feel the weight of the gun and was glad I had been working out with the guys in the gym. At this rate I'd soon be ready to take on Les in an arm wrestle.

At the entrance to the first room, Navarro and the specialists stacked up in a line and on his signal charged through one after the other. I winced, thinking this was totally insane. A single enemy fighter could have taken them all out with a grenade or a burst of machine-gun fire.

I followed them in straight away, biting my tongue and keeping my mouth shut. I wasn't an officer in the US Army; I was no longer an officer in anyone's army. It would have been madness to start debating tactics in the middle of an action anyway. But it was always a concern to me that American tactics were so very different to those we practised in the British Army. If you were clearing a house with a section of eight Brits, two would go forward into a room while the rest gave cover. Once the room was secure, the next assault pair would take the next room and so on. Nearly ten years previously in the US I had worked with paratroopers from Fort Bragg, Rangers from Fort Lewis and Marines from Camp Lejeune, and had had the same knee-jerk reaction back then as I had that day beside the Tigris. I knew their drills, I just thought they were suicidal.

It was not so much that you risked losing five or six men instead of two, but tactics like this soaked up nearly three times as many men and unless you were assaulting buildings with three or four platoons it would be the same team that would have to clear the building, one room after the other. As we moved away from the squad covering the entrance hall and into the rooms along the corridor, there would be fewer eyes watching the hallways and other doorways, and more important-ly at no stage would we be able to leave behind men to keep each room clear. A fundamental certainty in street-fighting is that the enemy will try and re-infiltrate buildings and will suddenly open up on you from rooms behind that had already been cleared. The only thing I could do was to leave the overall strategy to Gus and concentrate on looking after myself and this squad.

Navarro and his men stacked to clear the next room and to show I was a team player, I lined up with the rest of them. In under a second we piled in. As the men orientated themselves and took positions, I pointed the SAW at the next door and found myself automatically snapping out orders.

'Keep away from the window,' I said to the specialist silhouetted against the empty window space. I pointed to the two nearest the doorway we had just come through. 'Take one side each and cover both ways up the hall in case someone's coming up behind us. Potter, your bayonet's about to fall out.'

The orders made sense and they reacted instantly. If there had been a picture of Saddam on the wall (which there wasn't as they'd been nicked or incinerated long ago), and I'd said, don't touch that, they would have understood why and left it alone. I also realised that they were slightly in awe of me, obviously assuming that as a private contractor I was some bad-ass, ex-Green Beret death-dealer. It was their lucky day; I was better than that, I had been a British officer.

Sergeant Navarro was on the radio to Gus and didn't seem concerned that I had taken command of the squad. In the next few rooms I tried to keep quiet and not usurp his command, only giving strong 'suggestions' when I saw the guys in danger. And to be honest I did not need to say much. These men were a world away from those 82nd troopers I had trained with a decade earlier. These were experienced soldiers who had seen months if not years of active combat. I didn't try to change their tactics. I adapted and was soon leading the way as we charged like headbangers into the next room and the next, through the ground floor and up the curving staircase to the floor above. I would run the whole exercise through my mind later and realised after the event how bloody stupid I'd been. I'd done my time. It was someone else's turn. This was what those paratroopers were being paid for.

It was long hot work. I was dehydrated and Moss shared his canteen with me. It took three hours to go through the villas and we didn't find a soul. Gus Gazzard couldn't understand how the terrorists had vanished so easily but we had a theory at Spartan that made sense when I told him. One way insurgents would be able to avoid the roadblocks and pop up in this area and across the river to mount mortar attacks on the Green Zone would be through the network of underground tunnels that were said to have been built by Saddam and his family members so they could move in safety to their villas.

'That's what our locals tell us, but they don't know where the tunnels are,' I said.

'So they say.'

We returned to the empty buildings to scout about for tunnels, to no avail. We did consider taking a look at the doll's house building, the biggest in the complex, but it looked as if it could fall down at any second and we didn't want to take any injuries from walls crashing down on the men. Death in accidents is as bad as death by enemy fire.

The Kiowas reported suspicious movement in a farm 200 metres further down the river. I returned the SAW to the gunner and we mounted back into the Humvees. We drove slowly through the walled garden with its fractured swimming pool and dead flower beds and out into another palm plantation behind the villa.

There were about a dozen families of squatters living in adobe shacks built from breeze blocks pilfered from the ruins and plastered in mud. They made roofs from dead palm fronds, which were the same colour as the mud, and from the distance they looked like piles of dung.

Up ahead there were two of these little shacks and 50 metres to the right of them, next to the river, and almost invisible behind the tall grass and reeds, were the flattened remains of a small villa.

The moment we emerged from the trees, we came under fire from the ruins. These guys were determined. They had not escaped through tunnels, they had been waiting for us.

The front Humvee gunner returned fire and as each vehicle behind pulled off to the side their gunners opened up as soon as they had a clear target; the sacred palm trees were shot to pieces. The two Kiowas banked hard and screamed overhead seeking cover. Ricochets and concrete fragments sprayed across the plantation, sparkling the river with splashes and landing across the two little houses. I wasn't thrilled. This was my neighbourhood. I didn't want to see any innocent Iraqis getting killed because they happened to be standing close to where the Americans were shooting. At the same time, these bastards were trying to kill me.

I dropped over the side of the Humvee as soon as it halted, shouldered my rifle and started firing back. I had a Heckler & Koch G3 with a mounted scope that I had ordered from the States over the Internet and had mailed to Spartan HQ in the CPA. Through the scope I could see nothing but the long grass, dust and muzzle flash where the enemy fire was coming from. I put the cross hairs on the last flash I saw and fired five rounds rapid, the heavy rifle thumping against my shoulder. I scuttled to the side to change firing positions and knelt to fire around the side of a palm tree. Although the .50 cals were turning the palms on the other side of the clearing into coleslaw, they were big, thick trees and I didn't think an AK round would penetrate.

The noise was overpowering. The air was thick with dust and the not unpleasant smell of cordite. With the amount of bullet strikes and tracer going in, it was clear to the Kiowa pilots what we were firing at and one of them came back up the river to point-blank range and nailed the ruins with a 2.75-inch rocket that exploded with an almighty boom. Then there was silence. It was the sort of silence you are aware of when a car alarm wakes you at night, wails for ten minutes, then goes quiet.

We waited. The dust coated our skin as it settled. I sucked in deep breaths and realised that I was dying of thirst again. We waited some more.

I caught sight of Gus signalling up ahead and saw squad leaders tilting their heads as they listened to orders over the radio. Leapfrogging each other again, squad by squad, we made our way cautiously towards the ruins. They had been completely blown to pieces. We found one dead body and three weapons and made them safe. If there were two more dead insurgents, their bodies were either deep beneath the rubble or they had evaporated in the air across the river and into the trees beyond.

The dead terrorist was wearing a grubby white tunic over baggy trousers and a chest rig with ammo pouches for his AK under a European-style jacket. Stuck in his belt there was a curved knife that looked like an antique and on his feet there was a pair of worn out flip-flops. It always came as a shock when you saw reasonably armed rebels without proper footwear. He couldn't have run if he'd wanted to without them falling off. After a good gun, you need a good pair of boots. The dead guy was 25, perhaps. He had been shot in the face and his flattened head looked like an empty rubber mask. His *shemagh*, skull and brains were spread out in the grass behind him. Two men were detailed off to get a body bag and bag him.

The Humvees had pulled forward. Half the guns were pointed at the two squalid shacks, windowless and poorly constructed; one had an ornate door, stolen from the villas, this conventional piece of carpentry making it all the more depressing. Next to the shacks I saw a sink, an air conditioner, a fridge and a TV stacked up in a pile, obviously looted from a villa as well, despite the fact that there was no electricity. They got their water from the two-inch pipes that irrigated the plantation and they shitted among the trees. The smell was overpowering, chickens, goat and human waste in a toxic mix that hung over the area and almost made me gag.

The Humvees lined up on the road next to the shacks as I patrolled with Gus and two squads on foot towards the shacks, eyes peeled, weapons in the shoulder. Children swarmed around us, six, seven, eight, it was hard to be sure, they were ragged urchins who didn't ask for money. There was a vegetable patch, a couple of goats and a few chickens that were stamping about screeching, unsettled by the fuss.

A man appeared wearing a filthy tunic and sandals made out of car tyres. He had a bushy moustache and thick stubble on his sunken cheeks. His big Adam's apple was rocking up and down and more noticeable were his wild red eyes. Like virtually every Iraqi I had met he looked worn and lined. He looked terrified and it became apparent to me that it wasn't us he was frightened of so much as the man who stepped out through the ornate door behind him smoking a cigarette. He was a young city Arab in a suit and white shirt with his belly hanging over his belt. He was wearing a *shemagh*, but it was clean and he had a gleaming black moustache and a freshly shaven chin. It was like royalty arriving at a party. We were all quiet for a moment. Gus Gazzard's interpreter translated.

The city Arab said he was a farmer. They were one family. He didn't know anything about the fedayeen. 'They are very bad men. We are happy you are here and you are all alive.' Blah. Blah. Blah.

'What the hell's this guy doing here?' I said to Gus. 'Look at these people.'

The children were still swarming around us. They were universally filthy and barefoot, dressed in rags. Some of the specialists had sweets which they gave out and these children snatched at them gratefully. This was poverty like I'd seen in Africa.

'Sarn't Navarro, search those rooms,' Gus pointed at the shacks. They moved inside cautiously, no headbanger stuff, and almost immediately Sergeant Navarro poked his head back out the door.

'Something here, sir,' he called.

Potter and another guy kept their rifles on the two men and I followed Gus into the shack. There was a hole in the floor covered by palm fronds. We pulled them to one side. It was a bloody great big hole the size of a cellar and stored there were about two dozen sacks. We called the interpreter in with the men and asked them what was in the sacks.

The Adam's apple on the skinny farmer's throat was throbbing even faster and the colour drained from his face. I could see him sweating. The other guy started shouting at the interpreter, who in turn translated that they had no idea what was in the sacks or how they got there. The farmer fell to his knees and started babbling.

'He say please. He have the children. Don't take away. He never seen this before. He swear to the God,' the interpreter relayed to us.

It was obvious that the skinny wretch was the dupe and the city Arab was hiding stuff in the camp, something the farmer would have had to accept or the terrorists would do something nasty to his kids. Dead bodies were turning up all over Baghdad every day, killed by the insurgents for co-operating with the Americans, killed by bandits for their money, killed for not co-operating with whoever held the guns. The Americans found women with their throats cut, and men shot in the head, executed on the side of the road. You couldn't count the dead Iraqis. There were just too many.

Sergeant Navarro was about to climb down into the hole to throw up the sacks, but I stopped him. I called to the guys in the squad to bring a couple of children into the shack. If there were any nasty surprises, the farmer would stop us. He didn't have the intense look of zeal that a suicide bomber would have, looking forward to dining with the Prophet in heaven that evening. He looked scared shitless. It was safe to climb down in the hole and that's what Navarro did.

The squad formed a line and passed the sacks, piling them in the road. Half of them contained soap flakes, the other half fertiliser: accelerants for improvised explosive devices. Insurgents normally used unexploded artillery shells and mines, which they adapted for bombs, but like any guerrilla army without a regular logistics chain, they also built their bombs from home-made ingredients.

There was absolutely no reason for the dirt farmer and his well-dressed friend to have 1,200 kilos of soap flakes and fertiliser. You don't need fertiliser for the palms, and as for the soap flakes, I would have been surprised if the man and his kids had ever seen a bath in their lives.

Once we got the sacks out, Sergeant Navarro found a couple of hundred metres of electric cable and a dozen light switches. There was no electricity here in the plantation shacks. Electricity was science fiction.

'Vamos a ver,' he said. Let's see. The sergeant was grinning for the first time as he tossed up a dozen maps of Baghdad.

They were highly detailed maps and marked on them were the Coalition bases and the essentials of the Iraqi infrastructure, electrical power plants, our water filtration facilities, the

oil refinery over the river, the deserted Iraqi police stations. We
didn't find any detonators or the initial charges of plastic
explosives, but they are the kind of thing that a bomber can bring
in and attach to the main body of the IED at the last minute.

While the Americans plasticuffed the two men, I took a stroll
around the smallholding. I had a fair amount of experience
looking for arms caches, and was keeping my eye out for any
obvious markers. Five minutes later I gave up. Why would they
have bothered to cache all the sacks in the hut and then build
another hideaway outside? I made my way back to join Gus.

The Americans were about to load the two guys into a
Humvee. It was at that moment that the farmer realised he was
being taken away and he went berserk. He snapped the plastic
cuffs, an almost impossible feat that momentarily stunned us
all, and started fighting like a man possessed. Sergeant Navarro
leapt up and caught him in a throat lock and the two of them
went down under a rush of six soldiers. It was like a cartoon.
Helmets and rifles came flying from out of this great cloud of
dust and bodies. Maybe I should hire this guy, I thought, I
couldn't believe his energy.

About five minutes later Sergeant Navarro finally choked
him unconscious and the farmer dropped his bladder and
bowels. They hog-tied his body with about ten pairs of cuffs.
I was positive that he wasn't a terrorist. I knew that.
Lieutenant Gazzard knew that too. He was just a man who
didn't want to be taken away from his children.

During the fight, the well-dressed guy just watched emotion-
lessly.

I looked back at the farmer. One of the Americans was
checking his breathing. Potter, to my surprise, re-appeared out
of the shack with another pair of trousers and after they had
cut off the plasticuffs on the guy's ankles, they started to
change him. I suppose they would have got mess all over the
Humvee otherwise.

'Gus, this guy's innocent,' I said. 'If he wanted to fight us,
he would have been shooting at us as soon as we came in.'

The interpreter backed me up. 'Yes, Yes. This man is a
farmer,' he said. 'He say there is no mother, he say please don't
take me from the children.'

'It's the greaseball here who has hidden the stuff,' I added. 'I bet you he's with the guys we've just shot. He probably co-ordinated the contact.'

Gus was sympathetic. 'There's a procedure, Ash. He's just resisted arrest. I have to take him in.'

He said he would take the farmer in, check him on the database, ask him a few questions and then bring him back to the squatter camp.

'I won't let him sit in jail and rot for a couple of weeks while he goes through the system.'

Gus told the interpreter to tell the kids that. I added my own warning: 'And tell them they are going to be good children. They are going to stay in their houses until their father returns later tonight.'

The last thing we wanted was for the farmer to return and find some of the kids had run off.

It was important to me to always maintain goodwill among the people. If the farmer was treated well, he was more likely to support the Coalition. Every man offended or shamed was another candidate for the insurrection. Iraqis will do almost anything for money, but it helps if there's goodwill.

The guy in the suit had remained relaxed throughout the brawl. This may seem sensible, in his position I would have done the same. But Iraq is a tribal society and watching another member of your tribe fight a dozen Americans without stepping in just wouldn't happen. They are proud, violent people with short fuses. He would have exploded and joined the fray. He knew the score. I was sure the patrol would take him back and they wouldn't find anything on his record.

'Check his ID again and again,' I said to Gus. 'He's not worried about being taken in. Even if he's innocent, he should be pissing himself with fear.'

I didn't need to mention that everyone in Baghdad had heard stories of what went on behind the walls of Abu Ghraib. It had been the notorious prison under Saddam where the secret police tortured prisoners and now, under American control, rumour had it that the same treatment was being dished out to 'enemy combatants'.

They loaded the unconscious farmer into the Humvee like a sack of potatoes.

They put the smart guy in another Humvee and he got angry for the first time as one of the troopers made him lie down. He was screaming abuse. He was being taken prisoner by the Great Satan, but seemed more concerned about getting dirt on his suit.

The noise stopped suddenly. Navarro looked suspiciously at the gunner inside the Humvee. 'Hey, specialist, are you standing on that prisoner?'

The gunner stepped down off something. 'No, Sarn't.'

At this stage they realised that one of the Humvees had a flat front tyre, possibly from a lucky bullet from the enemy. I was astonished to find out that they did not carry spares but apparently this was routine. They hooked a tow-strap to another Humvee and prepared to set off with the two prisoners and two dozen sacks of fertiliser and soap flakes. There was enough to fill a van, enough to destroy a building.

They took me back to the villa and Seamus told me to get a move on. We were going to have to hurry if we wanted to get into the CPA gym before the evening rush hour. I would have to write up the incident later.

I spoke to Gus next day. He had kept his word. After four hours' interrogation, he returned the farmer to his children with a bunch of PX goodies and a sheep bought from the company petty-cash fund. The nearby farmers were hugely impressed and I was pleased to see a little progress in the hearts and minds campaign. I had already learned from our local informants in Karrada that the squatter was simple-minded. He hadn't known who the Americans were and, as I had suspected, he was only storing the sacks under threat by the insurgents.

The guy in the suit was far more interesting and had been passed up the line to Brigade headquarters. He wasn't Iraqi but a Syrian jihadi from a well-off family, which fitted the pattern.

Jihad, literally 'fight', is a slippery concept with infinite interpretations, peaceful as well as violent, and deriving from the fundamental religious duty of all Muslims to spread the teachings of Islam. Since the invasion of Iraq by the United States the jihad in Iraq attracted volunteers from all over the Arab world and for different reasons.

In Saudi Arabia, Syria and Egypt, jihad in Iraq found resonance among both the rich and the middle classes, much as writers and intellectuals were attracted to the International Brigade in the Spanish Civil War. For the vast majority of Muslims in the Middle East, Islam permeates every facet of their lives and defines them as individuals. An attack against other Muslims is thus perceived by many as an attack both against their religion and also against themselves in a way that would never be understood by Western strategists and politicians.

After a lifetime of indoctrination in how America helped Israel persecute their Palestinian brothers and was plotting against Islam worldwide, young Muslim men from many countries were clamouring to get into Iraq to wage holy war against the 'American-Jewish pigs'. Among the poor from all these countries there were also cash incentives to come and fight the *Amerikiyeh*; but especially in Yemen, which provided half the inmates at Guantánamo. The volunteers came from the dire poverty in the Arab world's most backward state. For anyone who wanted to escape poverty and make their families proud, jihad was practically the only option.

TWENTY-ONE

I mmediately after the war in the spring of 2003, journalists, peace activists, aid workers and even a few tourists were travelling around Iraq unescorted. Defense Secretary Donald Rumsfeld and Foreign Secretary Jack Straw had spent the rest of 2003 praising Iraq's progress. But a year on from the invasion, none but the foolhardy moved without PSD escorts and accommodation in secured and fortified hotels such as the Al Hamra and the Palestine.

Between September and December 2003 the rate of attacks dropped off by nearly two-thirds, and the first few months of 2004 were relatively calm. We could train our guard force in safety and pop into the Green Zone without any dramas; Seamus had pulled yet again and was currently shagging a Military Policewoman with a thing for handcuffs. We were lulled into thinking that military operations in co-ordination with diplomatic initiatives were making headway; either that or the insurgents had suffered crippling losses.

Unfortunately, it was only the calm before the storm.

I woke every morning to the voice of the muezzin calling the faithful to prayer over the loudspeakers in Aradisa Idah. On the eve of Ashura, 1 April 2004, the Shi'ite mosques across the city erupted in an explosion of hysterical shrieking and ranting that went on all night and we didn't manage to get any sleep at all. Not for the first time, Les threatened to take his wire cutters to the speakers on our local mosque. The trick, he said, wasn't just to cut them but to hack out large sections of the wiring so they would take a few days to repair.

Ashura had effectively been banned in Iraq under Saddam, and next day when the Shi'ites celebrated their holy festival for the first time in decades, cold-blooded surprise attacks were launched on unarmed Shia worshippers in Baghdad and Karbala, killing more than 140 and wounding some 400 people. The Jordanian Sunni Abu Musab Al Zarqawi was named as the most likely perpetrator behind the attacks. Blood was flowing in the streets again. This time it wouldn't stop. At Christmas 2003 the level of attacks had dropped to an average of eighteen per day. By summer 2004 there would be 180 a day, ten times as many. Al Zarqawi would be killed in an American bombing raid in June 2006, but his legacy lives on and now, at the time of writing, Iraq is closer than ever to civil war.

The insurgents had been observing Coalition Forces, re-grouping, and re-organising themselves. They had developed new tactics and there were new groups with diverse objectives and a new commitment to attacking foreign troops, PSDs, foreign interests, as well as each other, right across the country. In the space of a few weeks there were suddenly dozens of private security contractors killed from companies across the board.

In arguably the most well-known incident involving the deaths of contractors, Blackwater lost two vehicles and four men in Fallujah. The bodies of the men were mutilated, burned, dragged through the streets by the mob and strung up on the bridge in the centre of town, the entire gory episode filmed by the insurgents and screened on televisions across the world. We watched the footage in silence, flipped channels and watched it again.

Four days after the Ashura massacre, on 4 April, Colonel Faisal stamped into our office meeting first thing in the morning pissed off about something, which was not unusual.

'The revolution is come. They are a fucking people!' He drew himself up to his full five foot four inches and quivered with rage and indignation.

'Calm down, mate, do you fancy a cuppa?' said Seamus. He was full of beans since he had spent the previous afternoon in plasticuffs.

Without being asked, Raheed, the *chai wallah*, popped up magically with a tray of sickly sweet tea for all of us.

Faisal was one of the nicest men I had ever met, but his pilot's training in England had ruined him as an Iraqi. He returned disgusted by the corruption he found in his own country, the rubbish in the streets, the medieval mentality of the tribal and ethnic groups. Everyone to him was 'a fucking people'. The Iranians, Kurds, Syrians, Saudis, Kuwaitis and especially any Iraqi who did not measure up to his standards; he hated them all with a passion.

Seamus was sitting at the table counting how many 'Vitamin V' tablets he had left. Sammy had revealed that Viagra was twenty times cheaper on the black market in Baghdad than in the UK, and brought in a bin liner full of packets for us.

I tried my usual negotiation with Raheed for a cup of *mai haar*, hot water, in which I could make up my own brew. Despite making us cups of tea every day for four months, Raheed was still dismayed that I only took one sugar in my tea instead of the eight or nine favoured by the locals. The biggest danger I was facing in Baghdad at the moment was diabetes.

'Oi, Ratty,' Les said. 'Hop it and bring our poof Rupert some English tea, awright mate?' Les called Raheed 'Ratty' or 'Rodentay' because he looked like a rat. One day someone was going to tell Raheed what it meant and he would kill Les in the middle of the night.

'*Na'am, Mister Les. Chai Ingilisi.*' Ratty winked at me. '*Wahed shekir.*' One sugar. He disappeared down the hall cackling away to himself. I knew he would slip in three or four sugars.

'Come on, Colonel Faisal,' said Seamus, looking up from his pills. 'Sit yourself down on the sofa and tell us what's wrong. Let me guess, half the guards at Site Echo decided to sleep all night and the other half didn't bother to turn up at all.'

'Sack the fucking lot of 'em,' muttered Les.

'No. No. No. I tell you the revolution is come,' said Faisal. 'This is very problem. The Mahdi Army, he take the south of the country over the night. This morning they are in charge

of Basra, Nasiriyah, Najaf, Diwaniyah, Kut . . .' he counted off
the cities on his fingers. Shit.

'*Yissss!*' Hendriks shook his head and absent-mindedly went
to light up a Gauloise before observing Les's glare. No
smoking in the office. We had to think about our health.

I was amazed yet again at the efficiency of the Iraqi gossip
network. The news that the Mahdi Army was on the move had
undoubtedly come up with drivers from the south. I wondered
if Mad Dog knew about this.

'Aren't they Moqtada al-Sadr's mob?' asked Les as I dialled
Mad Dog on my IRAQNA. 'I don't know why they haven't
caught that cunt yet.'

Moqtada al-Sadr was the charismatic son of a clerical
dynasty and controlled Sadr City, a Shia district that had
tolerated Saddam. According to Shia tradition, the Mahdi is
the twelfth Imam. Shia preachers were teaching that the spirit
of the Mahdi was returning and the Americans had invaded
Iraq, not for WMD or oil, but to destroy the Mahdi. The
supporters of Moqtada al-Sadr believe him to be the son of the
Mahdi, or the Mahdi spirit, and al-Sadr had said in speeches
that the Mahdi Army could *never* be disbanded because it
belonged to the Mahdi. There is no reasoning on questions of
faith, and the blind allegiance of al-Sadr's followers was just
one of many complex facets of a multi-faceted culture where
the very notion of establishing a Western-style democracy in
what was a cauldron of medieval beliefs and Byzantine social
structures wasn't merely optimistic, it was foolhardy.

It was fortunate that Mad Dog McQueen was still at
breakfast since phone reception in Task Force Fountain's office
was terrible, much like the rest of the palace. He answered on
the second ring.

'Ash, how are you doing, buddy?'

'Hello, mate. Are you lot aware of what the Mahdi Army's
up to?'

'You bet. I was just about to call you guys. There's been
fighting in Sadr City all night. Look, I got a briefing right now,
I'll fill you in as soon as I got some more.'

I stuck the phone back in my pocket. 'The Americans know,'
I said.

'Must be serious,' said Hendriks.

'Sadr City's been at it all night.'

Sadr City was a large block of Shia slums in the northeast of Baghdad, a murderous no-go area and where Ibrahim bought most of our weapons. It was strange that I had not heard any shooting the previous night; maybe I had got used to it. Most nights in Baghdad you would lie there listening to explosions and distant gunfire. You would wonder what poor sod was catching it and also when the buggers were going to stop. After all, people were trying to sleep. The biggest worry was that if the explosions got too close you might actually have to get out of bed and do something about it.

Seamus called Spartan HQ and spoke to Angus. They already knew about the Mahdi uprising from their own Iraqi network. We agreed to lock down and suspend all movement until further notice.

The timing for a Shia revolt couldn't have been worse. Coalition Forces that morning had launched Operation Vigilant Resolve, attacking Fallujah with a full division of US Marines comprising 1MEF (1st Marine Expeditionary Force) and units from the Iraqi Civil Defence Corps (ICDC), so Sunnis in Baghdad were running around causing havoc in support of their brothers in Fallujah. To make matters worse, it was also the anniversary of Saddam's downfall. We decided it was probably a good idea to stay indoors and watch some DVDs. It looked like the weights bench and rowing machine on the roof were going to get a good seeing-to.

Two days later, the Brits were back in control in Basra, but there was no other good news. The Spanish contingent was still fighting in Diwaniyah, and the offensive in Fallujah, planned long before this revolt broke out, had drawn many US resources away to the west. CF units in Baghdad were stretched and had been fighting running battles in Sadr City. Night vision equipment was giving them the advantage but only just.

We sent out the order to our guards at external locations that they were to hide their uniforms and weapons and wait until they received a report from us that the fighting was over. The Mahdi Shi'ites and the enraged Sunnis were shooting anything that looked vaguely official, and the CF were shooting any local with a gun, including in some cases their ICDC allies. According to Mad Dog, the previous night at least one ICDC unit turned on the Americans they were working with, and there had been a deadly short-range firefight in the street. No statistics yet but apparently the Americans recovered from the surprise and dealt with them with brutal efficiency.

Faisal and Sammy both dropped in for dinner every night and stayed until midnight. It was touching since we knew that they both had a long drive back through the city where the streets were a death trap and coming across Shia, Sunni or Americans could end up with them being killed. We knew that they were keeping an eye out for us but naturally both denied this vociferously.

By contrast, Colonel Ibrahim seemed to be delighted with the progress his brother Shi'ites were making and, despite living close by, disappeared early from the office every day. We wondered if he was off helping them plan their ops. I checked our guard force ammunition status with Ali, a Sunni, who confirmed that no ammo had gone 'missing'. It was well known that we had an armoury and ammunition store, so we let everyone know that we took the keys from Ali every night to avoid the possibility of someone kidnapping his family to coerce him into allowing them access.

One night Sammy and I were talking alone on the roof and he passed me a piece of paper with lines of Arabic script.

'This my address. Keep here.' He tapped the pass-holder around my neck. 'If there is very problem and you are alone, you must take taxi and come. I am ready. I will take you to Jordan.'

I looked at the paper and handed it back. 'Thanks, Sammy, but I can't keep it on me. If I'm killed or captured and the enemy finds your address, they will come for you and your family.'

'Pah.' He made a gesture of dismissal, then laughed. 'If they kill you and look for me, that is good. I will not have to go look for them and kill them.'

'I'm not joking, Sammy, you've got your wife and half your clan living at your place. I can't take this, it's too dangerous.'

He slipped the address into my chest pocket. 'Mister James, trust in Allah and tether your camel. I am ready.'

Defence of the house was our main priority. Every morning, sitreps (situation reports) came in by email and by telephone of PSD houses like ours being attacked by small arms and RPGs. Hart, one of the private security outfits, had a house overrun in Kut. The PSDs fought their way to the roof and waited in vain for the local Ukrainian CF to come and get them. One of the team, a South African named Bran Grayfield, was killed and had his head cut off.

Photos and news had come out from Najaf where, on the first day of the revolt, Mahdi forces had been repelled by Blackwater ex-Special Forces PSDs fighting for nearly four hours from the roof of the CPA building with a handful of MPs and Marines. Running out of ammunition and with wounded men on the roof, it was a Blackwater civilian helicopter that flew in under fire to drop off ammo and evacuate a wounded US Marine. It was one of the rare times that the Marines and private security had fought side by side and a nice twist that it was hired guns that came riding to the rescue.

It was unlucky that we were three men down during the spring madness. Cobus and Etienne were home on leave and Dai was stuck in Jordan because he couldn't cross the desert during the troubles. The poor sod was in the Grand Hyatt eating Chateaubriand and lying beside the pool all day. To add insult to injury, he called one evening to say that he was going to take a two-day trip to Petra to see the sights.

We stockpiled extra ammunition and water on the roof and spent more time on the range. We added fitness to the shooting competitions, for example, running up and down the sand berms. We discovered that we Brits had the edge on the Yaapies and started winning some of our money back. Wayne immediately stopped taking part, saying that gambling was un-Christian.

We chased up sand hills, put rounds into targets and lifted weights in the spring sunshine on the roof. I was just getting into the routine when at three o'clock one morning there was a deafening roar of gunfire that sounded as if it were coming directly from the other side of the sandbags I'd stacked up against my window. I rolled out of bed shouting 'Stand to,' and could hear the words being echoed from Seamus and Les's room down the hall.

We were all veterans of both real contacts and hundreds if not thousands of hours of surprises in training exercises. Fifteen seconds after the first shots, everyone in the house had grabbed their armour and rifles and was piling up the stairs to the roof. Les and I were first up. I flipped off my safety and covered the doorway while Les unlocked the steel grille in case there was already someone up there waiting for us.

The door opened on to an empty roof and we ran out, crouching down below the wall. Our neighbour, an Iraqi policeman, was on his roof firing out magazines on full automatic into the night. The dark streets were full of running figures shouting in Arabic and waving weapons above their heads.

I tracked one of them with the illuminated cross hairs of my scope for a couple of seconds before realising it was one of our own guards. He was not wearing his baseball cap. I hissed a warning to the others and everyone acknowledged. In the cold of night it was common for the guards to wear their own coats and hats. The intruders appeared to be on the run, but in the dark, with our guards all over the neighbourhood, it was impossible to tell who was friend and who was foe.

We scanned the streets and rooftops for any potential firing point for thirty tense seconds. Then another thirty seconds. Occasionally one of us would see a suspect figure and indicate to the others with urgent whispers or hand signals. In every case, we eventually identified one of our own guards.

I glanced at the others, spread around the roof. Wayne was fully dressed, including his boots, which was odd; Seamus and Hendriks had boxer shorts and bare torsos under their armour, while Les was stark bollock naked under his. I was wearing a long-sleeved white T-shirt under my vest. Not a great idea when fighting at night. I considered trying that thing that women do where they remove their bra without taking off their shirt. Forget it. I unclipped my lock knife and reached up under my body armour. Ten seconds later my white shirt was in shreds on the ground.

We had been on the roof for five minutes now and the only shots we had been able to identify had come from the policeman who was still busy doing the Beirut unload, that is 30-round bursts into the walls of all his neighbours' houses, one magazine after another. I wondered just how much ammo he had stored up, and also why there was still no sign of any enemy. Knowing Iraqis, I didn't think it would be long before the neighbours got their rifles out and started firing back at the policeman's walls and windows.

'I think that cunt's just shooting at shadows,' said Les as he caught my eye.

I nodded in response as we both stood up.

BANG BANG BANG. BANG BANG BANG BANG BANG.

A volley of shots from out of the darkness slammed into the sandbags next to me. Someone was out there, and he wasn't a bad shot.

In a nanosecond we were both kneeling with our cheeks welded to our rifle stocks and our eyes trained through spaces in the hide-from-view screen.

The policeman eventually got bored or ran out of ammunition. When he packed up and went to bed, we spent a sleepless night co-ordinating a search of the area with our Kurdish house guards but found nothing. The following day we were exhausted and went to bed early.

The policeman living next door either had enough ammo for a war or had slipped into Sadr City during the day to stock up. At any rate, at midnight he was back on his roof shooting at the stars again. We spent another sleepless night without seeing more than a few shadows zipping through the dark and taking a few incoming shots that slapped into the sandbags. I was wondering whether the tactic wasn't to kill us, but intimidate us, to remind us that nowhere in Iraq was safe.

On the third day, to our utter amazement, the elusive Steel Dragon escort service turned up with a column of Humvees to drop off Mad Dog with his First Sergeants Gareth Evans and John Jenkins.

'Intel says that the shit is on tonight,' said Mad Dog. 'Thought you could use the company.'

'Did you bring a crate of booze?' Seamus asked him.

'The palace is dry. Muslim country, buddy.'

'So you've come here for our fucking booze, then, is that what you're saying?'

Mad Dog grinned and his two sergeants stood there shuffling their feet. They were never exactly sure whether we were joking or not.

Mad Dog strolled into the kitchen and I threw him a can of Stella.

'You do know you're stuck here,' I said. 'There's no way we can get back to the CPA.'

'Can't think of anywhere I'd rather be,' he said. 'There was something I wanted to tell you guys, there hasn't been a senior officer killed or captured by anti-Coalition forces yet. If it gets bad, you let the CF know there's a full colonel trapped here and believe you me the goddamn cavalry will arrive pronto with shitloads of firepower.'

I pulled a couple more beers out of the fridge for John and Gareth. You could tell that these guys liked working for Mad Dog McQueen.

I was glad to see they were fully armed. It had been extraordinary for us to discover that many US officers posted to the CPA had not been issued rifles, only M9 pistols. We had solved the problem for our TF Fountain buddies by supplying them with AKs. Other soldiers at the CPA had armed themselves on the black market in the same way and the generals were royally pissed off seeing so many of their countrymen openly strolling around with Kalashnikovs. The alternative was to leave their men unarmed whenever they went outside the wire.

That night an attack came at about 9.00 p.m. after we had just polished off another excellent roasted lamb with garlic prepared by the Yaapies. I was getting a taste for it. I was on the phone telling Krista how safe it was and not to listen to the bad news on TV – you know how the press likes to make things look worse than they are – when a firefight erupted right outside the door.

Cue silent pause.

'Can you hear that?' I crossed my fingers.

'Yes,' she said in a tone of voice that suggested I was lucky not to be back in London where she could have got her hands on me.

'I think Les dropped something in the kitchen. I'd better go and help him sort it out,' I said breezily. 'Call me tomorrow.'

Sammy and Faisal were still at the house and were right in front of me as we sprinted up the stairs. Up on the roof I realised I was again wearing a white T-shirt. It went the same way as the other one. Mental note: bin all white T-shirts.

Anyone seeing us on the roof would have thought it strange and enjoyed the irony: former Iraqi officers and American soldiers manning the sangars side by side when less than a year ago they had been at war with each other.

There was shouting two streets away and a crowd including many of our guards appeared to be converging on one house. Since the enemy had disappeared so quickly on the previous two nights, we suspected that the shooter lived in the neighbourhood, and we had placed pairs of guards hidden in alleyways to try and triangulate the firing point.

Hendriks, Les, Sammy, Colonel Faisal and I ran out and found the policeman from next door and half the neighbour-hood surrounding the same house. Everyone was armed. Everyone was screaming at the tops of their voices. Sammy and Faisal strode into the crowd and joined in. Les was muttering oaths and Hendriks scanned faces with his icy eyes, daring anyone to go for their weapons.

I called Mad Dog with a sitrep and he informed me that the 1st Cav, the nearest CF unit, was on the way.

Sammy and Faisal eventually cleared a path through the mob and found a sheepish but angry young man and his father standing outside the open door to what turned out to be their house. The policeman was screaming at them in rage and waving his AK in their faces. I dragged Sammy away and told him to tell me what the hell was going on before the Americans turned up and slotted the lot of us.

It turned out that those three nights of shooting and chaos had nothing to do with the insurgency, Fallujah or the rise of the Mahdi. The young man had wanted to marry the policeman's daughter and the policeman was having none of it since she was still only thirteen years old. The youth felt insulted and had shot up his house in the dark. Our house happened to be in the way.

'And did the policeman know who he was from the beginning?' I asked Sammy.

He indicated the crowd. 'Of course, yes, everyone knows,' he said.

Sammy explained that the policeman had not wanted to inform us in the Spartan compound in case we told the *Amerrikee* and they took the boy off to jail. His neighbours would then consider him a traitor or a collaborator, which would not be good for the policeman's health. This was, said Sammy, 'a private matter' between the two families. In spite of the rage and shooting, neither side had really wanted to harm the other because that would have started a devastating family feud. Now everyone in the street was just pissed off that they weren't getting any sleep at night.

The 1st Cavalry in a patrol of four Humvees now turned up looking for Colonel McQueen. The guys looked edgy when they stepped down from their vehicles but they calmed down when they saw our white faces and ID badges. As a result of the problems we'd had in identifying the guards that first night, our lot at least were all now wearing their baseball caps and FPS armbands.

We were standing about chatting to the sergeant in charge of the patrol and unsure what to do next, a common occurrence in these situations, when Mad Dog appeared in full uniform with his AK-47. The sergeant stared at him in amazement and his jaw literally dropped open when Mad Dog briefed him on the situation and then walked off into an alley again, in fact back to a second helping of our barbecue, but to the watching US troops in 1st Cav apparently continuing his one-man patrol of Baghdad at night.

I suggested quietly to the sergeant that they should lift the love-lost boy and take him back to the patrol base for half an hour and then allow the policeman to come and pick him up. That way, the youth would have a nasty shock and to the family and neighbours it would appear that the policeman had used his influence to rescue their son. 'Hearts and minds,' I whispered and the sergeant pushed his helmet back from his brow. 'Yeah, that one,' he replied.

The 1st Cav troopers appeared bemused by the whole situation and I told them that probably half the bodies they found every morning from the night's fighting came from similar feuds unconnected with the occupation.

With that sorted we disappeared back into the house to clear up. Tonight was film night and we were going to watch *American Pie 3: The Wedding*. Colonel Faisal and Sammy had loved the first two films in the series.

After finding himself a local hero, the policeman decided that placing a couple of dogs in the garden would serve as an early warning in case of future domestic disputes. But his mad kids spent most of the day throwing rocks at the dogs so most nights it took them until well past midnight to settle down again. We learned to sleep through it. It was an improvement on the day that the policeman had purchased a car alarm and the entire family would line up in the evenings and take it in turns to set the alarm off as a form of family entertainment.

The insurgents for their few successes had suffered terrible losses every time they tried to shoot it out with Coalition Forces or contractors and would now fall back on more traditional guerrilla tactics. Together with the CF and, sadly, the general Iraqi population, we would now face danger from increased rocket and mortar bombardment, and from the biggest killer of all, improvised explosive devices, IEDs.

TWENTY-TWO

Before the US invasion of Iraq, Saddam Hussein knew that a stand-up fight with the technologically superior Americans could only end in defeat and had activated a widespread training programme at guerrilla warfare centres. Even if Iraq was not prepared for an all-out war, it was prepared for an insurgency.

After the war, ex-Iraqi soldiers immediately armed themselves with weapons they had cached all over the country, and there were more than a hundred major arsenals and ammunition dumps left unsecured by the victorious Coalition. Not only the old Republican Guards and the Fedayeen Saddam, but anyone with a donkey cart was able to arm up with thousands of tons of weapons and ammunition. Many simply sold the weapons on the black market to private military contractors like ourselves who had come to combat their activities.

The insurgents couldn't risk deploying artillery pieces in the field and set about converting their vast stores of high-explosive shells into IEDs, usually wiring them up to a small piece of plastic explosive. They had lacked expertise in the early months, but the rebels learned quickly and were getting plenty of practice putting Coalition Forces, private security firms and the civilian population under constant attack from VBIEDs and roadside bombs.

Convoys were now running into complex ambushes where the killing area stretched for up to two kilometres and essential goods were being blown up or robbed. If the cooking gas, heating oil, electricity or the precious benzene ran out, the people of Baghdad kicked up a fuss. If the flow of drinking water was interrupted they went incandescent with rage. They knew the consequences of an outbreak of cholera and typhoid. As the Water Boys we had the support of the people in Aradisah Idah and when they found an IED they let us know about it.

The security market worldwide was now worth $100 billion a year, and while Adam Pascoe was in Washington trying to get a bigger slice of the market, Angus McGrath was the in-country manager.

There were several stakeholder organisations with the power to hand out contracts including the Iraq Reconstruction Management Office (IRMO), Iraq Project and Contracting Office (PCO), United States Agency for International Development (USAID), the Corps of Engineers Gulf Region Division (GRD), the Ministry of Municipalities and Public Works (MMPW), the Ministry of Water Resources (MWR), the Amanat of Baghdad and a handful of charities.

Overall security strategy for water resources was still unco-ordinated and haphazard. Two water engineers, one Dutch and one German, together with two of their Iraqi police escorts, had been killed on the Hilla Road, near Karbala, a dodgy area where a Western PSD team wasn't just desirable but essential. Having said that, I knew of small engineering sites operated by Fluor where one security company had the contract to protect the site with Iraqi guards; another firm had the contract to actually bodyguard the engineers; and yet a third had the contract to PSD them back and forth on the highways.

Angus was hoping that a recent double win in March by Amec, a British company partnered up with Fluor, for reconstruction contracts in the power and water sectors worth $1.6 billion would be an opportunity for us to gain more contracts. In the meantime, our team in Aradisah Idah was concentrating on not getting walloped.

About a hundred days after the death of Jacko Jackson and the maiming of Steve Campbell Spartan HQ had taken delivery of several armoured vehicles and had issued us with a BMW saloon car and a GMC 4 × 4 SUV. Both vehicles were armoured to B6 standard, i.e. up to 7.62mm rifle or machine-gun fire. We'd heard from other teams that after a couple of bursts from a machine gun, rounds would start to penetrate, especially through the windows and at the joins. They were excellent protection from IEDs and shrapnel, however.

Next day, Seamus accidentally discovered another disadvantage. He rolled the GMC on to its side doing J-turns out by the range. Dai and Hendriks were inside the cab with him and even with their combined strength they were unable to push the door open; it weighed about 200lb and was now horizontally above their heads. The passenger compartment was completely armoured and cut off from the boot, unlike in most designs I'd seen, so there was no way out at the rear. Cobus and I had to clamber on the side of the GMC, open the side door and drag the guys out. Not something you wanted to do in a contact, assuming that the other team members had survived.

There were a number of other disadvantages, the first being that you cannot shoot out of an armoured vehicle. You have to de-bus first, and then shoot. So in any contact we would have to rely solely on the roads being sufficiently clear to drive out of the killing area before the armour started to fail, a period measured in seconds. On the highway this might be possible maybe, but the jammed roads of Baghdad were unlikely to allow us that luxury. Also there was the problem with profile. The BMW was fine, there were plenty of those on the road, but the GMC was huge, obviously American and stood out like a sore thumb amongst the locally used Japanese and Korean models. The bad guys would be able to identify us from a long way out.

Currently we were operating a semi-covert profile. We would take two cars at all times for mutual support, but unlike standard PSD drills, we blended in with the traffic with two vehicles no longer trying to stay together as if attached by an invisible rope. We just moved in the same general direction keeping in touch with radio comms. We did not go as far as some other teams and dress up as locals, but we did have tinted windows on the side and rear. The windscreens we kept clear so that we could display flags as we approached CF patrols or bases.

There were dozens of American PSD packets moving around with pairs or trios of identical vehicles, driving in a distinctive manner, carrying massive HF antennas and bristling with guns. They were doing themselves an enormous disservice by creating 100-metre exclusion zones around their convoys. The rear gunners would shoot up the road in front of the traffic behind to ensure that no one got close enough to detonate a vehicle-borne IED, never mind the poor farmer on his donkey cart who takes a ricochet, never mind hearts and minds. These packets often had big signs on the back of their CAT trucks telling people to keep their distance in Arabic, although by now everyone in Baghdad knew that if you were coming up behind a CF patrol or a PSD convoy, you stayed away or you got shot.

It made the convoys even more obvious since they created huge voids in the traffic flow. It gave them some defence against VBIEDs, but it was a shit way of avoiding IEDs planted under or next to the road because the trigger man could see them coming from miles away. Bombs planted in parked cars would inflict a terrible toll on men and vehicles over the next few months.

Even with bombs a daily reality on the streets of Baghdad, we still didn't fancy the new GMC. It would have attracted too much attention for one thing and, for another, it was an up-armoured model not purpose-built for PSD tasks with brakes and suspension under specification for the three and a half tons of armour and chassis. Now we had it we didn't want to send it back and kept it parked up at the back of the villa as our last-ditch bug-out vehicle. We would discover in the summer that when the electricity and hence the air conditioning failed in the house and it was still 45°C at night, that you could sleep in the GMC quite comfortably with the engine running and the air-con on full power.

Armour was a good idea though and we tasked our Iraqi welder to find us some steel plating for our CAT truck. We tested it on the range and found that we needed a thickness of at least 12mm to stop AK rounds. You could get away with two 5mm plates bolted together with rubber spacers, but the outer layer degraded under fire and the weight saving was negligible. I also doubted that it would stop 7.62 long from a PKM. One day the welder came in very excited with some 6mm steel plate. Sammy translated that he had just stolen it from an old Iraqi army base. After my initial disbelief I took it down the range and found that it had been specially tempered. Everything bounced off it, 7.62 short, long and NATO, as well as 5.56mm. Nothing marked it at all. We were in business.

Our trusty Nissan Patrol received an armoured compartment and doors as well as head-plates, all of which were invisible from the outside. The vehicle was both bulletproof and IED-proof; we cut in gun ports and were then still able to retain the ability to shoot from inside the vehicle. Our BMW received a modification in the form of a solid steel 'nudge' bar we welded directly to the chassis. Painted black, it looked just like a normal bumper, but would allow us to ram our way out of most situations without risking damage to the engine.

Fortunately our covert profile and good route selection would mean that we would not be running into trouble any time soon.

Unfortunately I was about to experience how the CF patrolled. They had no choice whether to go high or low profile. You couldn't disguise a Humvee.

Order had been restored to Baghdad after operations by Coalition Forces against Sadr's militia, including the bloody four days after the initial revolt in which the enemy lost 302 KIA and 234 WIA for CF losses of 11 KIA and 86 WIA. That was just in Baghdad. CNN showed very little of the successes and was obsessed with gay marriages in Massachusetts so we were constantly on the phone to Mad Dog for intel updates.

The incoming 1st Cavalry wanted a local guide to show them the water infrastructure sites around Baghdad. Colonel Hind volunteered his help, by which he meant Spartan's help. Angus had agreed as this would put Spartan in closer contact with local military commanders and engineers, as well as Iraqi officials being groomed to take over security and management.

When Angus called Seamus and suggested I volunteer, I knew my old buddy from the Dukes expected a subtle business offensive if I got the chance.

What happened was I spent ten hours a day for ten days on the road, being passed from unit to unit as we patrolled from sector to sector. With just under a hundred hours on the road with the CF, I suppose I should count myself lucky that we were only contacted four times.

In those ten days I experienced a wide variety of US vehicles, rattling around in Bradleys, heavily armoured Humvees and gazing in awe at the blue-force tracker system when in a command Humvee. I watched a satellite photo of Baghdad streets with mobile icons depicting CF vehicles moving up and down them. It was so detailed I was sure that if I stuck my arm out of the window and waved I would see it on the screen.

One afternoon I was patrolling through the Zafariniyah district with a National Guard unit from Florida; friendly, good soldiers. We were driving the old, load-carrying Humvees, the same vehicles Gus's platoon had been using, but without the benefit of steel plates welded along the side. I sat in the rear bay of the lead vehicle with a couple of guardsmen with our backs against the wooden slats of the sides. I was just thinking that this would be a shit vehicle to get blown up in when we turned into a street leading to their FOB (Forward Operating Base) and the First Sergeant called back from the front.

'OK, Ash, we'll be back at the FOB in two minutes.'

As we pulled into the street I did a double take. The hair stood up on the back of my neck. It was a busy midweek afternoon in central Baghdad, but for two or three hundred metres, the street was deserted. A clear combat indicator. To even the most junior British soldier who had done a week in Northern Ireland, mental alarm bells would have been going off.

'Something's wrong. Stand by.'

I did not ask the driver to stop since we might already be in the middle of the killing area for a shoot. I did an automatic Belfast sweep of the area, looking for command wires and potential IEDs. As a route regularly used by the CF – in fact one of the FOB's gun towers had direct line of sight of the street – any IED would have to have just been dropped by the side of the road. They would not have risked the time needed to bury it. By some miracle, there was no rubbish in the street, no debris, no piles of building materials. The road was bare and there were no drainage culverts to stick things under.

My G3 was in my shoulder. I scanned the empty windows and rooftops over the top of the scope with the safety off. If someone popped up with an RPG I would only have a split second to drop him before he fired. The two soldiers with me knew I was serious. The colour had gone from their cheeks, but they were doing their job, aiming their own rifles at the houses as we sped by. I kept peering ahead, looking for potential IEDs, when I saw a fat Iraqi in a brown leather jacket stepping out from a doorway up ahead. I pinned him in the cross hairs on my rifle and was sorely tempted to pull the trigger. 'You bastard,' I hissed. The fat guy had two cameras strapped around him and was videoing us with a third camera. He was a self-styled journalist, one of the vultures filming attacks for the insurgents to post video footage of CF troops getting blown up on the Internet.

Beyond him was a major road junction that was empty of traffic from all the roads leading into it. Beyond observing that there were no cars/VBIEDs parked there, I could not see an obvious suspect device. I concentrated on keeping my sights on the cameraman. He was waving at us to slow down.

'Stop, stop, stop,' I shouted at the driver over the engine and the noise of the slipstream.

'Fuck that, we ain't stopping for him,' the First Sergeant shouted back, misunderstanding my reasoning. 'We're nearly there.'

I was certain that there was an IED on the junction and, if I was going to die, then that fucking cameraman was coming with me. I leaned completely over the side of the Humvee and took aim as we drove towards him. He dropped the video camera and held up his hands, backing away. We were nearly at the junction.

'Get down,' I roared at the two men with me.

There were sandbags on the floor of the vehicle. One of the guys dropped flat. The other kept his weapon on fatty, the same as me. The soldiers in the two vehicles behind us had realised something was up and were also covering him. The SAW gunner had taken his weapon off the cab and was resting it on the side wall, also pointing it at the cameraman. My Humvee driver zoomed over the junction and I made a split-second decision not to shoot. I was very conscious of the men in the vehicle watching my actions. To all intents and purposes I would be murdering an unarmed civilian and there were three Humvees full of witnesses. I grabbed the guardsman sitting up next to me, pulled him down into the sandbags and waited for the BOOM.

Nothing happened. We kept on driving. After a couple of seconds I poked my head up, feeling foolish. The cameraman was running into a doorway as the third and final Humvee in the convoy cleared the junction.

It was at that second that the junction vanished from view in a deafening explosion and we were enveloped in a huge cloud of dust. A lightning crack of concussion went through the vehicle and our bodies. All the windows in the street shattered. Seconds later, machine-gun fire came through the dust from the other side of the junction, high and wide, and the Americans in the gun tower answered back in kind. We were already turning into the FOB gates and the FOB reaction platoon hit the streets immediately.

Half an hour later I still had a ringing in my ears as I said goodbye to the National Guard and got ready to head out with the next unit. We had been wondering whether the bomber had delayed detonating the device because he knew we would have shot the cameraman that same instant. Or, just as likely, it could even have been the cameraman himself who had been holding the bomb trigger. Afterwards I spoke to the soldier who had been in the back of the lead Humvee with me.

'You know, if you hadn't been there I would have shot that fucking cameraman.'

'That's funny,' he said. He was an older man, smiling broadly. 'I'd been thinking the same thing.'

That night I complained to Seamus that I had too much paperwork backing up and wanted someone else to do the last two days of patrols. Obviously none of the Yaapies could go since the task required using a digital camera – 'white man's magic', I informed them loftily. I nominated Dai who, as a Welshman, was far more expendable than a former officer like myself.

He went off the next day cursing as always and returned thrilled that he had spent the day in the cupola of an Abrams manning the .50 cal. The day after, he came back and told us he was in love, having spent the whole day with a gorgeous female captain from a Civil Affairs battalion. We all laughed at this feeble fabrication until someone mentioned the name of the captain to Mad Dog and he confirmed that she was a well-known 'hottie' in the CPA.

In the meantime water pipelines were now being blown up by insurgents who had mistaken them for oil pipelines, but armed villagers started keeping an eye on the pipes and that problem soon diminished. As the warmer weather approached, more roadside bombs began to appear in our area. We informed Spartan HQ and Colonel Hind, then got on with the task of retraining our guard force in the correct actions to carry out when they discovered an IED.

Les and I had the two offices closest to the main entrance to the villa and we grew sick and tired of the Iraqi employees bouncing in very pleased with themselves saying 'Look what I found, Mister,' then placing an active detonator and ticking timing device on your desk.

We built a bomb pit out in the fields and the guards instructed visitors bearing gifts to place suspicious devices there and leave it for the American EOD Team (Explosive Ordnance Disposal), better known as the bomb squad. The guards themselves were under strict instructions not to touch anything; just to retreat to a safe distance and call for help. With Sammy translating, the guards sat and listened to our instructions on the 'confirm, clear, cordon, control' drills, but the next day would happily go off and prod and poke at whatever dubious device they could find.

That week we'd had two potentially tragic incidents. The first, in the desert at site 'Juliet', the guards had intercepted and captured a suicide bomber in a Peugeot stuffed with explosives.

This was excellent news. When I had asked them where the vehicle was so that I could task the bomb squad, I listened in disbelief as the shift captain told me they had secured the vehicle by driving it back to their own site. It was parked outside the office. In fact, he proudly told me that he was looking at it through his office window 'right now'.

We called the EOD Team and the Americans dealt with the device in a controlled explosion, which is normal, but still trashed the site office.

In the second incident, one of the landowners near us had sold some land to farmers and, as part of the deal, had agreed to clear the head-high grass from the site. While the Iraqi bulldozer driver he hired was working, he dug up an IED from its cache and pushed it 100 metres down the field wondering what the 'donk, donk' noise was as it banged against the big metal shovel.

When he finally got out to take a look, he realised it was a bomb and his first thought was ... the money. If the Americans came and sealed the area all day, he wouldn't get paid. So he continued working right next to where he'd dumped the bomb, thundering back and forth for the next four hours. Then he started to worry that he would get into trouble for disturbing the forensic evidence, so he finished the job, pushed the barrel all the way back where he'd found it and propped it up in its original position. He was pleased with his day's work and went to inform our guards.

When Les and I arrived on the scene we astutely judged that the device was not affected by vibration. Les took a close look and disarmed it in thirty seconds. You see in movies some guy sweating bullets as he stands over a bomb with wire cutters staring at a fistful of wires pondering which one to cut. It's good movie tension, but removing the detonator is all he needs to do.

We still had to brief the American EOD Team. The officer when he arrived wanted to know how we had been so sure that there were no booby traps on the device.

'Just a lucky guess,' Les replied.

'You guys ...'

'That's why they pay us more than you lot,' said Les. 'Here,' and he gave him the detonator.

The bomb squad drove off in their convoy of Humvees and the landowner paid the bulldozer driver for his work without argument. They lit cigarettes. The sun was going down and a ribbon of dirty orange light stretched across the horizon. We all shook hands and it appeared in those few moments that things were getting better. But it was a false feeling, the kind of sensation that can catch you off guard. The Coalition Provisional Authority had made a lot of promises, but the death toll since the invasion was rising not falling and the Iraqi people didn't blame the rebels for resisting the occupation but the Coalition for being there at all.

Attacks on foreigners and 'collaborators' were better co-ordinated, bolder and more widespread. Aid workers, at first welcomed, were becoming a target for kidnappers, a useful source of income when NGOs paid the ransom, a new brand of television porn when their bodies turned up mutilated or beheaded. There were two dozen terrorist organisations using kidnap as a weapon and a hundred criminal gangs in it for the money.

The Green Berets, based ten minutes from our villa and with whom we had become friendly, had been in Fallujah as part of the operation to suppress insurgents in the city. The US Marines had arranged a ceasefire and handed over the rubble to Iraqi security forces. The whole thing was a total mess, not just from our point of view, but from the Green Berets who'd been there in the middle of it. Over beers and barbecued lamb they regaled us with tales of leading Iraqi Civil Defence Corps troops into Fallujah against the insurgents, and also tales of ICDC refusing to fight and deserting. Nothing was ever simple.

More interesting to us was the intelligence that the insurgents hated the foreign fighters for their religious rhetoric, arrogance and the ill-treatment of local women. They were trying to kill Americans, but at the same time they were happy to lead American Special Forces to foreign fighters and on occasions killed their brother Muslims themselves. In one incident, the Iraqis in Fallujah identified a house that was smart-bombed by CF aircraft and the 28 killed were all Saudi and Syrian.

More importantly, now that the Green Berets were back in Baghdad we made a plan to bug out to their villa if things got

bad and we were cut off from the CPA. They had an
emergency operating room for casualties, the ability to call in
a helicopter medevac, and also enough weaponry to retake the
city single-handed.

TWENTY-THREE

R a'eed was an engineer trained in Munich and the manager at the filtration depot a couple of kilometres southeast of the city, a fifteen-minute drive from the villa. He was a softly spoken, clean-shaven man who wore half-moon spectacles and was, for an Iraqi, unusually calm.

He was hurried into my office by Sammy and Colonel Faisal and that day the quiet man was screaming at the top of his voice.

'We have very problem,' Sammy translated.

Colonel Faisal started muttering about 'fucking people'. I put down my coffee and wondered what else was going to go wrong. I had spent the morning with Sammy instructing workmen on some repairs that needed to be done on the villa and was not convinced that they would be able to do the work without constant supervision.

Sammy explained that a bomb 'with a thousand wires' had been planted on a valve pump at the heart of the filtration depot. Pipes could be replaced quickly. Pumps had to be reordered from the makers in Germany and required import permits. Even if the CPA could rush through the permits the pumping unit still had to be ordered, built and shipped; a possible delay of months before the plant was operational again.

This was an inside job. The filtration depot was huge. The bomber had known exactly where to place the explosives. If the bomb went up, it would close the plant and oil the wheels of the insurgency. The insurgents didn't have to defeat the CF militarily in the field to win the battle, they just had to prove that the Americans were incapable of running the country.

Seamus had heard Ra'eed shouting, you couldn't miss it, and pushed his way into my office.

'IED,' I said. 'Looks bad.'

He pulled out his phone. 'Wheels up in five, Ash,' Seamus said, and I went to muster the team while he called Mad Dog.

The standard drill was to call our TF Fountain masters with a GPS of the grid. They passed this on to the bomb squad, and they put it on their worksheet for the day.

The guard on the villa's main gate made a show of hurrying and we screeched out of the compound in a three-car packet, one Iraqi, one Brit and one South African. Sammy drove the lead vehicle in Mig pilot style, so we did the fifteen-minute drive to the plant in ten minutes.

The depot was surrounded by apartment buildings and covered a wide area with numerous pumping stations, a big car park and a high fence. We ordered the guards to turn off mobile phones and radios in case one of their transmissions detonated the device.

In spite of the urgency, Seamus and I followed convention and stood around for five minutes greeting the guard captain and his shift supervisors. *How's your wife? Has she had the baby yet?* Colonel Faisal and the shift supervisor lit cigarettes and chatted, which gave the supervisor prestige in front of his men and reminded everyone that Colonel Faisal was the guard chief. Finally trays of *chai* turned up and we sat down to talk business.

With the courtesies over, we sent guards out into the neighbourhood with instructions to tell the locals that there was a bomb in the plant and everyone was to stay indoors, but not to worry, the *Amerrikee* would be there to deal with it in an hour or so. We assumed the insurgents would be listening in on the local chatter. Knowing the CF was on the way, they would hopefully delay detonation and aim to score a double hit: destroying the machinery and killing a few Americans at the same time. The delay would give us the chance to gather intelligence before the bomb squad arrived.

The worker who had discovered the bomb was waiting to be interviewed and the shift supervisor had seen the bomb for himself. Both confirmed that they had not seen a command wire leading to the pump. The device would almost certainly be fired by a timer or by remote control, but you check every contingency.

Dai and the Yaapies remained outside sitting in the wagons with the air-con running. They were keeping an eye on the main gate for the Americans, not that we expected them any time soon. The bomb squad was tasked all over the city and may have had thirty incidents to deal with before they got to us.

In the British Army the standard practice is to clear the area of all personnel, but also to gather as much information about the device before the bomb disposal officer arrives. This would include a description and a detailed drawing. We had adopted this in our drills and added a digital photo or a video shot to the package. Ra'eed's hands were shaking when I got him to draw the exact location of the bomb. Effectively, if this device went off, the whole plant would be out of action.

Half the guards were deployed around the perimeter, radios and phones turned to off. The rest clustered outside the office, curious to see what we would do.

Mad Dog called Seamus on the IRAQNA to say the EOD Team had been tasked but were unlikely to arrive before 1900 hours. By this time it would be dark. If possible we should try and get a photo of the device in daylight to give to EOD when they finally turned up.

It was unfortunate that Les Trevellick was on leave. He was an engineer and had extensive experience as an instructor in demolitions. I was the next nearest thing we had to an expert, which wasn't that near at all. I volunteered to go forward and take a video shot of the bomb.

'You'll need to go dressed up as one of the guards,' Seamus said. If the bombers saw a Westerner they would be even more likely to set off the bomb.

'Good thinking.'

Sammy went out to find a guard about the same size as me. Most Iraqis are smaller and he returned with an older man in his fifties. When Sammy told him we wanted him to undress and exchange clothes with me he shook his head and babbled away to Sammy. I recognised two words out of the torrent: *mukhosh*, which meant 'bad' or 'wicked' and *haram*, which meant 'forbidden', in the religious sense. It was bullshit. I had seen our radio operators wandering around all night in their baggy underwear and string vests.

'Offer him ten bucks,' I said. '*Ashr dollar*,' I waved a note at him.

'OK, Mister.' The old fox smiled a mouthful of brown broken teeth at me and took the ten dollars. '*Shukran*.'

'*Afwan*,' I replied. You're welcome.

I stepped out of my boots, socks, belt kit, vest, shirt and trousers and stood there in my boxers. The guard hid behind the table and removed his clothes slowly like a stripper in a club. I pulled on his trousers, his dish-dash, which probably got washed once a week but smelled as if unlaundered for a year, and buttoned up the tattered cardigan with its guard armband. I was already sweating before Sammy covered my hair with the guard's grimy *shemagh*. He tied it properly, then tucked a fold in across my face so that only my eyes could be seen. Thankfully the headcloth stank of stale cigarettes and covered up the aroma of the rest of the clothing. The supervisor sat the guard down in his string vest and shorts and gave him a cigarette and a cup of *chai*. He looked pleased with himself, the hero of the moment.

'You look about as Iraqi as Claudia Schiffer,' said Seamus.

'You haven't read my reviews when I did Shakespeare at Brasenose.'

'Well, you'd better make this a star performance, mate. Be careful and make it quick.'

I slipped into the guard's plastic sandals and grabbed his systematically neglected AK-47. The mag was full of Iraqi ammo. I stuck the magazine back in place, slung the rifle over my back, and stuck the video camera under the dish-dash.

Outside, Colonel Faisal was giving orders to the guards to set up cordons around the plant and keep civilians away until the *Amerrikee* came and defused the bomb. I understood the last word, *Y'allah*, let's go. The guards shuffled off in groups to their places around the plant and I slipped out of the office and shuffled off with them. I headed inwards towards the pump with another three guards. We split up as we approached the part of the plant where the bomb had been placed.

I dawdled along with sloping shoulders across the open area where the bad guys would have a clear shot if they didn't think much of my acting and spotted me as one of the white-eyes. I paused to scratch my arse and continued, dragging my feet in the flip-flops as I followed the pipes along the ground to the pump. I became nervous as I drew closer, imagining for a moment that the bomb was on a timer and was about to go off.

I turned the corner and, when I saw the device, the first thought in my mind was: *Jesus Christ, Krista, I am so sorry.* The possibility that I wasn't coming home from Iraq and that Krista would have to bring up Natalie on her own suddenly, in that second, seemed very real. I had told her lie upon lie and she would never understand how I had put myself in this position of extreme danger. At least she'll get £250,000, I thought, and with all the money sloshing around Baghdad it suddenly didn't seem very much.

There was at least a wall protecting the position. I ducked down behind it and checked to see whether the bomb location was overlooked by windows or high points from the surrounding buildings. It is said that a fault is deliberately woven into every carpet made in the Arab world since only Allah is perfect. The fault in this plan was that, having set the bomb, the insurgents didn't have a clear view of the location.

It was late afternoon, the sun still high. I could feel the sweat running down my back. I took deep breaths to get my adrenaline under control, pushed Krista out of my mind and went to have a look at the device.

I was *reasonably* certain that I couldn't be seen. Always double-check, then check again. I scanned my surroundings, concentrating on everything I could see and from where I might be seen. OK. I was secure. I sat down with my back to the wall and spent a few minutes just looking around.

In Yugoslavia the Croats had been cunning bastards and if you came across a mine or an IED you could bet that there were half a dozen traps around it ready to go off at the slightest provocation. I had been looking out for wires, pressure pads and infrared projectors on the way up to the site and seen none. The bare concrete at the centre of the filtration plant provided no nooks and crannies for these little devices to be tucked into. Still, it pays to be safe and I waited a full five minutes until I was sure that my eyes had run down every wall top, side and bottom; I counted the corners to make sure I did not miss any. It appeared to be clear.

I pulled the camera out, opened the view screen and aimed the lens. I zoomed into the pump so that I could see as much as possible on the camera before I went any closer.

On top of the bomb there was a mobile phone connected to a circuit board about half the size of a cigarette packet with tape holding the whole mess together. Five lines of detonating cord ran along the pipes to five lumps of C4 or PE4 plastic explosive. This spider-like arrangement was the 'thousand wires' Sammy had described.

I couldn't at first work out why a mobile phone was being used to trigger the device. If you wanted to sabotage the plant, why not just set a timer and run, as they normally did when blowing up pipelines? Mobile phones were expensive, prestige items in Iraq, too valuable to waste without good reason. The only explanation was that whoever had set the device wanted the ability to detonate at a time of their choosing. Our suspicions back in the site office had been correct, they were going to wait until the EOD team turned up to try and kill them as well as blow the pump. The more bomb squad officers they killed, the more bombs they could set without interference.

I wondered if I could defuse it myself?

I had another quick look around to make sure that I really was in dead ground and then slowly approached the IED. Then I realised something else that had been bothering me. Calling this an IED was a misnomer. It wasn't improvised at all, it was a professionally laid demolition charge. A sense of familiarity had been nagging at me as I looked at the charges and realised that it had been set up exactly as I would have done it on my demolitions course in the army; a single detonator clipped to det cord, an explosive in itself, and then det cord running out to the PE (plastic explosive). An amateur might have used five different detonators, or stuck the dets straight into the PE, but whoever had set this up had done it by the text book.

I thought about Krista and little Natalie for a second and then wondered about the American EOD technician who was going to turn up later. At the end of the day, I had to be able to look myself in the mirror and I knew that if I let a man walk to his death when I could have done something about it, then I would always regret it.

There was probably an hour of light left in the day. *Let's do it.* I placed my rifle against a pipe and pulled the *shemagh* off my face. I don't know how Arabs wear those things all the time. They're restricting somehow. I couldn't see any better taking it off, but it was like I was back in my own skin. On camera I said what I intended to do. I thought about leaving a message to Krista but couldn't think what to say. I placed the camera around the corner so that if the bomb went off it might be protected by the wall. At least the tape might be found in one piece, so they would know what I had tried to do.

What I needed to do first was to get the detonator away from the det cord. If I could do that then I was in the clear. My main concern was whether there was something on the detonator that would initiate the device when I tried to remove it. I was unfamiliar with the mobile phone setup. But it appeared pretty basic. There were wires running from the circuit board to the mobile phone. This appeared to be the only electronic interface between the phone and the detonator, which was clamped to the det cord. I could see the chip clearly from both sides. There didn't seem to be any anti-tremble devices attached. I didn't want to touch the phone in case there was something unpleasant inside it.

What often kills members of the bomb squad isn't the device, but something placed nearby to catch anyone who tries to disarm it. I studied the floor around the pump. I was standing on solid concrete. There was nothing. No trip wires. I checked again. I was certain I couldn't be seen by a sniper.

I checked the det cord as closely as I could, looking for anything that might indicate it was anything other than what it appeared to be. There were no threads, hairs, fibreoptic cables, discolorations. Nothing. Then I checked it again.

This is it. I'm going to do it.

I stilled myself, took a breath and unclipped the detonator from the det cord. *Christ*, I thought to myself, *that's how by the book this guy is, he even had the correct clip to join the two together.* Even back in the army I had often had to make do with tape.

Not this time, you tossers!

I still didn't want to touch the mobile phone. I also wasn't sure how far away the detonator had to be from the det cord and the device before it was safe. I was able to stretch the thin wire connected to the detonator about twelve inches from the nearest bit of det cord. Was this far enough away or not? I wracked my brain but if I'd ever been told this vital piece of information, I couldn't remember.

In that case I still needed to move this stuff away from the det. My next order of business was to remove all the plastic explosive from the pump. I could see five lumps of the stuff moulded in at joints along the pump with det cord running through each one. If the bomber had been trained by the British Army, he would have knotted the det cord in the middle of each lump of explosive.

With my knife, I sliced through the plastic along the line of the det cord, opened it up and, sure enough, there was a knot tied in the centre. *Good man*, I said. I made another mental note for later. I cut slices all around the knot to make sure the det cord was not attached to anything else hidden within the PE and then lifted it out. There was nothing.

It took me about five minutes, which seemed like an hour, and I could feel the sweat pouring off me. I released a breath I didn't know I'd been holding. One bastard done. Four more to go.

Just because there weren't any nasty surprises hidden inside the first chunk of plastic didn't mean there wouldn't be any in the next. I moved carefully but with a bit more confidence and ten minutes later, I had removed all the det cord from the other four chunks of plastic. The main pump was still ringed in det cord. If detonated, it would still damage the pump.

It was highly unlikely that there was a high-tech sympathetic wire running parallel to the det cord. I looked it over again for strange bulges that might have been disguised dets, but there was nothing. Having gone this far, I went the rest of the way and cut away as much of the cord as I could. Finally, all I was looking at was the initiation device itself: the telephone, the little circuit board, the detonator twelve inches away on a thin wire and the duct tape holding it all together. There were a few clumps of det cord sticking out from the duct tape around the phone. If they did go off, I thought, all it would do was make a scorch mark on top of the pump and blow the telephone. It might take a man's hand off, but no more than that.

I had done the donkey work. I didn't know anything about mobile phone techniques and the guys from the bomb squad would be able to deal with it, maybe even just stand back and shoot it with a shotgun, the most common way of dealing with initiation devices. It is destructive, but leaves the main body of the explosive inert. I lumped the plastic explosive together, five balls, each about the size of an orange and covered now in dust. It would have filled a shoe box, enough PE to blow the pump and all the pipes to pieces for a considerable distance.

My heart was beating like a drum. My hands were wet and I was surprised to realise that the dish-dash was drenched in sweat. I retrieved the camera, took a shot of what I'd left for the EOD Team, then slumped down behind the wall to catch my breath. I'm not getting paid enough for this, I thought. Krista can never ever, ever find out.

Now I'd gone this far, it wasn't the moment to get slotted by some keen-eyed sniper. I hid the camera, spent a minute arranging the shemagh, stuck the AK lazily over my shoulder and, like Robert De Niro method acting, shuffled back up the road to the office.

The tic on Seamus's neck was vibrating like crazy.

'Did you fucking fall asleep up there, you cunt?' he demanded. 'What the fuck have you been doing for twenty minutes?'

So I told him.

He dropped down in a chair. 'Good on you, mate, fucking well done. But don't do it again,' he warned.

'Is there any tea, mate? I'm gasping.'

'Get this man some fucking tea,' Seamus said, and all the Iraqis in the office scurried about trying to look busy.

I exchanged *clothés*, as Sammy called them, and someone appeared with syrupy sweet *chai*. Now that the adrenaline was wearing off my hands were shaking slightly. I took a cigarette to calm down and amused the Iraqis in the room as I coughed my way through it.

We chatted with Ra'eed, the shift supervisor and the guard captain about the work at the plant. The guards needed new jackets. They'd all been issued with at least two, but they'd lost them, or sold them. We told them we were getting new Czech bullets for the AKs and assured them that the pay would be on time this month. It had been late over Christmas and late pay made unhappy guards.

At around seven, with the sun slipping behind the apartment buildings, the Americans turned up, four Humvees with at least five guys in each. Two EOD guys, a warrant officer and another guy, came in the office looking exhausted. They'd been on the road all day. The warrant officer was quietly spoken and, like many specialists, wasn't too gung ho. I briefed him on what I'd done. He raised his eyebrows without making any comment, but when I showed him the before and after shots on the video he whistled out through his teeth. 'Good job. That'll be no problem at all. No problem at all. We got a GSM jammer transmitting right now in the Humvee.'

Along with Spartan and the Iraqi guards, we now had twenty fully armed Americans with .50 cals and Mk19s. The guys in the turrets on top of the vehicles were panning the surroundings and looked deadly serious. One of them told me that EOD techs were being actively targeted by the resistance, just as I had suspected. I was definitely not going near any more demolitions ever again.

The warrant officer felt confident and wandered off on his own to the pump. He'd only been gone about two minutes when he returned holding the telephone and the detonator separately. It was just what it had appeared to be, no traps,

just the phone hooked up to the detonator. Fuck it, I thought,
I could have saved him the bother.

We went out, everyone shook hands, and the Americans
drove off to the next job.

Colonel Faisal turned to me and Seamus. 'Fucking people,'
he said.

'The Americans?' Seamus asked.

'No, my fucking people.'

It turned out that when he'd inspected the guards he'd
discovered that out of a shift of fifty men, eight were absent
and twelve weren't even on the books at all. It was the usual
Iraqi corruption at work. Twenty men had been missing and
when the site captain had realised that we were coming to
investigate the IED, he had run around trying to find bodies. It
was possible that the twelve strangers were who they said they
were, relatives of the real guards. They had the ID cards of the
missing guards, and Iraqi ID papers confirming the same
family name. We did know that in Iraq it was common for
brothers or sons to come in and cover for absentees, but we
strongly forbade it since we could imagine the chaos if
someone carrying Spartan ID and weapons shot some civvies.

The problem was the missing eight men. The shift supervisor
had signed his morning return to confirm that there had been
100 per cent attendance at roll call. It was always possible that
he just did not want to pass on bad news to his bosses, a
common Iraqi trait amusingly similar to Donald Rumsfeld's
staff, but more likely they were ghosts in the system. They were
either nonexistent employees and he was pocketing the pay, or
they had 'bought' the jobs in return for a kickback to the
supervisor of, say, $20 a month, to sign them in for every shift
so they never had to actually turn up and could have full-time
jobs elsewhere.

We had had the same problem just that week when trying
to hire a cook. We'd grown bored with cooking our own
evening meals. We interviewed and accepted an old man but a
complete stranger turned up the next day. It turned out that
the old man did not want to work evenings, but accepted the
job because it was a potential source of income he could sell
to someone on the street.

We sat the stranger down and informed him that we were not happy and his employment would depend on passing our security vetting. He agreed. We put a guard with him to make sure he didn't poison us, showed him the fridge brimming with food and told him to cook dinner for seven men; if he had any questions he should just use the phone to the office. When we got in at 8.00 p.m., we were starving and there was no dinner. The cook had spent the whole day sitting smoking fags and doing nothing because no one had actually specified what it was we wanted him to cook for dinner. The phone was right next to him but he hadn't thought to call us. Also the guard had been told, 'He is going to start cooking, watch him', but seemed to think it completely normal that the cook then sat down for seven hours and smoked four packs of cigarettes without doing anything.

On returning to the house from the filtration depot, the Yaapies set to work cooking dinner, lamb and rice, and I inspected the building work.

The walls and floor in the bathroom had been beautifully tiled, but the workmen had waterproofed the surfaces by smearing the tiles with filthy concrete and then installed the fittings by bashing holes in the tiles. Bare wires hung from the lighting and were wired directly into the mains next to the shower. The main cable from the national grid entered the house through the shower room and when I pointed out the potential danger to the electrician he promptly wrapped the fizzing lump of live wires in black tape.

Where the builders had put up a new wall, they bricked straight through the chainlink fence at the back of the office. At the back of the house, where we had five washing lines strung up, the middle two were in the way of the wall, so they bricked over them. I took some photos showing the inside and outside of the walls with the washing lines going through them. It's a good thing the 'cook' wasn't sitting there, smoking, because they probably would have bricked him into the wall as well. Two days later the steel gates fell off since they had been welded directly to the concrete wall. When Les came back off leave he was going to have a fit.

'Come and get it,' yelled Hendriks.

We filled our plates in the kitchen and piled into the sitting room to jostle for places in front of the big-screen television. Tonight was the final of *For Love or Money 3*, where some American guy has to dismiss all these potential girlfriends based on whether he thinks they are really in love with him or are just pretending in an attempt to win the prize money. We cranked up the volume to drown out the noise of the Blackhawks thundering overhead. In this episode the guy had just sacked a lovely, distraught young lady who was genuinely in love with him and the last girl was about to reveal that actually she did not like him, it was all about the money. Forget about bombs in Baghdad – this was real drama.

TWENTY-FOUR

In 1258 Genghis Khan's grandson and his Mongol horde conquered Baghdad by walking in through the front gates. It had been a hot day and the Baghdad guards had propped their helmets up on the walls with their spears and were having an afternoon siesta. I sympathised with that long-dead Baghdad military commander as I watched the Iraqi guard outside my office nod off on his plastic chair, fag in mouth and rifle under his seat.

I had arrived back three days earlier from a great leave in which Krista had told me that she had fallen pregnant from the leave before that. We had done our sums and budgets and worked out that I could finish working for Spartan at the end of this tour and stay with her until she gave birth, before seeing about getting another contract.

My three days had already been filled with the usual Iraqi madness. In fact it had started on the flight out to Amman where the eighteen-year-old student sitting next to me talked of her plans to travel the world. When I said I was going to Baghdad she asked whether it was on holiday or business. I told her I was a tourist with an interest in Mesopotamian archaeology.

At Queen Alia airport I chatted to other PSDs about pay and leave in the queue of security men checking in to fly to Baghdad. As usual we all eyed the South African stewardesses, the last decent-looking women we'd see for a couple of months, possibly before we died, and as usual the pilot arrived over the BIAP, stood the plane on one wingtip and dropped 12,000 feet in three tight spirals, levelling out literally three seconds before the tyres kissed the runway.

I arrived at the office straight into a mess of contacts from the previous few nights. Our guards at Site Juliet had been unable to return fire because they had shot all their bullets weeks ago after Iraq beat Portugal at football, but had been afraid to request more ammunition. At Site Bravo, they had sold their ammunition and at a third site, Golf, they did have ammo but had not wanted to fire back on contact since they recognised the attackers as cousins of two of the guards and didn't want to start a feud. We were still working out whether or not to pay compensation to the families of four guards killed at Bravo because although they had died on duty, they had been killed in a shoot-out inside the site, feuding with each other.

The second morning I found myself having to draw up yet another radio training package after a more serious mortar incident overnight at Site Alpha. Radios had been lost when guard vehicles had been hijacked and we were sure that the enemy listened in on our radio traffic. Sure enough, that night the guards ended up correcting enemy fire on to their own position, i.e. one mortar bomb landed way off target, not surprising as it was pitch black, the enemy had set up one kilometre away and was using the lights of distant radio towers as aiming markers.

'Help, Alarm! They are shooted mortars at us! It explosions 500 metres to the south.' Thirty seconds later another bomb landed, closer.

'Help! This explosions only 200 metres away, they are come closer, but now to the south and the east!' I could just picture the insurgent listening to the radio and adjusting the dials on his mortar. Thirty seconds later five bombs hit the compound directly on target.

'Help! They are killing us! The explosions shoot directly the building! Fire is everywhere!' Thirty seconds later, fifteen bombs hit the compound, again exactly on target, and the enemy withdrew.

Normally during emergencies no one could hear the callsigns under contact because two of the guards on more powerful base stations would be overspeaking everyone chatting about what they had for dinner, or someone would find it really cool to press transmit and hold his walkie-talkie next to the car radio so we could all listen to his favourite song.

Major Razak came in looking gloomy with his report that morning. First, Nabeel, his driver, had been arrested for carjacking. He had confessed to twelve car thefts and four murders. He had been driving around in our vehicles with our weapons permits, a shame because he was a damned good driver. Next, the road to Site Delta was currently impassable since a benzene pipe alongside it had been hit the day before. The insurgents had not done that much damage but the repair crew had. Although they were in the middle of a large lake of petrol mending a pipeline full of residue petrol and fumes, this 'experienced' repair crew failed to take any precautions. As soon as the welder sparked up, the fumes and then the lake ignited and exploded in a huge fireball. The locals estimated it would be at least 24 hours before the tarmac had cooled and re-solidified enough for us to use the road.

Coalition Forces, and particularly the Americans, received a lot of negative reports in the press and on TV. I was disappointed to see that the insurgents often came off in a sympathetic light. The prime example was coverage of the siege of the Imam Ali mosque in Najaf, where Moqtada al-Sadr and the active remnants of the Mahdi Army were holed up. Constant TV coverage forced the CF and the Iraqi National Guard (ING) to pussyfoot around outside because they were afraid of offending people by attacking such a holy place.

The correspondents never showed that al-Sadr had been using this holy of holies to store ammunition and weapons. Security forces were kept outside during negotiations and, while CNN and Sky News showed the terrible conditions the defenders were forced to live in, the Mahdi Army rounded up policemen, councillors, local elders, and even Shi'ite clerics who had made the mistake of denouncing al-Sadr. Away from the cameras, inside the mosque, these innocent men were beaten, tortured, sentenced in al-Sadr's courts, then garrotted, beheaded or shot. When the siege lifted the Iraqi National Guard discovered more than two hundred bodies piled up in rooms.

During this time, dozens of people died after kidnaps, beatings and torture including Dublin-born Margaret Hassan, married to an Iraqi and an aid worker living in Iraq for thirty years. Her body has never been found. But the murder of Margaret Hassan and many other innocent people was over-shadowed in the world news by the torture of Iraqis in the infamous Abu Ghraib prison by Americans. When our Iraqis saw the photos they agreed this was terrible behaviour, but said by no means was it torture. They had lived under Saddam and all had stories of real cruelty involving eye-gouging, gang-rape and power tools.

Moyed, Colonel Faisal's driver, took off his shirt to show us holes in his armpits where he had been hung on meathooks and beaten for disobeying orders in the army. When the news came out that the prisoners were being released from Abu Ghraib, the local village elders were horrified. 'These are bad people! Just kill them instead,' was the typical suggestion.

When I guided 1st Cav units around Baghdad, in one of the contacts the soldiers had refused to fire because they didn't have clear targets, and again in another because the fire was coming from a mosque and they preferred to sit it out and trust their home-made armour. That was never reported, but I suppose 'American Soldier Doesn't Shoot Mosque' doesn't make a good headline. Nor did I see much publicity about the children used as camouflage for suicide bombers, or even *as* suicide bombers as in the case of one poor child with Down's syndrome and another in Kirkuk who was only ten years old. The enemy had learned how to use the press as another tool. No one seemed to query why so many journalists and press teams, even Ameri-cans, were now being released after being kidnapped. It wasn't out of mercy, because often their Iraqi drivers would just get slotted by the side of the road, instead the insurgents realised the importance of staying on the right side of the press.

I was just as much a victim of press bias as anyone. I had arrived in-country believing the propaganda that the CF were trigger-happy thugs, and although that was unfortunately true in some cases, the overwhelming majority turned out to be professional, dedicated and sympathetic soldiers doing a tough job under extremely difficult circumstances. I now had the utmost respect for all of them.

I was not divorced or isolated from daily life in Baghdad. I was living and working with Iraqis, working class and middle class, from the illiterate to the well educated, and it was depressing listening to their daily tales of loss and fear. None of them, from the highest to the lowest, paid any attention to the international propaganda about the 'Coalition of the Willing'. It was clear to them all that this was a primarily American and partly British occupation. Christian armies were in power in their country and harsh and unforgiving treatment of civilians by Coalition soldiers at checkpoints only brought back memories of the Ba'athist regime.

Chatting with Sammy and Colonel Faisal over beers through many long evenings brought out a surprising view of the United States from the Iraqi perspective. Although many Iraqis saw the chaos around them as evidence of American incompetence, many former military officers, including Sammy and Faisal, dismissed that argument. They thought America was unarguably the most powerful country in the world. The Iranians had fought against Iraq for eight years and had been beaten, at least from their point of view. The Americans had walked through them in three weeks. There had been an anti-aircraft unit on the base where Colonel Faisal had flown from. He told us that the gunners didn't have to activate their radar scanners to attract hostile American aircraft. Even turning on the equipment to run a diagnostic check was enough to have radar-seeking missiles dropping out of the sky.

It was inconceivable to them that such a powerful country could let Iraq crumble into medieval anarchy with hundreds of thousands of people living with no utilities, fuel, food or medical aid. Not through incompetence. To them it was a deliberate plan, orchestrated to punish the Iraqi people. They had no doubt of that, and just wanted to know how much they needed to be punished before this time would end.

Without a free press under the former regime, Iraqis passed on their news through hearsay and rumour; a rumour could zip through the city and across the country in a single day. Even with the abundance of new newspapers in 'free' Iraq, the rumours still did the rounds; like the CIA was flying in Afghan fighters and Saudi suicide bombers to punish the Iraqis and make them look bad to the outside world. When suicide bombers killed 180 Shi'ites celebrating Ashura in March 2004, the crowd attacked CF troops sent to give medical aid because the immediate assumption was that the bombers had been aided by the Americans.

They believed the CIA had paid looters to take hospital equipment which had been shipped directly to Israel. It was said that Israel had been behind the invasion as part of a plan to claim holy Jewish land. Did I not know that the two blue lines on the Israeli flag represented the Nile and the Euphrates, and that the Jews claimed everything between the two rivers? Did I not know that the Kuwaiti military had followed Coalition Forces into Baghdad to torch everything in their path? Actually, I did. That was not a rumour. The Kuwaitis and the 'Free Iraqi Forces' brought in by the CF as part of the 'Coalition' had been documented doing very little in the way of combat with the Republican Guard but a lot of looting and destruction.

Oh, and American sunglasses gave them X-ray vision through clothing allowing them to dishonour Iraqi women.

Despite their insistence on the plot to punish Iraq, they found nothing contradictory when they also stated that the Coalition Forces, and especially the CPA, had 'shown weakness', a huge failure in their eyes. Sammy and Faisal cited the non-arrest of Moqtada al-Sadr as an example.

Sammy constantly said that a leader must be strong. It became clear from conversations with him and with Spartan's Iraqi managers and officers that they did not want democracy for the present. After thirty years under Saddam they could not adjust to this idea of 'freedom'. Arabs respect strength and if a strong dictator came along, that was quite possibly what they needed. No one had liked Saddam because he was a murderous tyrant. Now a benevolent tyrant, that was what they were talking about. By mid-2004, when everyone was heartily sick of the blood and dying, Colonel Faisal confided to me that if Saddam were released and put back in charge, most Iraqis would welcome him.

Sammy and Faisal were both Sunni, which gave me an insight into the Sunni loyalty towards Saddam Hussein among the insurgents. They didn't like him, they despised him, but without Saddam they faced a future as a persecuted minority; a poor one to boot. All the oilfields lay under lands occupied by the Kurds to the north and the Shia to the south. Despite a worldwide press frenzy condemning abuses of prisoners at Abu Ghraib, all Iraqis would demand to be held by the Americans rather than the up-and-coming Iraqi security organisations. The Americans might take photos of you, maybe even slap you around. But that was not torture to people who had lived under Saddam's secret police. If the police or army, predominantly Shia, got hold of you and you were a Sunni, you had a good chance of never being seen again. For some reason the press never seemed to report the rooms full of dead, starving and tortured Sunnis being uncovered in Iraqi security bases. These men would weep with relief to hear that they were being taken to American prison camps.

At the same time, for many Iraqis their first encounter with an American was to be flattened on their faces on the street and searched in front of their women and the crowd. Even if it was better than being tortured by the Shia, every insult, beating and abuse of an Iraqi by an American, or a Brit for that matter, was an unforgivable insult and virtually always resulted in another recruit for the insurgency.

It would be too simplistic to blame insensitive Coalition troops for fanning the flames of the insurgency. I had done my research before leaving for Iraq to make sure I knew what I was getting myself into. As far as I could see as a former infantry officer, the occupation troops had from the start been dealt an awful hand to play by their superiors.

Summer passed into autumn with our only dramas being the dozen or so incidents a week with the guard force. After the June 2004 handover of power to the Iraqis, the CF had been renamed the MNF, or Multi-National Force, the CPA was now the US Embassy, and the Green Zone was the International Zone. They did not rename the Green Zone Café, where we had spent many pleasant evenings, because that had been blown up along with the street market in the CPA. Our misgivings about giving large numbers of Iraqis free rein around the Green Zone had been well founded. The CF and then the MNF had refused to use explosives search dogs around Iraqis in case they offended them.

Ramadan had arrived with the usual deadly laser breath from our fasting Iraqis and the even deadlier flurry of insurgent attacks. In the first three weeks of October 2004 there were 55 VBIEDs in Baghdad alone. The night I arrived from leave the CPA was hit by 75 mortar and rocket strikes.

More relevant to us was that Badger had brought us three immaculate PKMs and a Dragunov rifle as early Eid presents. He had an ex-Para mate working on a contract in Taji airbase guarding enormous warehouses stuffed full of former-regime weapons. Apparently every day an OGA, aka CIA, plane took off fully laden with weapons to God knows where. Undoubtedly Badger had squirrelled away several items for himself to trade later but these titbits were a welcome addition to our arsenal. We had already traded our RPDs for para M249s and our G3s were under our beds; we carried M4s on the streets now. This was a big improvement since we each normally carried about 300 rounds per man and 5.56 weighs just under half of 7.62 NATO.

The brakes weren't up to slowing all the armour on the BMW and during October I crashed twice and was banned from driving, although that became academic one morning in the early hours when Dai tried to mount an 18-inch kerb at 140mph. He had been attempting to avoid running through a CF patrol at night which had their lights off. After crawling from the wreck, Dai and Les were nearly shot by the same patrol until they were identified as friendlies.

To celebrate the end of Ramadan, we sent our officers out to the various sites with sheep as gifts and roasted two of them with our guards at Site Juliet, the closest. We left early in the soft-skinned Peugeot to rush home and catch *Baywatch* in

Arabic. On the way, two young guys pulled pistols and blazed away at point-blank range as we passed. Dai fired back half a mag as we sped off and after inspecting the damage to the car back at the villa he pulled out a flattened 9mm round that had embedded itself in the driving seat headrest where he had been sitting. It had hit the 1cm-wide metal support. A few millimetres left or right and it would have zipped straight through the cushion and into the back of Dai's head.

We called Colonel Faisal and Sammy to let them know and they told us they were on their way back to the villa with an escort of guards from Juliet. We had gone back to watching the episode where Mitch falls for his hot, Swedish au pair, and forty minutes later Sammy turned up as we were getting ready to hit the gym at the CPA.

'Colonel Faisal, he is dead,' he said simply. Then he began to cry quietly.

Sammy had left early to join us but had heard shooting behind him. He had wheeled his car around and retraced his route back to Colonel Faisal's car. It was on fire and all the men inside were dead, Moyed, the driver, who had been tortured by Saddam's henchmen, Abeer, a guard, and in the back Faisal and Senior Lieutenant 'Handcrusher' Usama, who had always tried to kiss Les whenever he saw him. Sammy had carried on driving back, looking for the escort of guards, but didn't find them until he arrived at the gates of Juliet where they were still waiting. They had been ordered not to move by Obi-Wan Kenobi.

'That fucking cunt!' Les was all for taking Obi-Wan down the range for an impromptu execution.

The whole thing stank. Faisal's group had been wearing civvies and had clearly been targeted. The rivalry between Ibrahim and Faisal had become more pronounced as we handed more power over to the Iraqis, and there had been death threats to Faisal in the past. Obi-Wan was Ibrahim's right-hand man. On our way back from Juliet, we had only been shot at by a couple of chancers, whereas witnesses said that there had been two cars full of men waiting for Faisal and Usama. Obi-Wan later came up with some crap excuse as to why he had ordered the escort to stay, but the sure proof as far as I was concerned was that Ibrahim refused to fire him. To add insult to injury, he promoted Obi-Wan to senior lieutenant to take over Usama's job.

Faisal had been an inspiration to the guards and his death had a crushing impact on both them and us. He had never abused his position and had refused to employ his relatives, since he regarded this as the 'bad' Iraqi way. He had shared many dangers and spent many nights 'just dropping by' for a drink with us on the roof. We had created a fair, uncorrupted and multi-ethnic, meritocratic guard force. But Iraq was seeping in now. The violence of the turf wars, the nepotism and the corruption would start taking root whenever we turned our backs.

So I was in a foul mood when I was summoned to the CPA to help Colonel Hind in one of his last presentations before leaving the country.

He had asked for my input for a briefing to a two-star general about insurgent threats and we had ended up having a vigorous discussion in the Embassy chow hall. I refused to call it an argument because that implied two opposing but in-formed views, and as far as I could work out Colonel Hind was woefully ignorant. The problem was he insisted on lumping together all enemy forces under the politically correct title of AIF or 'Anti-Iraqi Forces'.

I tried to explain that the situation was more complex than that. Much of the rural 'AIF sabotage' against infrastructure targets was carried out by the very same tribes hired as guards in order to extort more money. When the sheikhs demanded more money to 'hire more guards', the biggest mistake was to pay them. The situation would quieten down again until either the sheikh wanted even more money, or the neighbouring sheikhs were furious that they were being paid less. Then, all the tribes would be out blowing pipelines and claiming that they needed to hire more guards. We knew who was blowing up the pipelines because (a) insurgents would not wander into tribal areas because the tribes would kill them and (b) the inexperienced tribesmen often blew themselves up setting the devices.

There are few things more tragic than going to a village to inspect corpses who are 'strangers I have never seen before', when the sheikh is after reward money for killing dead terrorists, and all of the grief-stricken women and half the men are there weeping and having to be pulled back from the bodies of the 'strangers'. The only solution was to penalise the sheikhs and deduct payments if any sabotage occurred in their areas. Under Colonel Hind, the reverse happened.

I also knew from an Iraqi oil engineer that an oil pipeline from Iran was regularly blown up by Iranian saboteurs from over the border coming in on motorbikes. He knew because his opposite number at an Iranian refinery had apologised. He said that when oil was pumped into the Iraqi pipes, the pressure dropped in the Iranian refinery, meaning that the workers had to stay late at work, meaning that their wives would complain, or they missed the football on the telly. So they would hop over the border, blow the pipeline, the valves would shut and they would enjoy high pressure and early afternoons off for several weeks until the Americans organised a repair crew. Nothing to do with the insurgency at all.

The bloodiest violence came from Sunni and Shia militias targeting each other's civilian populations and religious leaders. Sunni Iraqis occasionally killed Sunni Arab foreign fighters and helped Iraqi and American forces to kill them in disgust at their bombings of civilians and also when their attempts to impose the strict fundamentalist values of the Salafis annoyed the Iraqis. Rival Shi'ite groups were also killing each other in blatant attempts to gain power in what were not much more than turf wars. Attacks on Americans and Multi-National Forces were just a bonus for these groups, but were not necessarily the main focus of foreign fighters motivated by either jihad or money.

'Well, it doesn't seem like a problem to me, we should just stay away and let these fuckers kill each other,' said Colonel Hind.

'So if there was a journalist here, you would be happy to give a statement for the record that in your opinion, the United States has no obligation to impose any sort of order or stop the slaughter of hundreds of Iraqi civilians every month?' He started gaping like a goldfish but I didn't let him answer. 'Well,

I can tell you, John, if you want to impress this two-star, there is one thing that it is essential you understand.'

'Oh, yeah?' He leaned forward attentively. That had got his attention all right.

'I bet you a month's pay that he is under pressure to come up with a way to tell Rumsfeld how to get the US forces out of here as soon as possible.'

The relentless pressure for an accelerated withdrawal of US troops was the primary reason for the 'Iraqification' nightmare. Every project managed by Westerners was facing a punishing deadline to hand over responsibility to the Iraqis.

'Your problem is that you cannot withdraw until the fighting dies down. How can you do that if you don't understand what these dozen different factions want?' I asked him.

'We don't need to know what they want, we just need to know that they die easy,' laughed some major I didn't know sitting next to John Hind. He blew smoke off an imaginary gun and everyone laughed.

'Well, that's just what's getting American soldiers killed every day. Did they teach you that at West Point?' I asked him quite calmly. 'It doesn't matter how many AIF you kill, there will always be more of them until you take away what they are fighting for. As a professional soldier I would find it difficult to prevent the enemy from achieving his objectives if I didn't know what they were to start with.'

Everyone agreed with that but they weren't happy with what I came up with next.

'So my first point is that you don't know what your enemies are trying to achieve, the second is that you don't know what you are trying to achieve.'

'What?'

'That's your problem, mate, half the American soldiers I've met think we're here because of 9/11, fighting Al Qaeda.' I pointed over my shoulder at the mural of the twin towers painted on the wall behind me.

'What the hell are you talking about? That is why we're here. We're fighting them here so that we don't have to fight them on American soil.' Colonel Hind glared at me in angry bewilderment.

There was a chorus of enthusiastic agreement from the officers sitting at the tables around us and I realised that we had attracted a small audience. Mad Dog and Gareth had joined us but remained silent. They had spent enough time listening to contractors' debates on the war to have open minds. In the US military, however, anyone not 100 per cent 'with the programme' was in danger of being labelled an unpatriotic enemy sympathiser. 'You're either with us or against us,' as Mr Bush had said.

So I educated them. I told them that Osama bin Laden had hated Saddam's secular Ba'ath party and had regularly referred to him as a devil in his speeches, and that vice versa, Saddam had banned Al Qaeda from Iraq.

'What's more,' I continued, 'after the Soviets withdrew from Afghanistan in 1989 there were thousands of mujaheddin with no one to fight, many of whom ended up in Al Qaeda. After Saddam invaded Kuwait in 1990, and allied forces were preparing troop build-ups in the Gulf, how many of you know that Osama bin Laden offered the use of Al Qaeda's fighters to Saudi Arabia to use in any conflict against Iraq?'

They were dumbstruck. Even Mad Dog raised an eyebrow.

'I'm not making this up. Go read a history book. Al Qaeda and Iraq hated each other. And if you want to talk about 9/11, none of the hijackers came from Iraq. Four were from various Middle Eastern countries. Does anyone want to tell me where the other fifteen came from? Can anyone tell me where Osama bin Laden is from? Where did the money for the op come from?'

No one said anything because they all knew the answer.

'All from Saudi Arabia.' I looked around. 'So why the fuck are we all sitting here in Iraq?'

Colonel Hind was puce. I wondered if I kept pushing whether he would have a stroke. The others seemed genuinely attentive so I carried on explaining why I thought the invasion of Iraq had nothing to do with fighting Al Qaeda.

The war on terrorism had been going very well in Afghanistan, I said. Small, elite units operating with good intelligence had greatly reduced Al Qaeda's command structure at the same time as conventional forces destroyed its fighters and resources in the field. Then in 2002–3, much of that elite force and their CIA colleagues had been transferred to Baghdad to chase down former Ba'athists on the Coalition hitlist. But the cost of removing manpower from Afghanistan to track Saddam's former commanders and ministers could be seen in the falling number of high-ranking Al Qaeda leaders then killed or captured. In 2002, the CIA issued a list of thirty Al Qaeda commanders whose unique experience and technical expertise were irreplaceable to the enemy. Of those thirty, in 2002, eight were caught or killed; in 2003, only five. In 2004 there was only one caught, trying to smuggle himself into Iraq.

Ms Frances Townsend, the Counter-terrorism and Homeland Security Advisor to the White House from May 2004, said that a clear measure of the United States' success against terrorism was 'every day that goes by that America doesn't suffer another attack'. In that case I would then also like to heartily congratulate Monaco, Luxembourg and the Kingdom of Bhutan for their successes against international terrorism.

To my mind a twofold strategy to deal with Islamist international terrorism made sense. First, deal with the hardcore leadership cadres. Secondly, reduce international recruitment for new militants. Numerous political leaders had agreed before the war that the invasion of Iraq would greatly increase the threat of international terrorism. It had given Osama bin Laden an overwhelming media victory; every subsequent terrorist act could now be justified as being in defence of Islam. There had been a worldwide increase in sympathy, political support, funds and recruits to Islamist cells who were widely dispersed and often unknown to the authorities. There had also been hundreds killed by bombings in Madrid, London, Bali, Istanbul and Egypt in direct response to the war in Iraq. So 9/11 clearly did not make sense as a reason. So why had they invaded? My little audience came up with the standard rationales and I shot them down.

WMDs? Rubbish. Report after report had failed to find any evidence before the war and so many of the famous satellite photos Colin Powell pointed out on television were now admitted to be 'mistakes'. The British case presented to Parliament was even worse, with excerpts from some student thesis several years old taken off the Internet put forward as 'intelligence'. Anyway, if you wanted to find WMDs, why not invade North Korea, which has a nuclear capability and a robust bio-weapons programme? Or Iran, which clearly does not need to refine uranium when they are sitting on top of an ocean of oil and the largest gas reserves in the world?

Regime change? Even more laughable. There were at least a dozen countries in Africa that had despotic tyrants brutalising their populations.

I told them that the Iraqis tended to believe three main avenues of thought which were just as ridiculous. That the US was there to physically steal the oil; to punish the Iraqis for the first Gulf War (for the defeat imposed on them by Saddam in the Mother Of All Battles – that got a laugh at least); or as part of some Zionist plot whereby the Hashemite royalty could move back into Iraq from Jordan and the Israelis could have Jordan, their spiritual homeland, before expanding ever on-wards to the Euphrates river.

Economic theories, at least, made sense and revolved around oil. In 2003 the US budget deficit was about $413 billion and the trade deficit $551 billion. So why didn't the US dollar and the economy collapse? I reckoned it was because all oil purchased from OPEC since 1971 was purchased using US dollars. Every country around the world constantly needs US dollars for their oil-dependent economies and therefore demand for dollars is constant and high. But Iraq had switched to selling oil for euros in 1999. When the euro became stronger against the dollar over the next two years, US analysts suddenly realised that there was a very serious problem. If any other country decided to move to euros and dollar demand dropped, the US economy would be in a shit state. Was that a good enough reason to invade? I don't know, but one of the first things the Coalition Provisional Authority did in Iraq was switch from trading in euros back to US dollars.

Many educated people would also say, as I had once said to Sammy, that maybe the plan was to flood the global market with Iraqi oil, lower the prices and break OPEC's monopoly on the world market. But since the invasion, oil had more than doubled in price and the plan had backfired. Or had it?

Because once I was in-country and saw the state of the
infrastructure and talked to a few engineers, it was obvious
that the Iraqi oil industry had been seriously neglected and
would need billions of dollars and years to get higher
production volumes. It is just my theory but there are two
famous oil men in the White House, the President and the
Vice-President; and all of a sudden the price of oil doubled, US
oil companies have been posting record profits for the last few
years. Dick Cheney's former employer, Halliburton, has been
awarded contracts worth billions in Iraq. And, a funny old
thing, but with world oil prices doubled, people would need
more US dollars to buy it. Strange that. I could also mention
that since they now governed Iraq, the US has also acquired a
de facto seat on the OPEC cartel through control of Iraq's
energy policy.

Maybe I am just too cynical. I also had thoughts about US
hegemonic ambitions. Modern-day economics had done what
the CIA had always dreamed of and destroyed communism.
Socialist-type governments in the Arab world – Egypt, Yemen,
Algeria, Libya – have had to adapt to free-market forces, and
at the same time had become less anti-American. But other
large, oil- and resource-rich countries that remained indepen-
dent of US capitalistic influence have also been threatened.
Venezuela, Iran and Iraq all fell into this category. Iraq got
invaded, Iran was suddenly labelled as an axis of evil just one
month after co-operating with the CIA and handing over
details of hundreds of Al Qaeda agents, and Venezuela and
their democratically elected President Hugo Chavez are reeling
against the ropes as America actively tries to undermine the
government. And by way of coincidence, Venezuela, the
world's fourth largest oil producer, and Iran, were also
thinking of switching to the euro.

I didn't bother to share these last thoughts with the men
around me. I had already shaken the pillars of their universe
by even daring to imagine that the war in Iraq might not all be
about 9/11 and fighting Al Qaeda.

'So if you're so goddamn clever, why did we invade *I-raq*?'
snarled Colonel Hind angrily. Everyone leaned in to hear my
answer.

'I don't know, mate,' I replied cheerfully. 'But I am just a
civilian. What I do know is that I should be able to go out there
and ask any soldier what he or she's fighting for and they
should know why they are here. But they don't.' I looked
around at all of them. 'And I'm sat here with a bunch of senior
officers and they can't tell me why there are American soldiers
dying out there every day. And that, gentlemen, is not right.'

I left Colonel Hind amid a little hubbub of discussion and
Mad Dog came to walk me out to the pool to meet Seamus
and Les. I shouldered my daysack full of books I had borrowed
from the welfare library next to the chow hall.

'Shit, Ash, you're in a gloomy mood today,' he said.

'Yeah, sorry, mate. I guess I am. I'm pissed off at seeing
ignorant pricks making insane decisions in here and then
having to face our Iraqis and see the disastrous consequences
on the streets the next day. I'm pissed off with the fact that
Colonel Faisal's killers are still out running free and I'm pissed
off with the fact that he,' I indicated Colonel Hind with a
backwards nod, 'is about to bale out back to the States and
leave you in charge of the Iraqification process so that when it
turns into a complete gangfuck –'

'Which it will,' he broke in.

'– which it fucking will. It will be on your career report, not
his.'

As we walked out past the smiling Ghurkha guards I realised
that I was also getting tired of Iraq in general. The team had
been out here for over a year now and maybe it was time to
go and work in another country. Somewhere with better scoff
too, because the food in Iraq was truly appalling. The danger
didn't bother me as much, because apart from just being part
of the job, someone took a shot at you – what, once a month?
But you have to eat three times a day. Part of me also had a
foreboding that as autumn drew into winter things were just
going to get worse.

TWENTY-FIVE

During the past twelve months we had trained a guard force and officer structure of 1,500 Iraqi nationals to protect Baghdad's water supply. After the general election in January 2005, that force would be reorganised and responsibility for security would pass from Spartan to the new Water Minister at the Ministry of Municipalities and Public Works.

Colonel Hind had once observed with rare insight that if the water failed there would be a nationwide uprising. This risk was appreciated at the State Department and, for this reason, Task Force Fountain was kept operational until spring 2005. It was, to my knowledge, the longest lived private security project funded by the US Project and Contracting Office.

The process of 'Iraqification' had been progressing throughout the year. What this meant was that contracts awarded to foreign companies were cut short before their tasks had been completed, often with disastrous effects and to the dismay and frustration of officials at the United States Agency for International Development and the Iraq Reconstruction Management Office, as well as their Iraqi counterparts.

Once the State Department, through the Project and Contracting Office, ceased funding reconstruction projects, I was certain that an almost complete breakdown in the country's infrastructure would occur; Iraq had still not recovered from Ambassador Bremer's de-Ba'athification order and the removal of tens of thousands of experienced civil administrators.

The new staff moving into the Iraqi ministries owed their posts more to their blood relationship to the respective minister than to operational competence. To me, the State Department and CF leadership were no better and operated an insular old-boy network. Many State Department civilians and senior US officers who had served in Iraq came with one eye on promotion and had tended towards writing reports that would both serve to make them look good and would be what their superiors wanted to read, Colonel Hind being a prime example. They were more concerned with their future careers than making a difference and drastically undermined the good work being done by the many hard-working officers and civil staff who were genuinely trying to help rebuild Iraq.

With the onset of winter the news spread among our guards that our contract was coming to an end and that responsibility for security would pass from Spartan to the new Water Minister. The guards seemed genuinely sad that we were leaving. We had treated them fairly, trained them and they had come to see that as Brits we deserved our reputation for being men of our word. Our guard officers were anxious about their future. They were worried that they would lose their jobs and be replaced by relatives of the Minister, as had happened in other ministries.

The guards themselves were less worried about their job security than their pay prospects. They were earning $150 a month and were concerned that once we had gone, their salaries would be cut back to the meagre levels paid to other Iraqi civil servants. Or more likely the Ministry would continue to pay the going rate, but that the old system would return, where the colonel would take $20 off every man's pay, the captains would take $10 and the shift supervisors $5.

Dai Jones and I both had leave due. Having missed Christmas at home the previous year, Seamus decided to keep us on the books but let us go back to the UK on 23 December and remain there without having to return and serve out the final few weeks of our contract. We would be leaving Seamus,

Les and four South Africans in Aradisa Idah. At the end of the contract, they would hand the villa back to Shakir Ahmad, the owner, and withdraw to Spartan HQ.

Seamus and Les both had other contracts to go to in the UK. The Yaapies were staying on at Spartan. As for myself, I had the choice of either a consultancy contract in Venezuela or a PSD contract in West Africa. The latter was with a new company called Erebus UK and I liked the look of them; set up by guys who had worked in Iraq, they seemed a sharp and professional crew that had their act together.

We said our goodbyes to the Iraqis with lots of kissing and hand shakes. Although Sammy and I had spoken of it often, when the time came to say goodbye we were both blinking back tears. He had risked his life to save ours the first time we met and we had since been together virtually every day for more than a year. I honestly could not say how many times Sammy and I had sweated together out on the range, how many white-knuckle journeys we had made with weapons tightly gripped ready for use, or how many nights he had sat sipping whisky with us on the roof, popping by 'just for a drink' whenever there was trouble in the streets and he wanted to make sure that we were OK. I found myself remembering the day our sides were splitting with laughter when I tried to persuade him that Les and Seamus were gay.

I looked at this tubby, older man with his hair combed over his bald patch, his shoes with holes in the soles, his trousers pulled up too high over his belly button, his blue eyes, his ginger moustache and his lined face that I knew as well as my own. And now, just as things were getting really bad, I was going to cut and run with my British passport and leave him in this shithole. Sammy's address was still tucked in my pocket. He was clutching my email address and promised to write *every day*. Sammy had made himself so useful that he would likely be kept on to help manage the guard force. But it would not be a happy time. The hated Shia Colonel Ibrahim was well connected with a senior aide within the Ministry and would have a senior role there.

'Maybe you find contract in the Africa and you need my help. You call me. I am ready.' He smiled. 'And when the problems is finished you will come back and visit to Iraq, Mister James.' He gripped my hand firmly. 'You are my brother. I wait for you.'

We had to hand in our M4s but I gave Sammy all my 9mm ammunition, my scope, fifteen full magazines and my G3. It was a good weapon and if he needed to he could sell it.

The guards all had presents for us, plaster of Paris statues, ceramic vases, revolving globes, 'crystal' swans, and 'gold' watches that were artfully made of plastic. Dai took his gifts out to the range and used them for target practice. I re-wrapped mine so that Mad Dog, John, Gareth and Sergeant Harvey would have presents to open on Christmas Day.

I had been in Iraq for sixteen months and was sick to death of lamb and the kind of rice you could not chew too hard on in case you cracked a tooth on a small stone. I'd had enough of the extremes of weather, the dust in the air, the corruption, the treachery, the ali-babas, queues at the gas stations and the heartbreaking, illiterate, hand-to-mouth poverty in a land that should have been one of the wealthiest countries in the world. I had found in Iraq generous and sometimes surprising moments of kindness and goodwill and witnessed once again a depressing capacity for human cruelty that I thought I had left behind in the Balkans.

We packed a few things and left most of our gear behind. In my daysack I had a few souvenirs, some old banknotes with the head of Saddam, my maps of Baghdad, the bravery certificates awarded ceremoniously to me at the CPA – 'mercenary medals', as Mad Dog had called them.

All too soon the guys were dropping us off at Spartan HQ and we were slapping the Yaapies on the back and swearing we would come and visit them as soon as their country discovered toilet paper. We shook hands with Les and Seamus, promising we would get together for beers back in Blighty in the New Year. Then the men who had shared my life, dreams and dangers for more than a year drove off and it was just me and Dai next to our pile of bags in the dust.

'Tell you fucking what, mate, I'm fucking not 'appy about this fucking next bit. Fuckin' Route Irish, mate, the most dangerous road in the fucking world,' Dai said with relish and lit up a fag. 'Last trip out after a year in Dad's Bag, I tell you, mate, we're bound to get fucking walloped.'

'Well, it's all right for you, isn't it? I mean you're Welsh and butt ugly. I'm the one that's going to get it.'

'Fucking twat.'

'I mean it, it's the Hollywood ending. Good-looking hunk gets it, while his beautiful, pregnant girlfriend and small child are waiting for him on Christmas Eve. I don't stand a chance. *Ally Akbar* KABOOM.'

We both laughed.

And then I became deadly serious. 'Mate, you're not going to smoke that in the wagon are you?'

It was Badger's team taking us up the BIAP road. It was their regular daily run and they went high profile, no point trying to disguise who you were when you were driving the one highway between the BIAP and the Green Zone. Being Badger's crew of thieving pirates his convoy now comprised three CAT trucks with three PKMs in each. The back seats were full of spare boxes of belted 7.62 long and the backs of the front seats were festooned with bandoliers of field dressings and grenades. There was steel plating on the doors and ceramic vest plates duct-taped behind the headrest of every seat. Our feet rested on spare AKs and pouches of AK magazines and in each rear gunner's nest was a spare RPK in case of stoppages. In the lead car Badger had a para Minimi in his lap ready to go through the front windscreen. Dai and I sat back to back in the rear seat of the middle vehicle and manned a PKM each.

This was our final drive up the BIAP highway. We'd driven this road a thousand times and I was convinced that this time we were going to get hit. Soldiers are a superstitious lot. The last journey, the journey home, is always the most stressful. We made ready as we left the Green Zone and every second of the ten-minute journey we were scrutinising every window, every bridge, every pile of rubbish, until we pulled through the CF checkpoint and stopped to unload weapons in the unloading drums.

We felt strangely naked without our vests and rifles but were relieved when we strode into the marble halls of the airport. At least it was open again and we no longer had to cross the

desert to Amman. Steely-eyed Ghurkhas were manning security but we decided not to congratulate ourselves until we were
eating our steak back in the Library at the Marriott.

Thirty hours later and a thousand miles from Iraq, I had
never been so happy to see the green fields and rain-filled skies
of England as we descended into Heathrow. I walked into the
arrivals lounge to see the two most beautiful women in the
world; Krista and Natalie, blonde and sparkling, both in red
coats with long tartan scarves, Krista tall and willowy with her
pregnant tummy just showing through her coat, Natalie the
perfect miniature in shiny leather shoes. She ran into my arms
and I swung her round in the air like I always did, playing
aeroplanes. Krista stood watching. She looked relieved, deeply
happy, more beautiful than ever. I was a lucky guy.

I was enjoying the journey back from the airport in our new
Range Rover, courtesy of my last pay cheque from Spartan,
soaking up the sights and sounds of home.

'Now you have come back, I think we should get married,'
Krista suddenly announced.

I was glad she was driving. I would have crashed the car. For
the last five years every time I had steered close to the subject
she had become angry and defensive, making it clear that it
was never going to happen.

'Sure,' I said, playing it cool. We drove on in silence. I
waited until we had parked up at home and then leapt out of
the car whooping and shouting. I fell to my knees outside the
driver's door. 'Will you marry me?'

'Get up, James! Your trousers will get dirty and the
neighbours are watching,' she scowled. 'And yes, of course.'

I asked her again as we gave Nat her bath and twice at
dinner until she got angry again and told me to stop being silly.
Then I asked her one last time as she lay dozing off in bed
against me, with the solid lump of her belly touching mine.

'Yes, James. I missed you so much. I wanted to marry you
for such a long time, but I was too proud and silly to admit I
was wrong. Now go to sleep.' She rolled over and drifted off
into slumber.

Tears of emotion pricked the backs of my eyes; I'm soft as
butter on the inside, me. I don't think I had ever been happier

in all my born days than I was at that one special moment. For the first time since I had met her, Krista had admitted that she was wrong about something.

The next day was Christmas Day and after we had opened our stockings in bed with Natalie, my mother and the rest of the family arrived to help get Christmas lunch sorted. I announced that Krista and I were going to get married and my mother just looked at me.

'Yes, James, I know. We have been planning it for a few weeks. I am trying to book a weekend this autumn. I am very happy for you, dear, but I really don't understand why you didn't ask the poor girl earlier,' she sniffed.

The house was full of family and friends and I took a moment to make some calls to people who didn't already know I was engaged. Dai's girlfriend answered to say that he was still hung over in bed. I called Seamus to wish him Happy Christmas. He congratulated me when I told him my news, but he sounded tired.

'How's work, mate?'

'Just the usual crap,' he said. 'We've just paid the guards yesterday and there's a rumour gone round already that we're not going to pay 'em at the end of January.' I remembered the plan to pay the guards early, partly as a deception plan for security in case the pay convoy got ambushed, and partly because Baghdad would no doubt be locked down between Christmas and New Year as the threat level soared. 'Sammy's on the case, but I don't think they're listening.'

'Are they listening to Ibrahim?' I asked and he chuckled.

'You know the score.'

Ibrahim would be weighing up what was more advantageous to him, to let the guards carry on believing they weren't getting paid or to tell them it wasn't true.

Mad Dog, John and Gareth had gone to the villa knowing they would be 'stuck' in Aradisa Idah for the entire period of the lockdown. Mad Dog had pulled a blinder and traded a bottle of whisky for a real Christmas pudding from the Brit encampment and had also arrived bearing cases of beer. They were about to watch *Shallow Hal*, a team favourite, then start working their way through the James Bond movies until they were all shit-faced and fell asleep. Everyone wished me Merry Christmas and congratulated me on my engagement.

I could see them in my mind's eye, gathered in front of the wide screen in the sitting room with their plates of roast lamb, every man with a pistol on his belt and rifles stacked next to the sandbagged door. The Yaapies would close their eyes and say a silent grace before eating and Seamus would continue bullshitting John and Gareth about the time he worked as Princess Diana's PSD.

As I looked around my own house, full of people chattering about their neighbours and holidays, I felt a sense of disorientation, that this was not the real world. It was just too frivolous. I felt an unexpected desire to be back in Baghdad. In the place that had become my home. But that was crazy, wasn't it? When I thought about my friends with weeks still to go before they could also relax, still in danger, I felt ashamed to be safe at home in London with a glass of champagne in my hand.

I could not understand why, but my heart felt like lead as I put the phone down. Krista came over with a bright smile.

'How's Seamus? Did you say Merry Christmas for me?'

I plastered a smile on my face and said he was fine.

I had promised Krista I was never going back to Iraq, but as the days passed I watched the news of the worsening situation during the elections, the fresh spate of IEDs and firefights in Baghdad, the CF patrols and private security contractors struggling to prevent the city going up in one last apocalyptic explosion. Seamus never said anything but I had known him for long enough. I knew they were feeling the pressure and were short-handed without Dai and myself.

One night Krista asked me what was wrong. So I told her that I felt bad about being home in London when my team-mates were still in danger. It was unfinished business and I wanted to go back for the last few weeks of the contract and see it through with them.

She fingered the new diamond engagement ring I had just bought and then looked me in the eye.

'I suppose you had better go then. I will be here when you get back,' and her eyes crinkled at the corners as she smiled and kissed me.

I still had my return tickets to Amman and Baghdad as well as all my Coalition ID cards. I emailed Seamus and simply told him that my leave terminated at the end of the week and I was reminding him that he needed to organise a pick-up for me from the BIAP on Monday morning, 9.30 a.m.

The reply came immediately. 'Transport's arranged.'

TWENTY-SIX

The Christmas madness had passed and Baghdad had settled back into being its usual murderous self by the time I arrived. The guards had been told that everyone would be paid with a Eid ul-Adha bonus when the TF Fountain contract officially ceased at the end of January. Security at the sites was being managed by Colonel Ibrahim and Major Razak, with our team out of the guns and jeeps division and now acting only as consultants.

Sammy had been emotional when I left Baghdad and there were fresh tears in his blue eyes when I gave him the gifts I had brought for his family.

'I knew, Mr James, I would see you again.'

'Four weeks and I'm out of here for good,' I replied.

He looked sad and I immediately felt guilty. We walked outside to Sammy's old Toyota. It was a chilly day with a stiff wind.

'It is a pity we did not visit the *melwiyeh*,' he said. 'You would be very happy. Iraq is a very beautiful country.'

'When it all settles down I'll come back with my family,' I said. 'By then you will be very rich and I expect you'll have three more wives.'

He laughed and held his plump hands to his chest. 'I am ready.'

* * *

At 11.30 on the last Thursday of January, the day before payday, Cobus raced into my office suited up with his vest and rifle.

'Ash, back to the house.'

'All right, mate, soon as I've finished this email.'

'No, Code Red, we have to go now.'

I had drawn up the evacuation plan and our standard drill, assuming a minimum of two hours' notice, was first to put a bullet through the hard drives in the computers, burn all documents then withdraw to the house to remove weapons, ammo and anything that might help the enemy. Cobus made it clear there wasn't time. Our emergency escape SOP was to grab weapons and bug-out bags and leg it to the emergency RV (rendezvous), in this case with the American Special Forces guys a ten-minute drive from the villa.

I grabbed my rifle and vest, chased out of the office block and followed Cobus across the courtyard. The rest of the gang was in the living room ready for Seamus's brief. The two cleaning women and eight of the Kurdish house guards were also there, hanging around translating but not really sure what to do.

Major Razak, a Sunni rival of Ibrahim, had radioed in that the guards were gathering to storm the house. The rumour that they were not going to be paid had broken out again. It was the last month of the contract now and, by Iraqi reasoning, that made perfect sense. We did not know where the rumour had started, but Major Razak reported that Ibrahim had promised to sort the matter out, not with us, but *with the minister*. Meaning that he had definitely blamed the non-payment on us white-eyes.

Razak had bravely gone to the five guard posts, one at each end of the street and three surrounding the office, and had confiscated the weapons. The guards had gone home to get their own AKs, buying us a valuable few moments. Most of our security guards were out at the water plant ten minutes' drive away. They were still armed and they were still using our radios. They were coming to get us and they would arrive in fifteen minutes. Major Razak had gone in search of Ibrahim and was now cut off.

We split up. Les went out to start the HAV while the rest of us chased about the house stocking up on ammo. Cobus and I grabbed sleeping bags and threw in cameras, wedding photos and laptops. There was no time for much more. We ran out to find Les cursing.

'I don't fucking believe this,' he said.

The gas had been siphoned from the armoured car, our emergency bug-out vehicle. We still had the old Peugeot, but it wasn't armoured and, even without the Kurds, there were seven of us. We wouldn't fit.

The two women stood there nursing their hands. The Kurdish guards seemed ashamed that the other guards, mainly Shia it has to be said, were coming for us. Their radios were still crackling.

'Mr Seamus, they are on the way,' one of them said.

'How long?'

'Very soon.'

Although the guards often flared up, it usually blew over without anything happening. But there was something different this time, we could feel it in the air. The mood was different. Seamus took a snap decision which was absolutely the right thing to do. He told the Kurds there was no point in them getting into a firefight. They would still have to live in Aradisa Idah after we had gone.

'Go home,' he said. 'Go home and come back later tonight and see if we're still here.'

We had a good relationship with these men. We had interviewed them personally before giving them their jobs. They had worked beside us, guarded us at night while we slept and learned a lot of fruity English from Dai Jones. There was no time for long goodbyes.

'Go. Go,' said Seamus, and slammed the door to the armoured car.

The Kurds looked relieved, and ran off, taking the two women with them. It was the last possible moment for a safe escape. We could already hear in the distance AKs being shot into the air, the sound of voices growing louder as the mob approached.

There was one more vehicle, an open pick-up truck used by the guards and almost certainly fully fuelled. It was parked behind the office block but to get to it would require leaving the compound and going around the perimeter wall. We'd run out of time. We could see our guards through the main gate. We raced back into the house and up the stairs. I was the last man up on the roof and threw the weighted end of the coil of razor wire down the stairwell, sealing that route off.

The plan was to escape across the roof, drop down on the office roof and then drop down to the waste ground where the pick-up was parked.

Over the black canvas cover-from-view sheet on the roof we could see a mob of nearly 200 guards. I was mortified that they were not taking cover; they were ignoring all the training I had drilled into them over and over again for the last year and were ambling down the middle of the road in a typically shambolic Iraqi fashion, shouting and waving their rifles. The intermittent shots in the air were intoxicating and with encouragement from the ringleaders the rest of the mob joined in. The gunshots set the dogs off. Our neighbour, the policeman with the beautiful daughters, now had three dogs and they were barking like machine guns.

I could see a few of the guards, including Ali, the armourer, and Ra'ad, the tea boy, trying to restrain the others, but Obi-Wan Kenobi was leading the pack and he was the first man to lower his AK and put a few rounds in the compound wall.

'I knew I should have sacked that cunt.' Les had already set up the PKM machine gun in one of the corner sangars and was hooking a box of ammo under it.

'Right, let's start moving now,' said Seamus. 'Wayne, Etienne and Les, you first. Les, grab the keys from the office and give us a shout when you get the vehicle started.'

The rest of the guards were following Obi. Their shots were wild, but they were coming in our direction and I sourly recalled the few guards at the range who'd had suspiciously good marksmanship skills.

Wayne took his knife to the black canvas screen at the back, ripped it apart and held it for Etienne and Les. Wayne followed as they slipped down the side of the building and clattered their way across the corrugated iron roof that gave shade to the vehicles. They dropped one after the other on to the office roof where they were immediately pinned down by the guards who had seen them.

'Warning shots,' Seamus yelled.

As our guards fired at us, we fired back over their heads.

Seamus gave Hendriks and Cobus a hard stare. 'And don't fucking shoot any of them until I give the order,' he said.

'Right, mate,' said Cobus.

Hendriks glanced at Seamus then returned his concentration back down the sights of his rifle.

We opened up with 'deliberate fire', one aimed shot every few seconds into the street six feet in front of the guards. The volume of shouting doubled but the shooting ceased as all our guards ran and threw themselves over the nearest garden wall.

I had slung my M4 on my back and taken hold of the PKM. It already had a full 200-round box underneath, which I kept as a spare, and stripped out a 200-round belt from another box and loaded that. I had a good view down the main street that led to the front of the house and also the alleyway down the backs of all the houses on our street.

As the guards started to reorganise themselves in the gardens, I let off a 20-round burst that stitched up the entire length of the street.

'Good, keep their fucking heads down,' Seamus said. He was covering the back of the house.

I could see Obi-Wan Kenobi rallying the guards to continue the assault. I put a closer burst along the street and he disappeared again. Hendriks and Cobus were picking their targets and putting single rounds so dangerously close to the guards they must have tasted the dust as they thumped into the walls beside them.

Les and the Yaapies were up and running again. The access door on the office roof was locked from the inside, so they hung off the side of the building and dropped down to the pick-up on the waste ground. They entered the building from the back, grabbed the vehicle keys from where they were hanging in Les's office and sixty seconds later Les's voice came over the radio: 'Truck's running. Move now.'

The guards were back in it again, aiming shots that ripped

through the black canvas screen, drilling neat holes like a pattern on a polka-dot tie. Rounds were pinging off the white painted walls of the villa and burrowing into the sandbags on each corner of the roof.

Obi, clever lad, must have twigged that we had been deliberately aiming to miss them and was taking his time aiming. He wasn't a bad shot, either. His rounds moved in a zigzag over the screen, and the other guards must have got their bloodlust up and joined the attack. Some of them were running towards the villa while the others covered them. Then they ran while the first batch put down covering fire.

My flare of pride in their drills didn't prevent me from putting bursts down the road in front of them as they were running. That stopped them for a bit. They may have known that we were not going to kill them but with the shitty state of medical care in Baghdad nobody wanted to catch a ricochet off the ground.

I came to the end of the belt.

'Magazine,' I yelled. I changed belts as Cobus and Hendriks started climbing down the back of the roof.

There was just the two of us now. I glanced at Seamus.

'I'm already on the gun, you get going.'

He paused for a second. It made sense.

'Don't be long, Ash,' Seamus said.

I let go with a long burst on the PKM as Seamus raced across the roof and through the slit in the canvas. I heard his boots clatter over the corrugated iron and ten seconds later he was down from the office roof to join the others.

Fresh holes were turning the black canvas sheeting into a sieve. The guards were coming down the back alley as well as down the main road. I swivelled rapidly between bursts, firing down the front of the house and then up the back, still trying to pin the guards down and still making bloody sure I didn't kill any of them. My heart jumped every time an incoming round slapped into the other side of the sandbags.

The guards were now behind the compound wall at the front and I knew the second I stopped firing, they would pile in. Seamus came up on the radio. 'Listen up, mate, we have to drive down to the end of the block so we can take cover around the corner. Make your way there through the gardens.'

'Roger that.'

I peeked through the holes in the canvas. Bursts of light from
the muzzle flash sparkled from sheltered spots and I could see
Obi-Wan Kenobi yelling encouragement to his troops.

From the amount of expended link hanging from the left side
of my gun I knew there was hardly any ammo left on the belt.
I put down two last bursts, the first in the direction of Obi to
keep him quiet, the second up the back alley. The gun was
empty. In three quick moves I had stripped out the bolt-return
spring from the PKM and was slinging it over the wall as far
away as I could, then I remembered there was no more ammo
on the roof so it didn't matter that I was leaving a functioning
gun to fall into the hands of the enemy. Enemy! I'd met the
families of half these guys. They didn't want to kill us. They
didn't know what they wanted.

I hammered across the roof, over the discarded sleeping bags
where we had put our valuables. A tiny part of me was smug
that I made a habit of keeping my own camera in my bug-out
bag which was on my back. I slipped through the slit in the
screen, over the corrugated iron cover and down on to the roof
of the office, skinning my shin from ankle to knee. Rounds
smacked viciously into the roof as I legged it across, totally
exposed. I hung down from the roof and dropped into the
policeman's garden. The dogs went mad barking and stretch-
ing on their chains but fortunately those chains remained
tethered to the wall.

'Moving now. I'm on my way,' I puffed over the radio.

I didn't exactly hear everything Seamus said in response but
gathered that they would not be on the corner I was heading
for, but were driving one block further away. If the guards
managed to surround the team and forced our hand, Hendriks
alone would have turned Aradisa Idah into a blood bath.

Blood was soaking into my trousers but I didn't feel any pain.
I didn't even think about it. I sprinted through my neighbour's
garden, vaulted the wall and ran through another garden.

I knew there would be a pause in the action. I didn't imagine
for one second that the guards were committed to an attack to
the death. The moment they discovered the villa was empty,
they would take out their anger and frustration by looting and

trashing the place. I puffed through the next garden and vaulted the last wall. I was wearing my vest, daysack and full fighting order, total weight about 25kg, but I had so much adrenaline I was flying like a gazelle. My helmet was in my bug-out bag. If I got the chance I'd get the fucking thing out and put it on.

The pick-up truck wasn't there. They had driven over one more block. The road was deserted. Just the mud-coloured buildings with shuttered windows and bolted doors. The smell of dust and cordite. I could hear gunshots still.

I went to the end of the street and, peeking gingerly around the corner, I could see the guards piling into the villa. I was about to go back in the opposite direction, when Sammy pulled up on the other side of the junction. He was hidden from the guards by a garden wall, but to reach him I would still have to cross the road fully exposed to the mob 50 metres away milling around the compound.

Sammy leaned out of the window and beckoned me across. I nodded and he began a three-point turn ready to hurtle off the way he'd come. I holstered my pistol, slung my rifle into position and took a deep breath. This was it. A cry went up immediately I bolted across the road. I fired off three or four rounds above the guards' heads and they all hit the deck.

I cleared the road and was diving into the back of Sammy's old Toyota as a flurry of wild shots crackled into the corner behind me. Sammy gunned the motor.

'Fuck me, Sammy, I thought it was your day off today?'

He lifted a radio handset from the passenger seat. He had been listening to the babble of guard chatter. Unbelievable.

I called Seamus: 'Get moving, mate, I'm in a car with Sammy.'

'Fuck me. I thought it was his day off.'

'That's what I just said.'

'Follow us, we'll head for the RV with the Americans.'

'Tell them I'm coming in with an Iraqi in a beaten-up yellow Toyota.'

'Roger that.'

We had got away by the skin of our teeth. Through the back window I could see a plume of smoke rising over the villa.

They must have set fire to the property after doing a thorough job looting it. The old pilot drove like he was at the controls of his Mig and before long I saw the pick-up in front with guns bristling at every window. I leaned over the front seat.

'*Shukran Jazeeren*, Sammy.'

'This is no problem. You are my brother.'

AFTERWORD

22 February 2006

The Al Askari Mosque, one of the holiest Shia sites, was blown up. Despite appeals for calm from the Grand Ayatollah Ali al-Sistani, in revenge attacks during the following two days, 130 Sunnis were killed and more than 200 Sunni mosques damaged or destroyed.

22 April 2006

Shia leader Jawad al Maliki was nominated prime minister of Iraq ending four months of political deadlock. He was given thirty days to form Iraq's first full-term post-Saddam government.

The deadlock was only broken when former premier Ibrahim al-Jaafari had a 'change of heart', reported Kurdish lawmaker Mahmoud Othman, after two separate meetings, one with the United Nations envoy Ashraf Qazi, the other with two men whose names will, in my opinion, dominate Iraqi and Middle East politics for many years to come: Ali al-Sistani, the most powerful Shi'ite cleric in the country, and our old friend Moqtada al-Sadr, the head of the Mahdi Army.

Kurdish leader Jalal Talabani kept his job as President in spite of past ties with the CIA, Iranian intelligence and Saddam Hussein. In this largely ceremonial post, Talabani is the first non-Arab president of an Arab country.

George W. Bush, facing his lowest poll ratings since becoming President of the United States, said the move towards establishing a new government in Baghdad 'will make America more secure . . . and as more Iraqi troops stand up, more Americans can stand down'.

With his usual keen sense of timing, Al Qaeda leader Osama bin Laden said in a tape broadcast by satellite TV Al Jazeera that the West's moves to isolate the new Hamas-led Palestinian government prove it is at war with Islam and that 'along with their governments, the people of the West bear responsibility for the Zionist crusader's war against Islam'.

24 July 2006

I could have written four or five books with all the things that happened to me and the guys at Spartan over eighteen months and what makes me sad is that now, twelve months on, nothing much in Baghdad seems to have changed.

Seamus and Les split their time between Western Europe and the USA. Badger does Afghanistan and Iraq. Dai still suffers from Tourette's syndrome but continues bodyguarding VIPs and celebrities all over the world. The Yaapies have all remained in Iraq but are finding things difficult due to pressure from the South African government. I plan to visit Mad Dog McQueen and see his famous gun collection in the near future.

Sammy – Wing Commander Assam Mashooen – saved his money to build a house for his family and parents. In spring 2005 his brother was kidnapped and he had to sell the house and take out a loan to pay the ransom.

Colonel Faisal is dead.

Major Razak was kidnapped, tortured and killed on video by an insurgent group in 2005. He had been a brave and loyal companion.

Colonel Ibrahim rides high as the Shias take power with a senior role at the Water Ministry, and rules his private army with a Ba'athist-like rod of iron.

John Hind got his promotion. He was posted to Washington and as a one-star general is a special advisor on Iraqi infrastructure security. Holy shit.

Looking at the violence today, which is becoming more and

more polarised between Shia and Sunni, I can only say that we all saw it coming because it was already happening.

In 2006, the Iraqi Body Count charity estimates that approximately 36,000 Iraqi civilians have died as a result of this war. They use multiple sources to confirm each death and are generally recognised to be the most accurate record. I believe that many more have died unreported. Many people will automatically assume that Iraqi civilians have been killed by Coalition Forces. The truth is the Iraqis have been and continue killing each other. So much for the claim that there had been 'no history of ethnic strife in Iraq'.

I hope the neo-cons in Washington have woken up now and got some oxygen to their collective brain.

In 1991 George Bush Senior did not finish off Saddam Hussein because there would have been a power vacuum with nothing to balance against Iran. Now Americans are having to come to terms with the fact that, having brought democracy to Iraq, the 60 per cent Shia majority population have voted for a Shia leadership.

How many times during the local elections did I hear CPA officials saying, 'I don't understand, they're voting for the wrong guy.' Well, it's a funny old thing democracy, isn't it? Unfortunately the world, and especially Iraq, is not full of people waiting to be freed so that they can act like little Americans. None of the projected strategies survived contact with the reality of Iraq because during the planning process no one really asked the Iraqis what they wanted.

At the time of writing Iraq has a largely a Shi'ite government, army and police force.

And Grand Ayatollah Ali al-Sistani, the most powerful Shi'ite cleric in Iraq, is an Iranian.

Unfortunately I cannot say when the troubles will end. In the UK we took 700 years from the signing of the Magna Carta to develop our democracy fully. The former republics of Yugoslavia have taken more than a decade to try and stabilise their economies and governments since their war finished.

Ten years or 700 years? I should imagine the Iraqis are going to take somewhere in between.

The worrying thing for me is that with all the anti-war rhetoric we now see in the media, future political leaders may not have the moral courage to launch another war when one is actually needed.

Islamists describe PSDs working in Iraq as anti-Islamic mercenaries, without looking at what the PSDs actually do. Coalition or Multi-National Forces may be prosecuting the war, but PSDs in Iraq for the most part safeguard the reconstruction crews and are helping to rebuild the country. The water purification plants I protected prevented outbreaks of typhoid, cholera and gastroenteritis and have directly saved the lives of thousands of Muslim children, the sick and the elderly. PSDs don't get paid to kill people. We get paid to save lives and stay out of trouble.

So, all you Islamists and fundamentalists out there, do me a favour and stop whining about how I am oppressing Muslims by escorting humanitarian supplies and medical aid workers to the local population, or journalists who publicise the plight of the helpless. At the same time maybe one of you can start a website explaining how blowing yourself up and killing a busload of Muslim schoolchildren or a marketplace full of mixed Sunni and Shia Muslims qualifies for paradise, exactly?

Although I love slagging off our old enemy, the French, I have to admit that I have been impressed by their soldiers on operations and one of the best guys I met in Iraq was a Frenchman; an experienced soldier of fortune who lives the kind of life other men dream of. Richard, wherever you are, you lunatic, I hope you are well. I am living a life with some remorse but no regrets. Roger and Vance, I hope you two are also well.

They will debate for decades whether it was right or not to invade Iraq. Personally I disagree completely with the reasons presented by Bush and Blair to justify the war, but I must also say that I fully support every soldier sent out there, American, British and other Coalition Forces, who should be proud of the outstanding work they are doing in often impossible situations.

The Erebus UK contract worked out well for me. Krista and I got married three months after our second daughter, Veronica, was born. We have all moved out and are living happily in Africa where I work full time for a private security company.

I still intend to return to Iraq one day and climb the *melwiyeh* in Samarra with Sammy. But it will be a cold day in hell before I eat lamb again.

James Ashcroft
July 2006
www.makingakilling.co.uk

INDEX